GAYS

· AND THE ·

MILITARY

G A Y S
· A N D T H E ·
M I L I T A R Y

Marc
Wolinsky
and
Kenneth
Sherrill,
Editors

J O S E P H   S T E F F A N
versus the United States

PRINCETON UNIVERSITY PRESS
· P R I N C E T O N , N E W J E R S E Y ·

Library of Congress Cataloging-in-Publication Data

Steffan, Joseph, 1964–
Gays and the military : Joseph Steffan versus the United States /
Marc Wolinsky and Kenneth Sherrill, editors.
p. cm.
Selected records and judgment in the case of Joseph C. Steffan v.
Richard B. Cheney, Secretary of Defense, heard by the United States
District Court for the District of Columbia.
Includes bibliographical references and index.
ISBN 0-691-03307-2 (cloth : acid-free paper). —
ISBN 0-691-01944-4 (pbk. : acid-free paper)
1. Steffan, Joseph, 1964–   —Trials, litigation, etc.   2. Cheney,
Richard B.—Trials, litigation, etc.   3. United States.—Armed
Forces—Gays—Legal status, laws, etc.   4. Equality before the law—
United States.   I. Wolinsky, Marc, 1954–   .   II. Sherrill,
Kenneth S., 1942–   .   III. Cheney, Richard B.   IV. United States.
District Court (District of Columbia)   V. Title.
KF228.S74S74   1993   355'.008'664—dc20   93-22692   CIP

This book has been composed in Adobe Utopia

Princeton University Press books are printed on acid-free paper
and meet the guidelines for permanence and durability
of the Committee on Production Guidelines for Book Longevity of
the Council on Library Resources

Printed in the United States of America

10 9 8 7 6 5 4 3 2

To Barry
Skovgaard
and
Gerald Otte,   for their love and dedication;

to Wachtell,
Lipton,
Rosen & Katz
and
Hunter College   for their patience and support;

and to
Joseph Steffan   for his courage and commitment.

CONTENTS

ACKNOWLEDGMENTS

IF JOSEPH STEFFAN had not had the courage of his convictions and a passionate commitment to justice, this book would have been impossible. He provided us with the opportunity to try to use our professional skills to end the United States military's policy of discriminating against gay people. All Americans are indebted to the courageous lesbians and gay men who risked their lives—physical and professional—to fight for our constitutional rights.

We want to thank the contributors to this volume for bringing their scholarly skills to this struggle. Academics do not often enter into the public realm in such efforts. We believe that our colleagues have acted in the tradition of those who contributed their scholarship to the struggle to end racial discrimination in the United States and that they have brought honor to their professions. Portions of Gregory Herek's testimony were adapted from his articles "Stigma, Prejudice, and Violence against Lesbians and Gay Men," in J. Gonsiorek and J. Weinrich, eds., *Homosexuality: Research Implications for Public Policy* (Newbury Park, Calif.: Sage Publications, 1991), reprinted by permission; and "Gay People and Government Security Clearances: A Social Science Perspective," *American Psychologist* 45 (1990): 1035–42 (copyright 1990 by the American Psychological Association, reprinted by permission). Portions of Richard Green's testimony were adapted from his article "The Immutability of (Homo)Sexual Orientation: Behavioral Science Implications for a Constitutional (Legal) Analysis," *Journal of Psychiatry and Law* (Winter 1988) (copyright Federal Legal Publications, 1988). We wish to thank Sage Publications, the American Psychological Association, and Federal Legal Publications for consenting to the inclusion of adaptations of these works in this volume.

We want to thank our home institutions, Wachtell, Lipton, Rosen & Katz and Hunter College of the City University of New York, for supporting our work. Their support was tangible; it also was moral.

Many of our friends and colleagues provided invaluable assistance over the course of this project. Sandra Lowe of Lambda Legal Defense and Educational Fund when this case was being litigated, provided indispensable assistance and great good cheer. Her interns at

Lambda, notably Robert Mower, provided essential research assistance. Dean Norman Redlich assisted on the briefs and in formulating the strategy for the case. Leona Perreault, Justine Kalka, Shera Goldman, Sheila O'Hare, Frederick C. Hollingsworth, and Michele Curcio of Wachtell, Lipton, aided us at every step of this process. We also received great research assistance, advice, and support from friends, colleagues, and students at Hunter College, notably Joan C. Tronto, Ana Oakes, Chris Goeken, Scott Sawyer, José Hernandez, Sarah Watstein, Tom Flanegin, and Judith Friedlander. Doug Strand, of the University of California, Berkeley, provided years of support, criticism, and data—all by electronic mail. Robert L. Hardgrave, of the University of Texas, was an extraordinarily constructive critic in his reviews for Princeton University Press. He understood, perhaps better than we, how our material could become a book.

We particularly want to thank Malcolm DeBevoise and Walter Lippincott of Princeton University Press for their belief in this project, their skill, professionalism, and patience.

Finally, we thank our lovers and other family members, who lived through this project and made certain that we, too, lived through it.

M.W.
K.S.
New York, 1993

THE MATERIALS in this volume were originally prepared for court and, as a result, reflected the unique style used in court documents. In order to make the volume more accessible and readable to the layperson, the materials have been edited to eliminate some of the technical elements of legal filings, such as case citations and captions, and to conform to the style and punctuation typically found in a book written for the general public. In a very few cases, sentences have been rewritten to make them clearer. The written testimony of the expert witnesses has also been edited to eliminate the recitations of the experts' credentials—which are, in each case, impressive—and some citations. Legal briefs have been shortened by the elimination of unessential material and procedural matters. In most cases, exhibits and appendices to the original court filings have been deleted. The one document that has not been materially edited is the district court's opinion upholding the constitutionality of the military's ban on gays. It is reproduced in its entirety, with changes only to the case citations and punctuation.

All notes and source citations have been moved to the end of the volume. A table of cases is also included at the end of the volume for those who wish to pursue their interest by reading the major legal decisions in the area.

Marc Wolinsky and Kenneth Sherrill

COLLECTED in this book are the most significant portions of the court record from a case known as *Joseph C. Steffan v. Richard Cheney, Secretary of Defense.* As with most court cases, at its heart lies the story of one person. Joe Steffan entered the United States Naval Academy in July 1983. Once there, he was quickly singled out as a model for his classmates. In his sophomore and junior years, he sang the National Anthem as a soloist on national television at the Army-Navy game. In his senior year, he was selected as a battalion commander, making him one of the ten highest-ranking midshipmen at the Academy, with direct command over one-sixth of the Academy's forty-five hundred midshipmen.

Six weeks before he was scheduled to graduate, Steffan was forced to resign from the Academy because he answered "Yes, sir" to the question "I'd like your word, are you a homosexual?" Once Steffan stated that he was gay, he was required to be discharged under Department of Defense regulations that assert that "homosexuality is incompatible with military service" because, among other things, the presence of homosexuals "adversely affects the ability of the Military Services to maintain discipline, good order, and morale" and "to foster mutual trust and confidence among servicemembers."

Litigation was commenced on December 29, 1988, in the United States District Court for the District of Columbia. The case was assigned to Judge Oliver Gasch, born in 1906 and appointed to the bench in 1965 by President Lyndon Johnson. The principal legal claim was that Steffan's discharge violated the constitutional guarantee of equal protection under the laws provided by the Fifth and Fourteenth Amendments. During the ensuing two years, the lawyers for Steffan and the government engaged in "discovery practice"—a process by which each side can request the other to produce documents and other evidence that is helpful to its case. Those proceedings resulted in two diversions from the merits of Steffan's claim.

In one, Judge Gasch dismissed the case when Steffan's lawyers directed Steffan not to answer questions about whether he had ever engaged in homosexual conduct. The court of appeals reversed, holding that the question was irrelevant since Steffan was discharged on the basis of his "status" as a homosexual, not conduct, and remanded the case to Judge Gasch for further proceedings. The second arose during a court hearing following the remand, when Judge Gasch repeatedly and derisively referred to Steffan and other gays as "homos." Steffan's lawyers filed a motion with Judge Gasch to have him remove himself from the case for bias. Judge Gasch denied the motion, holding that a "reasonable person" would not conclude on the basis of his remarks that he was prejudiced against gays and lesbians generally, or against Steffan in particular. The court of appeals refused to issue an order requiring Judge Gasch to remove himself from the case.

After this wrangling, Judge Gasch was asked to rule on the merits by both sides when they filed cross-motions for summary judgment. Essentially, on a motion for summary judgment, each side has an opportunity to present evidence showing that it is entitled to "win"—i.e., to have "summary judgment" entered in its favor—without going through a trial with live witnesses. The evidence typically consists of sworn statements called "affidavits" or "declarations" and source documents provided by the parties. In theory, the district court is required to deny a motion for summary judgment if there are any "disputed issues of material fact," that is, if there are any factual issues in dispute between the parties whose resolution would affect the outcome of the case. If there are disputed issues of material fact, a motion for summary judgment must be denied and the case must be decided on the basis of a trial with live witnesses.

An Introduction to Equal Protection Law

On his motion for summary judgment, Steffan claimed that the Defense Department regulation barring the service of gays should be subjected to heightened or "strict" scrutiny under the equal protection clause. A brief outline of equal protection law is in order here. Governments routinely and by necessity must make distinctions between classes of individuals. Under the equal protection clause, the fact that these distinctions are made, indeed must be made, by the political branches does not itself constitute a constitutional violation. So, for example, the fact that the Congress may decide that a family of four that resides in Chicago and earns more than eight thousand dollars per year is not entitled to food stamps does not violate the equal protection clause because it is "rational" to discriminate in distributing limited government resources between the very poor and those who, while they may be needy, are not quite as poor.

More rigorous scrutiny is required, however, when the distinction made by the political branches involves a classification that is "suspect." For example, while it may be rational to discriminate on the basis of income in determining eligibility for food stamps, on its face it is suspect to discriminate on the basis of race in distributing food stamps because one would presume that African-American, Asian-American, and Caucasian families of the same size, residing in the same city, and earning the same income are equally needy. When government bodies do discriminate on the basis of characteristics that have no apparent relation to the subject matter in question, the possibility is raised that the government action was motivated by a naked desire to discriminate against an unpopular group. Government action of this type is at the heart of what the equal protection clause is designed to prohibit.

The notion that courts should subject laws and regulations that discriminate against groups that are politically disadvantaged to more rigorous review under the equal protection clause can be traced back to Justice Stone's seminal footnote in the Supreme Court's decision in *United States* v. *Carolene Products Co.* (1938). In that footnote, the Supreme Court suggested that "prejudice against discrete and insular minorities may be a special condition, which tends seriously to curtail the operation of those political processes ordinarily to be relied upon to protect minorities, and . . . may call for a correspondingly more searching judicial inquiry." Thus, the central idea of the body of equal protection law that has evolved since *Carolene Products* is that because certain disfavored groups— "discrete and insular minorities"—are disadvantaged in protecting their interests through the political process, there is a correspondingly greater responsibility on the part of the judiciary to scrutinize laws that discriminate against those groups.

Equal protection analysis thus requires two steps. The first is to determine whether the group in question constitutes a "suspect" or "quasi-suspect" class, i.e., to determine whether the group bears characteristics that make it more likely that the political process will work to unfairly single out the group in question. If a group constitutes a "suspect class," the government must show that the classification is necessary to promote a compelling government interest. If the group constitutes a "quasi-suspect class," the government must show that the challenged justification is substantially related to a legitimate state interest. If neither a suspect nor a quasi-suspect classification is involved, the government must show only that the classification is rationally related to a legitimate government purpose. Whatever test is applied, the government must always show that its interest is "legitimate." In defining what is a legitimate interest, the Supreme Court has ruled that the government cannot rely on irrational prejudices or private biases to justify discrimination against a disfavored group.

In deciding whether a group constitutes a suspect or quasi-suspect class, courts have focused on essentially five questions:

1. Has the group suffered a history of purposeful discrimination?
2. Is the group defined by a trait that frequently bears no relation to ability to perform or contribute to society?
3. Is the trait defining the class "immutable" or, in other words, is the trait a product of an accident of birth?
4. Has the group been saddled with unique disabilities because of prejudice or inaccurate or absurd stereotypes?
5. Does the group burdened by discrimination lack the political power necessary to obtain redress through the political process?

Some concrete examples will help illustrate these concepts. Slavery and its legacy plainly reflect the fact that blacks have suffered a history of purposeful discrimination in our country's history. An individual's race has no relation to his or her ability to contribute to society. Race is an immutable characteristic defined by genetics. Blacks have been unfairly and inaccurately stigmatized by stereotypes that characterize them as lazy, prone to criminality, and hypersexual. And blacks historically have been disadvantaged in their participation in the democratic process. Accordingly, it is no surprise that the Supreme Court has determined that blacks constitute the paradigmatic suspect class.

Women constitute the paradigmatic "quasi-suspect" class. Like blacks, women have suffered a history of discrimination and are saddled with stereotypes concerning a woman's "proper place" in society. Women historically have been underrepresented in the political process. And sex, like race, is an immutable characteristic. However, unlike blacks, sex does have a bearing in some respects on one's ability to perform. To state the obvious, women, unlike men, bear children. Less obvious, but no less true, is the fact that women tend to live longer than men. Some Supreme Court justices have argued that since men and women admittedly have biological differences, a legislature's "discrimination" between men and women in a way that takes the differences between the sexes into account is not necessarily invidious. And so, over strong dissents, the majority of the Supreme Court has held that an intermediate level of scrutiny is appropriate in reviewing government action that discriminates on the basis of sex.

Equal Protection and Gays

It is within the framework of this analysis that Joe Steffan, on his motion for summary judgment, argued that gay men and lesbians, like blacks and women, constitute a "suspect" or "quasi-suspect" class and that the Department of Defense regulation barring the service of gays in the military should be subjected to heightened scrutiny. Surprisingly, there is very little decided case law in this area. The Supreme Court has never spoken on the subject. A few lower courts have held that the class of individuals defined by people who engage in homosexual *conduct* does not constitute a suspect class, the obvious reason being that conduct by its very nature is not immutable; someone can always choose to refrain from engaging in certain types of sexual activity. Still fewer lower courts have focused on the question of whether the class of individuals defined by people who have a homosexual *orientation* constitutes a suspect class. The most notable discussion is in the concurring opinion of Judge William A. Norris in *Perry Watkins* v. *Secretary of the Army* (1989). Prior to the *Steffan* case, no court to our knowledge was ever presented with rigorous evidence from recognized experts in the social and biological sciences discussing each of the five factors that the courts have identified. The written testimony of those experts constitutes the bulk of this volume.

The use of expert testimony from physicians, biologists, and social scientists in constitutional adjudication is not new. In the series of cases that led up to *Brown* v. *Board of Education* (1954), for example, the legal team headed by Thurgood Marshall (who was then a lawyer for the NAACP Legal Defense Fund) presented evidence from a number of psychologists and educators concerning the adverse impact of racism on the development of black schoolchildren. This evidence was no doubt a critical element in convincing the lower courts and ultimately the Supreme Court that separate is not equal and that segregated schools violate the constitutional guarantee of equal protection under the laws. So, too, the Supreme Court decision in *Roe v. Wade* (1973), much of which was recently reaffirmed in *Planned Parenthood of Southeastern Pennsylvania v. Casey* (1992), rests in part on biological evidence concerning the viability of the fetus outside of its mother's womb during the gestation period.

The basic premise of the American legal system is that cases must be decided on the evidence presented in court. At the most elementary level, the accused is innocent until *proven* guilty. Constitutional litigation, in theory, is no different. That is particularly so in an equal protection case, where the task of the court is to determine whether governmental discrimination is founded in reason or in prejudice and stereotype. Indeed, equal protection law uniquely calls on the judiciary to assure that the majority does not tyrannize a disfavored minority.

Of course, there are a number of instances in which the judiciary has failed to live up to these ideals. In 1896, for example, the Supreme Court in *Plessy* v. *Ferguson* held that the equal protection clause did not prohibit segregation as long as blacks were provided with "equal" facilities. And in response to the hysteria that followed Japan's attack on Pearl Harbor, the Supreme Court held in *Korematsu* v. *United States* (1944), that the military could force American citizens of Japanese ancestry into relocation camps.

The decisions in *Plessy* and *Korematsu* no doubt reflect judicial acceptance of the accepted "wisdom" of their times. Until relatively recently, the "accepted wisdom" has been that homosexuality is an illness and that gays and lesbians are evil or morally corrupt. Since World War II, that "accepted wisdom" has been challenged by scholars working in virtually every field. Large segments of society remain unconvinced by—or at least unexposed to—this scholarly literature. As one would expect, many, if not most, judges fall into this category.

Writing on the subject of human sexuality generally, Judge Richard Posner has observed that sex and sexuality "are emotional topics even to middle-aged and elderly judges" and, as a consequence, "the dominant judicial, and I would say legal, attitude toward the study of sex is that 'I know what I like' and therefore research is superfluous."[1] Judge Posner's observations no doubt apply with even greater force to homosexuals and homosexuality. Judges have assumed that because the culture of nineteenth- and twentieth-century England and America has condemned homosexuality, that has always been the case—the Judeo-Christian tradition has uniformly (and rightly) held homosexuals in contempt. The most notable example of this is Chief Justice Burger's concurrence in *Bowers* v. *Hardwick*, the 1986 Supreme Court decision holding that the right of privacy does not extend to private, consensual homosexual acts. In his concurring opinion, Chief Justice Burger rested his legal conclusion on the factual assertion that "millennia of moral teaching" have condemned homosexuality. As Judge Posner so ably demonstrates in his book, society's attitudes toward homosexuals and homosexual love have varied widely over the centuries, and Justice Burger's factual assertion is both superficial and inaccurate.

The evidentiary record developed in the *Steffan* case was intended to educate the district court, the court of appeals, and possibly the Supreme Court on the extensive scientific literature concerning lesbians and gay men; to show the judges why gay people are gay, how religious and moral attitudes toward gays and lesbians have evolved, how and why society has developed incorrect stereotypes about gay men and lesbians, and why lesbians and gay men have been relatively unsuccessful in advancing their agenda through the political process. In short, the evidence was designed to convince the judges *on the evidence* that their own views on gays are shaped by society's prejudice and incorrect stereotypes and that an educated judiciary has a unique role in protecting lesbians and gay men from discrimination in the military and elsewhere.

An Overview of the Evidence

Following this introduction is the legal "brief" submitted to Judge Gasch on Steffan's motion for summary judgment. The brief provides more factual background about Steffan's discharge from the Academy and a fuller discussion of equal protection law. Most important, the brief shows how Steffan's lawyers used the expert testimony that they submitted to the court to support their legal argument that gays constitute a suspect class and the military's ban on the service of gays cannot withstand judicial scrutiny. The brief also shows that the rationale underlying the "accepted wisdom" concerning the suitability of gays to serve in the military is identical to the "accepted wisdom" concerning the suitability of blacks to serve in any capacity other than mess attendants and stewards.

The evidence comes next. The first affidavit is from John Boswell, a professor of history at Yale University. Boswell's testimony discusses social attitudes toward homosexuality from ancient Greece to the present and focuses in particular on the fact that while certain sexual *practices* have been condemned, no religious or moral code has ever made judgments on an individual on the basis of sexual *orientation*.

The next declaration is from Richard Green, a professor of Psychiatry at the University of California School of Medicine, Los Angeles. Green's testimony focuses on the key issue in equal protection law as it applies to gays: whether homosexual orientation is an "immutable characteristic."

The testimony of one of the co-authors of this volume, Kenneth Sherrill, follows. His testimony develops a theoretical model for measuring the relative political power of a given group. He then applies this model to the characteristics of the gay community in the United States today and identifies the factors that have disadvantaged gays politically.

As discussed above, one of the factors that courts have looked at in determining whether a classification is suspect is whether the group has been saddled with disabilities resulting from prejudice and inaccurate stereotypes. Gregory Herek, a psychologist on the faculty at the University of California at Davis who has written extensively on the social psychology of prejudice against gays, addresses this subject. He also discusses the scientific evidence refuting the notion that homosexuality is an illness and shows that homosexual orientation has no bearing on an individual's ability to perform or contribute to society and gays are not a special security threat.

The final expert declaration is from Robert Rankin, a professor of psychiatry at both the University of California at Davis and the University of California at San Francisco Schools of Medicine who is also a retired Navy captain with nineteen years of service. Rankin discusses the evidence showing that gays have historically served and are currently serving in the military without incident and that many gays in the military are tolerated by their superiors. In a related vein, the evidence concludes with an affidavit from Kate Dyer, former executive assistant to Congressman Gerry Studds, and letters from foreign military establishments that permit gays to serve in their armed forces. All of this evidence is designed to refute the proposition that "homosexuality is incompatible with military service."

The government's response follows. What is perhaps most notable about the response is not what it says, but what it does not say. There is virtually no attempt to present any evidence on whether homosexuality is immutable, for example, and no attempt to introduce evidence justifying the military's discriminatory policy. All of this is pointed out in the brief submitted on Steffan's behalf in response to the government's memorandum. That response also included a short supplemental affidavit from Richard Green, who refutes a few small points made by the government in its brief and who advises the court of recent developments in the field of brain research that lend further support to Green's conclusions.

The volume concludes with Judge Gasch's opinion upholding the constitutionality of the military's ban on gays. It stands as the proof of Judge Posner's generalizations concerning judicial closed-mindedness in the area of sex and sexuality. The expert evidence is ignored and, in its place, the court relies on anecdote, two book reviews, personal preconception, and prejudice. Perhaps most remarkable is Judge Gasch's interjection of the specter of AIDS as a grounds for discriminating against homosexuals, grounds that the military itself refused to advance in support of its regulations.

Following the issuance of Judge Gasch's opinion on December 9, 1991, Steffan's lawyers appealed that ruling to the United States Court of Appeals for the District of Columbia Circuit. No action was taken on the appeal for almost one year. During that period, the issue of gays in the military erupted on the national scene, as President Clinton was pressed by some to make good on his campaign promise to lift the ban with an executive order, and by Senator Sam Nunn and the military to maintain some version of the ban.

During the course of the Senate hearings on the ban, it became apparent that gay men and lesbians are to many a despised minority. One colonel testified that he would not want his gay son to enter the military because he would be afraid that his son would be assaulted by servicemembers who hate gays. He made this point not to argue that in lifting the ban, the military would have to work to reduce prejudice against gays as it has worked to reduce prejudice against African Americans and women, but to argue that the military must cater to this extreme form of homophobia in order to preserve good order, morale, and discipline. The Senate debate thus proved the importance of the role of courts in protecting minorities from the potential excesses of majoritarian rule. Constitutional principle can be compromised in the political arena in order to achieve a politically popular or expedient result. An independent judiciary stands as the bulwark against such compromise. And so the battle continues in the courts for Steffan and his lawyers as the fight to end discrimination against gay men and lesbians in the military and elsewhere moves forward.

G A Y S
· A N D T H E ·
M I L I T A R Y

Memorandum of Law in Support of Plaintiff's Cross-motion for Summary Judgment and in Opposition to Defendants' Motion for Summary Judgment

THIS memorandum of law is respectfully submitted on behalf of plaintiff Joseph C. Steffan in support of his cross-motion for summary judgment and in opposition to defendants' motion for judgment on the pleadings or, in the alternative, summary judgment.

Preliminary Statement

In the spring of 1987, plaintiff Joseph C. Steffan was a model midshipman at the United States Naval Academy. Selected to be a battalion commander in his senior year, he was six weeks away from graduation when a promising career in service to his country was abruptly terminated. This unfortunate and unnecessary result came about because Steffan remained true to the United States Naval Academy honor code and truthfully answered "Yes, sir" when he was asked, "I'd like your word, are you a homosexual?" No one ever claimed that Steffan's sexual orientation interfered with his performance at the Academy or his three summer tours of military duty. And no one ever claimed that Steffan engaged in homosexual conduct, in or out of uniform, on or off duty.

For purposes of the Navy's regulations, Steffan's character and record of service are all irrelevant. All that is relevant is Steffan's status as a homosexual, a status that is an intrinsic part of his makeup, as intrinsic as his race or hair color. In the defendants' eyes, nothing Steffan could do or refrain from doing would allow him to graduate, save his career, or qualify him for continued service, once he truthfully answered his commander's question.

The United States Court of Appeals for the District of Columbia acknowledged in *Doe* v. *Casey* (1986) that this Circuit has not decided "whether an agency of the federal government can discriminate against individuals merely because of sexual *orientation*." The *Doe* Court also acknowledged that this is a "difficult issue." What makes it difficult is the fact that the regulations require that individuals who perform well, even superlatively, in their positions be discharged not because of what they do, but because of what they say, think, and feel.

Without any proof whatsoever, defendants ask this court to find that these regulations have a legitimate and rational basis as a matter of law. Just ten days ago, however, in *Pruitt* v. *Cheney* (1991), the Ninth Circuit squarely rejected the position that defendants advance here. *Pruitt*, like this case, presented an equal protection challenge to military regulations that require the discharge of servicemembers solely on the basis of homosexual orientation. The district court granted a motion to dismiss Pruitt's complaint, holding that the military's regulations withstood constitutional challenge as a matter of law.

The Ninth Circuit reversed, reinstated Pruitt's equal protection claim, and held that the military must "establish *on the record* that its policy ha[s] a rational basis." The Ninth Circuit also held that the plaintiff in that case had to be afforded "the opportunity to contest that basis." Accordingly, in light of *Pruitt*, defendants cannot prevail on their motion. See Point 1 below.

Given that defendants have not sought to prove that there is a rational and legitimate basis for the regulations, their motion must fail under *Pruitt*. Indeed, as shown in greater detail below, plaintiff should be granted summary judgment on his equal protection claim because not only have defendants *failed* to offer any such proof, they *cannot* do so.

One contention that the military has offered for its draconian policy is that gays are subject to blackmail. It is an argument that literally can be traced to the cold war "red scare" of the 1950s. Given that pedigree—and given that an individual who openly acknowledges his sexual orientation to his superiors cannot be blackmailed—it is no surprise that Secretary of Defense Richard Cheney recently admitted that the security concern was an "old chestnut" that was no longer valid and that this supposed security concern does not preclude civilians from serving in even the most senior positions in the Department of Defense. Nor is it a surprise that the Navy admitted twelve years ago, in *Berg* v. *Claytor* (1977), that its regulations were not and could not be justified on this ground.

Blackmail aside, the other asserted justification for the ban on gays is that the mere presence of homosexuals in the armed services disrupts military order, discipline, and morale. It is a justification that cannot withstand any level of scrutiny. Gay men and women have served in the military with distinction and without incident throughout our country's history; indeed, throughout recorded history. As Secretary Cheney recently acknowledged, many thousands of gay men and women are now serving in the military in positions from the highest to the lowest reaches without incident. American servicemembers currently serve with openly gay soldiers and sailors from any number of our allies, including Israel, Germany, Spain, France, the Netherlands, Sweden, Denmark, Finland, Brazil, Norway, and Japan—none of which precludes the service of gays and all of which have found that homosexuality is not "incompatible with military service," as defendants claim.

The military's justification founders on more fundamental grounds, however. For when one asks the question "Why does the presence of a gay person disrupt military order?" one gets a remarkable answer. The answer is that gay men and women are viewed as being disruptive because some soldiers and sailors are so prejudiced against homosexuals that they cannot serve with them. Thus, in the defendants' view, gays must be excluded not because they cannot be good soldiers, but because their fellow soldiers harbor irrational biases against them, biases that are not sanctioned by any accepted legal or moral principle.

These arguments, too, have an ignoble origin. During World War II, blacks were largely excluded from the Navy, serving only as mess attendants. In those branches of the military where they were permitted to serve, blacks were relegated to segregated units. The stated justification for that policy was *precisely* the same one that defendants offer here: integration would damage morale, discipline, and good order. The underlying rationale for the policy is also familiar: black soldiers could not be permitted to serve with white soldiers because whites were prejudiced against blacks.

Today, with a black man serving as the chairman of the Joint Chiefs of Staff, we know that the asserted justification for such blatant racial discrimination made no sense. We know also that no court today would ever sanction the exclusion of blacks from the Navy on the ground that the irrational prejudices of white sailors makes it necessary to relegate blacks to positions as mess attendants in order to preserve "good order" and "morale." This case requires this court to confront precisely the same kind of irrational prejudice applied to a different group.

The fundamental tenets of our Constitution preclude discrimination against one group of individuals in order to cater to the prejudices of others. Indeed, it is precisely because gays constitute a distinct and insular minority that has suffered a history of purposeful discrimination and that is defined by an immutable characteristic that the regulations at issue must be subjected to a heightened level of scrutiny. See Point 2.A below. Even if no special scrutiny is applied, however, the regulations banning gays must fail because they are not related to any legitimate state interest.

As discussed in Point 2.B below, it is well recognized that "[p]rivate biases may be outside the reach of the law, but the law cannot, directly or indirectly, give them effect." *Palmore* v. *Sidoti* (1984). Similarly, the Supreme Court has not hesitated to strike down regulations that are based on overbroad premises and stereotypes that bear no relation to an individual's actual abilities. The application of these principles mandates the conclusion that the discrimination at issue here should be held invalid. See Point 2.C below.

The justifications for the Navy's regulations suspect, defendants are left to argue that they must be left alone because courts must "defer" to the judgments of military officers. But there is a big difference between deference to judgments based on reason and blind abdication to "judgments" based on irrational prejudice. Assuming that any deference is due, its limits are far exceeded here. No case that defendants cite supports the notion that an individual or group whose conduct is blameless can be discriminated against with impunity because bigots wedded to archaic stereotypes may be offended by their presence. To the contrary, the same cases that defendants cite also stand squarely for the proposition that "'our citizens in uniform may not be stripped of basic rights simply because they have doffed their civilian clothes.'" *Chappell* v. *Wallace* (1983), *quoting* Warren, *The Bill of Rights and the Military*. See Point 2.D below.

Quite apart from the patent unconstitutionality of the regulations as a whole is the unconstitutionality of the treatment that Steffan himself received at the Academy. Six weeks away from graduation, he was made the subject of whirlwind discharge proceedings that were initiated and concluded in the space of one week. The treatment that Steffan received stands in stark contrast to the treatment that the Academy accords to midshipmen who are deemed to be uncommissionable in their senior years for other reasons unrelated to their performance. The record shows that the Academy as a matter of policy and practice permits midshipmen in these circumstances to graduate even though they cannot continue on into active service. It also shows that the military has wide discretion in the timing of the initiation of administrative discharge proceedings and that, once initiated, the discharge of a commissioned naval officer routinely takes four months or more to conclude.

The same principles of equal protection that invalidate the military's regulations as a whole invalidate the discriminatory treatment that Steffan suffered. See Points 3.A and B below. They also mandate that the Academy's actions be held to be violative of the Administrative Procedures Act, 5 U.S.C. §§ 701 *et seq.*, as arbitrary and capricious. See Point 3.C below.

Statement of Facts

A. Joseph C. Steffan

Plaintiff Joseph C. Steffan entered the United States Naval Academy in July 1983, shortly after he graduated from high school in Warren, Minnesota, as the salutatorian of his class with eight varsity letters. Once he arrived at the Academy, his promise was quickly recognized. His first-year evaluation called him "gifted" and predicted that he would "excel as a whole-man over the next three years." During a tour of duty in the summer between his freshman and sophomore years, Steffan was identified as having "excellent potential to perform well as a nuclear submarine division officer." During his sophomore year, Steffan was praised as an "outstanding performer" who had "exhibited excellent leadership" and who was "an asset to the Academy" who "should continue to do well in the future."

In his junior year, Steffan was selected to serve as the regimental commander of one-half of his class of one thousand midshipmen and was described as a "model for his classmates and subordinates." That year, and again the following year, Steffan sang the National Anthem as a soloist on national television at the Army-Navy game, earning a citation from the superintendent of the Academy in the process. An evaluation of his performance during a tour of duty in the summer between his junior and senior years stated that Steffan's "training is best characterized by his constant dedication to superior performance" and that he "will undoubtedly make an outstanding naval officer."

In his senior year, Steffan was selected as a battalion commander, making him one of the ten highest-ranking midshipmen at the Academy with direct command over one-sixth of the Academy's forty-five hundred midshipmen. He served at that time as the president and cantor of the Catholic Choir and premier soloist of the Glee Club. In the spring of 1987, all expected that Steffan would be awarded a bachelor's degree in May, enter the navy's prestigious nuclear submarine program, and pursue a career for which, according to one evaluation, the sky was the limit. It was not to be.

B. The Initiation of Discharge Proceedings

On or about February 13, 1987, the Naval Investigative Service (NIS) commenced an investigation on Joseph Steffan after it received a report from the Academy that Steffan had admitted to another midshipman that he, Steffan, was gay. Steffan learned of the investigation in mid-March 1987 when one of Steffan's friends at the Academy, Wes Wilson, informed Steffan that he had been interviewed by an NIS special agent. A few days after his conversation with Wilson, Steffan approached a chaplain at the Academy, Byron Holderby. Steffan told Chaplain Holderby that he was gay and that he believed that he was being investigated by the NIS. Holderby offered to intercede on Steffan's behalf and speak with Captain H. W. Habermeyer, Jr., the commandant of midshipmen, to see if Steffan could be allowed to graduate.

Holderby failed and a few days later, on March 23, Steffan approached Habermeyer himself to get more details as to why he was being investigated and what charges were to be filed against him and to seek permission to meet with the superintendent to request permission to graduate. After some discussion, Habermeyer asked Steffan, "Are you willing to state at this time that you are a homosexual?" Steffan responded, "Yes, sir." Habermeyer told Steffan that it was unlikely that he would be permitted to graduate from the Academy. Habermeyer then asked Steffan what he would want to do in that event, and Steffan stated, "I guess I would have to leave the Naval Academy." Deviating from the normal requirement that seventy-two or more hours notice be provided, Habermeyer told Steffan that he would arrange for a Brigade Military Performance Board to convene the next day to review Steffan's "performance" in light of his statement.

Later that same day, Steffan was given formal notice that a Brigade Military Performance Board would be convened at noon the next day. The notice was accompanied by a letter dated March 23 from the Sixth Battalion officer, G. D. Moore, to Habermeyer, which, according to the notice, would be presented as "documentary evidence" to the Board. The letter itself stated that Steffan had "acknowledged that he is a homosexual, and as such, he should be separated from the Naval Academy." Attached to the letters were two memos from Habermeyer. The first recounted Habermeyer's conversation with Chaplain Holderby in which Holderby reported that Steffan had stated that he is gay. The second recounted Habermeyer's conversation with Steffan in which he acknowledged that he is gay. Also attached was a Navy psychologist's evaluation reporting that Steffan's "self-identity is as a homosexual," that his homosexuality "appears to be a preferred orientation to which he has adjusted," and that he "has an excellent track record and appears to have adjusted quite well at the Academy."

C. The Brigade Military Performance Board Hearing

A Brigade Military Performance Board was convened the next day, March 24, with the deputy commandant, Captain Konetzni, presiding. Before Steffan entered the Board room, Konetzni threatened him, stating that he should not answer any questions put to him in an adversarial manner and that if he "did not go along with the proceedings of the performance board without taking an adversarial stance, that the Academy had within its means the ability to make life much more difficult for [him] than it already was."

In accordance with Academy regulations, Konetzni advised his fellow Board members that they could only consider "the documents and testimony presented to the board today in open session" and that "[e]ach case must be decided on its own merits based on the evidence before the board." Konetzni then dispensed with the requirement of Academy regulations that a resume of Steffan's record be presented, observing that Steffan's "performance here as a midshipman . . . has been outstanding." He proceeded to read into the evidentiary record the recommendation of the Sixth Battalion officer that Steffan be discharged because he had acknowledged that he is gay, Habermeyer's two statements, and the Navy psychologist's report.

This concluded, Konetzni asked Steffan the only question posed at the hearing concerning the substance of the charge against him: "I'd like your word, are you a homosexual?" Steffan responded, "Yes, sir." The Board then went into secret deliberations. When it reconvened, Konetzni reported that the Board had voted to change the "A minus" evaluation of Steffan's military performance over the past three and a half years to an "F" and to recommend to the commandant that Steffan be discharged from the Academy. Later that same day, the Brigade Military Performance Board sent a memorandum to Habermeyer that stated that "[b]ased on his own admission [that he is gay] and the evaluation by the clinical psychologist, the Brigade Military Performance Board recommends that Midshipman Steffan be separated from the Naval Academy due to insufficient aptitude for commissioned service."

D. The Academic Board Hearing

Habermeyer transmitted a letter dated March 26 to the Naval Academy's Academic Board reporting the Brigade Military Performance Board's recommendation that Steffan be separated from the Academy. Habermeyer recounted that Steffan had admitted to the Board that he is gay and concluded that "[b]ased on his own admission and the evaluation of the clinical psychologist, I recommend that Midshipman Steffan be separated from the Naval Academy." On the basis of this recommendation, an Academic Board was scheduled to convene on April 1. Prior to the Academic Board hearing, on March 26, Steffan told the conduct officer, Major Funk, that he wanted to transmit a statement to the Academic Board along with the recommendation of the Performance Board. Funk refused to permit plaintiff to do so and advised plaintiff that he would have to wait until the Academic Board met to make a statement.

Steffan was given formal notice of the Academic Board hearing on March 30. Attached to the notice was Habermeyer's March 26 letter recommending discharge on the basis of Steffan's statements concerning his sexual orientation.

The Academic Board convened to consider Steffan's case on April 1 as scheduled. The superintendent of the Academy presided and, at the opening of the session, either read or summarized Habermeyer's March 26 letter recommending Steffan's discharge on the basis of his statements that he is gay. Steffan next read a prepared statement in which he asked that he be permitted to complete the academic requirements needed to obtain his diploma. The superintendent responded that there was nothing that the Academic Board could do to allow Steffan to graduate. After Steffan protested that the Board did have the discretion to permit him to graduate, the Board went into closed session. Barely five minutes later, Steffan was informed that the Academic Board had unanimously voted to recommend his discharge on grounds of homosexuality. There was not even a suggestion that Steffan was being discharged on the basis of homosexual conduct or that he gained admission to the Academy through false pretenses.

Steffan then met with Major Funk, who pressured Steffan to resign. Funk told Steffan that an appeal would be useless and that if he were discharged involuntarily, his discharge certificate would include a code that would indicate that Steffan was gay and that his academic and career prospects would be adversely affected. Under the pressure of numerous threats, suspended from class, with no hope that he would be permitted to graduate and faced with an Academic Board recommendation from which an appeal would be futile, Steffan submitted an involuntary resignation from the Academy on April 1.

Argument

Point 1. Defendants' Motion for Judgment on the Pleadings or, in the Alternative, Summary Judgment Should Be Denied.

Plaintiff was discharged from the Academy pursuant to servicewide regulations promulgated in 1981 as Department of Defense (DOD) Directive 1332.14. The regulation was adopted in part in response to the decision in *Matlovich* v. *Secretary of the Air Force* (1978). Prior to the adoption of DOD Directive 1332.14, the services *permitted* the retention of homosexuals. In *Matlovich*, the D.C. Circuit held that if the military did decide to discharge a gay servicemember, it would have to articulate a reason as to why the discretion to retain the member was not being used. The military's response was DOD Directive 1332.14, which sharply limited the authority to retain gay servicemembers and, in a departure from past practice, made discharge essentially mandatory.

DOD Directives 1332.14 and 1332.30 plainly and clearly discriminate on the basis of sexual orientation. An individual is not automatically disqualified from military service just because he or she engaged in homosexual conduct. Rather, the regulations provide that a servicemember who engages in such conduct may be retained if the conduct was a departure from the servicemember's "usual and customary behavior," "is unlikely to recur," and did not involve "force, coercion or intimidation." As a corollary, a gay servicemember may be discharged without any proof or allegation of homosexual conduct. Indeed, that was precisely the case here.

The Supreme Court has never ruled on the question of whether discrimination on the basis of sexual orientation is violative of equal protection of the laws in violation of the Fifth Amendment. In a related context, however, the court of appeals for this circuit has cast serious doubt on the validity of such regulations, holding that justifications offered for regulations of this type must be examined to determine whether they are merely "a smokescreen hiding personal antipathies or moral judgments." More recently, in *Doe* v. *Casey*, the court of appeals noted that the question is open in this circuit:

> Although this circuit's decision in *Dronenburg* v. *Zech*, and the Supreme Court's recent decision in *Bowers* v. *Hardwick*, hold that homosexual *conduct* is not constitutionally protected, they did not reach the difficult issue of whether an agency of the federal government can discriminate against individuals merely because of sexual *orientation*.

On their motion, defendants ask this court to uphold the constitutionality of their regulations as a matter of law. They offer no proof, expert or otherwise, to support the rationality of their regulations. Their motion must fail.

Just ten days ago, in *Pruitt* v. *Cheney*, the Ninth Circuit reversed a district court that followed the path defendants urge this court to follow. *Pruitt*, like this case, involved an equal protection challenge brought by a gay servicemember who was discharged solely on the basis of her homosexuality. The district court in *Pruitt* granted the military's motion to dismiss Pruitt's equal protection claim, holding that as a matter of law there was a rational basis for the regulations and that "its right to discharge homosexual servicepersons is . . . firmly supported in the law."

On appeal, the Ninth Circuit reversed the dismissal and reinstated the complaint, holding that the military could not merely assert that its regulations have a rational basis. Rather, the Circuit Court held that the government "must establish *on the record* that its policy had a rational basis." The court went on to hold that if the government did submit any evidence to support its claim that the regulation has a rational basis, the plaintiff would have an "opportunity to contest that basis."

Pruitt mandates that defendants' motion for judgment on the pleadings or, in the alternative, summary judgment be denied. As in *Pruitt*, defendants here offer no proof to support the rationality of their regulations. Rather, defendants' position is that the "rules requiring plaintiff's separation are valid as a matter of law" and hence that they are not required to show any rational basis for the regulation. *Pruitt* plainly and correctly holds that defendants' motion cannot be granted.

Point 2. DOD Directives 1332.14 and 1332.30 and Their Progeny Should Be Declared Unconstitutional insofar as They Discriminate on the Basis of Sexual Orientation.

As shown above, in the absence of proof, defendants' motion for judgment on the pleadings or, in the alternative, summary judgment may not be granted. Plaintiff submits, however, that on the basis of the proofs submitted on his behalf, the Court should declare Department of Defense Directives 1332.14 and 1332.30 and their progeny to be violative of equal protection insofar as they require the discharge of servicemembers on the basis of homosexual orientation. The D.C. Circuit, in *Doe* v. *Casey*, has held that the constitutionality of regulations that discriminate on the basis of homosexual orientation presents a "difficult question." It is difficult because the regulation penalizes a group "for their status [as homosexuals] rather than their conduct," something that the Eighth Circuit, in *Gay*

Lib v. *University of Missouri* (1977), found to be "constitutionally impermissible."[1]

In deciding the "difficult question" before it, this court must consider and apply the basic principles of equal protection law. The Supreme Court has established a sliding scale of scrutiny that a discriminatory regulation must withstand in order to pass muster under the equal protection clause.

At a minimum, a statutory classification must be "rationally related to a legitimate government purpose" in order to withstand challenge. E.g., *City of Cleburne* v. *Cleburne Living Center, Inc.* (1985). Where the classification involves a "suspect class," however, the regulations can be upheld only if they "'are *necessary* to promote a *compelling* governmental interest.'" *Dunn* v. *Blumstein* (1972), *quoting Shapiro* v. *Thompson* (1969). In applying this test, a court must consider whether a less restrictive alternative is available to promote the compelling governmental interest.

An intermediate level of scrutiny is applied where a "quasi-suspect class" is involved. Under that standard, the government must show that the challenged classification is "substantially related to a legitimate state interest."

As shown in Point 2.A below, homosexuals as defined by their orientation constitute a suspect or quasi-suspect class. Accordingly, the Academy and DOD regulations that require the discharge of gay individuals solely on the basis of their status cannot withstand the strict scrutiny that is constitutionally mandated. Even if this court were to find that gay people do not comprise a suspect or quasi-suspect class, plaintiff submits that the challenged regulations must fail. Defendants cannot defend the regulations by claiming that they are necessary to cater to private prejudice in order to preserve discipline, good order and morale. See Points 2.B and 2.C below. Finally, as shown in Point 2.D below, there is no basis for this court to defer to military regulations of the sort at issue here.

A. Homosexuals Constitute a Suspect or Quasi-suspect Class.

The notion that courts should not defer to the political branches when certain groups of people are disadvantaged by the government was first expressed in *United States* v. *Carolene Products Co.* In its seminal footnote, the Supreme Court suggested that "prejudice against discrete and insular minorities may be a special condition,

which tends seriously to curtail the operation of those political processes ordinarily to be relied upon to protect minorities, and . . . may
call for a correspondingly more searching judicial inquiry."

The central idea of the *Carolene Products* footnote and its progeny
is that government may not disadvantage some minorities simply
because they are unpopular and that, when this happens, the political process has broken down and more rigorous judicial scrutiny is
therefore appropriate. In developing a method for identifying those
situations in which courts ought to be suspicious that government
activities might be based on prejudice and not be the result of the
normal functioning of the political process, the Supreme Court has
identified five factors that alone or in combination demonstrate a
group's character as a "discrete and insular minority," and thus trig-
ger "heightened" judicial scrutiny of the classification:

—Whether the group has suffered a history of purposeful discrimination.
—Whether the disadvantaged class is defined by a trait that "frequently
bears no relation to ability to perform or contribute to society."
—Whether the trait defining the class is "immutable."
—Whether the group has been saddled with unique disabilities because of
prejudice or inaccurate or absurd stereotypes.
—Whether the group burdened by discrimination lacks the political
power necessary to obtain redress through the political process.

There is no way to analyze the equal protection issue using the
guidelines established by the Supreme Court and reach any conclusion other than that discrimination based on sexual orientation is
inherently suspect. Indeed, courts are increasingly recognizing that
laws that burden homosexuals as a class should be subjected to
some form of heightened scrutiny. See *Watkins* v. *United States Army*
(Judge Norris's concurrence); *Jantz* v. *Muci* (1991); *Seebol* v. *Farie*
(1991). "Only by abandoning the established tests of suspectness,
and retreating to some other formulation is it possible to achieve
some other result." *Jantz.*

1. Gays Have Suffered a History of Purposeful Discrimination.

Lesbians and gay men "have historically been subjected to discrimination both pervasive in its scope and intense in its impact." *Jantz,*
citing *Rowland* v. *Mad River Local School Dist.* (1985) (Justice Brennan, dissenting from denial of certiorari) ("homosexuals have historically been the object of pernicious and sustained hostility"). Gay

persons suffer discrimination in jobs, housing, and custody of children, and "are forced to deny or disguise their identity in order to enjoy rights and benefits routinely accorded heterosexuals." The prejudice to which gays have been subjected is also revealed by the fact that gays, like blacks and Jews, are often the subject of bias-related violence. See Affidavit of Sherrill, par. 59–66.

2. Homosexual Orientation Bears No Relationship to an Individual's Ability to Perform or Contribute to Society.

It is simply not disputable that homosexual orientation bears no relation to an individual's ability to perform or contribute to society. Joseph Steffan's exemplary record attests to that. So does the record of gays who have achieved prominence in every field of human endeavor, from the arts and literature to sports, science, business, and the law.

The scientific literature bears out this obvious conclusion. As discussed in detail in the accompanying declaration of Dr. Gregory Herek, a recognized expert in social psychology, experts long ago abandoned the notion that homosexuality is an illness or that it is associated with psychopathology. See Affidavit of Herek, par. 35–49. As Dr. Herek points out, the accepted view of psychiatric experts is that "'[h]omosexuality in and of itself is unrelated to psychological disturbance or maladjustment.'" Ibid., par. 38. Indeed, a study that defendants sought to conceal in discovery establishes that homosexuals as a group are better adjusted than heterosexuals. See M. McDaniel, "Preservice Adjustment of Homosexual and Heterosexual Military Accessions: Implications for Security Clearance Suitability" (PERSEREC 1989).

Confronted with the overwhelming empirical evidence refuting the linkage of homosexuality with psychopathology, psychiatrists and psychologists have radically altered their views of homosexuality. In 1973, the American Psychiatric Association removed "homosexuality" as a diagnosis from the third edition of the *Diagnostic and Statistical Manual of Mental Disorders* (*DSM*-III), replacing it with the more restrictive "ego-dystonic homosexuality." In 1986, even the ego-dystonic homosexuality diagnosis was eliminated; consequently, the 1987 *DSM*-III contains no diagnostic category for homosexuality. The American Psychological Association endorsed the psychiatrists' actions and has worked intensively to eradicate the stigma historically associated with a homosexual orientation. American Psychological Association, *Policy Statements on Lesbian and Gay Issues* (1975, 1987). See Affidavit of Herek, par. 26, 40.

3. Homosexual Orientation Is an "Immutable Characteristic."

All available scientific evidence also confirms that homosexual orientation is an "immutable characteristic." The affidavit of Dr. Richard Green, a nationally recognized expert on the etiology of human sexual orientation, is conclusive on this point. In his affidavit, Dr. Green reviews studies that consider genetic influences, hormonal influences, brain differences, and childhood development. He concludes from this evidence that "sexual orientation is largely determined by genetic, neurological, hormonal, and environmental factors prior to birth," that "homosexual orientation is not consciously chosen but rather . . . [is] a basic part of an individual's psyche" and that "sexual orientation is set by early childhood." See Affidavit I of Green, par. 3, 87.[2]

In his declaration, Dr. Green also reviews clinical studies of attempts to "reorient" homosexuals into heterosexuals. He concludes that these efforts have "yielded exceedingly poor results." Ibid., par. 3. The American Psychological Association's "Fact Sheet on Reparative Therapy" similarly concludes that "[n]o scientific evidence exists to support the effectiveness of any of the conversion therapies that try to change sexual orientation." Ibid., par. 81.

Judge Norris, in his *Watkins* concurrence, addressed this issue succinctly:

> Although the causes of homosexuality are not fully understood, scientific research indicates that we have little control over our sexual orientation and that, once acquired, our sexual orientation is largely impervious to change. Scientific proof aside, it seems appropriate to ask whether heterosexuals feel capable of changing *their* sexual orientation. Would heterosexuals living in a city that passed an ordinance burdening those who engaged in or desired to engage in sex with persons of the *opposite* sex find it easy not only to abstain from heterosexual activity but also to shift the object of their sexual desires to persons of the same sex? It may be that some heterosexuals and homosexuals can change their sexual orientation through extensive therapy, neurosurgery or shock treatment. But the possibility of such a difficult and traumatic change does not make sexual ori-

entation "mutable" for equal protection purposes. To express the same idea under the alternative formulation, I conclude that allowing the government to penalize the failure to change such a central aspect of individual and group identity would be abhorrent to the values animating the constitutional ideal of equal protection of the laws.

4. Gays Have Been Saddled with Unique Disabilities because of Prejudice and Inaccurate or Absurd Stereotypes.

There can be no question that homosexuals have been saddled with unique disabilities because of prejudice and inaccurate stereotypes. Homosexuals have been portrayed as sick hypersexuals who will use their positions to sexually exploit and harass their subordinates and engage in open and offensive sexual conduct. All of these stereotypes are belied by fact. Most significantly, as Dr. Herek discusses, these same stereotypes have historically been applied to validate prejudice against other disfavored minority groups. See Affidavit of Herek, par. 20–25. Homosexuals, like Jews before them, have been labeled as threats to children, again, without any basis in fact. Ibid., par. 24.

As Dr. Herek explains in his affidavit, social psychologists agree that prejudice against gays can be understood by the same social scientific theories and measured by the same methodologies as prejudices against other minority groups. So, for example, anti-gay attitudes are more likely to be held by individuals who are older and less educated, who reside in the midwestern and southern United States, and who have had little or no contact with gay men or lesbians. See Affidavit of Herek, par. 8, 9. Anti-gay attitudes are also more likely to be held by individuals who have a general intolerance for stigmatized groups and are correlated with racism. Ibid., par. 11. And anti-gay bias can be changed with the same types of strategies that have been effective in combatting prejudice against women, blacks, Jews, and other minority groups. Ibid., par. 33–34.

Defendants will no doubt argue that opprobrium against individuals on the basis of homosexual orientation is not invidious prejudice but, rather, the enforcement of moral norms. Any such contention cannot withstand scrutiny, however. As shown in the accompanying affidavit of John E. Boswell, A. Whitney Griswold Professor of History and Chairman of the History Department of Yale University, no religious or moral teachings endorse discrimination on the basis of homosexual orientation or stigmatize an individual on that basis. To the contrary, to the extent that any judgment is made at all, Western moral traditions uniformly focus on conduct, not status. And as Judge Norris observed in his *Watkins* concurrence, "homosexual orientation itself has never been criminalized in this country." Nor could it be.[3]

5. Gays as a Group Are Relatively Politically Powerless.

Relative political powerlessness, the last element, is aimed at finding evidence that prejudice has resulted in keeping the group out of full participation in the political process. Courts typically look at two factors to find evidence of political powerlessness: (1) the extent to which the group in question appears to have been successful in protecting its interests through the political process; and (2) the extent to which the group is represented in the nation's policy-making bodies. In both areas, the evidence that lesbians and gay men are relatively powerless is incontrovertible.

First, the gay community is certainly a "discrete and insular minority," with limited power to effect political change. "Because of the immediate and severe opprobrium often manifested against homosexuals once so identified publicly, members of this group are particularly powerless to pursue their rights openly in the political arena." *Rowland* (Justice Brennan dissenting from denial of certiorari). Indeed, lobbyists and litigants who advocate equal treatment of gay and lesbian persons have enjoyed little success: only a handful of states and a sprinkling of municipalities protect gay persons from discrimination.

Not only have lesbians and gay men been unable to secure their interests in the political process, but not surprisingly, they are woefully underrepresented there as well. The Supreme Court in *Frontiero* held that women are relatively politically powerless despite being a technical majority of the electorate because they "are vastly underrepresented in this Nation's decisionmaking councils." The Court based its conclusion on the fact that there had never been a woman president; that there had not yet been a woman on the Supreme Court; and that there was not then a woman in the United States Senate (although there had been women in the Senate in the past); and that there were but fourteen women in the House of Representatives.

If women were underrepresented in 1973, lesbians and gay men are virtually unrepresented in 1991. There has never been an openly gay president. There have been no open lesbians or gay men on the Supreme Court or, indeed, on any federal court. There are no openly gay United States senators, and there never have been any. There are currently two openly gay members of the United States House of Representatives, Congressmen Gerry Studds and Barney Frank, both of Massachusetts. There were no openly gay members of Congress before 1984 and both Congressman Studds and Congressman Frank made their sexual orientation public only after being elected. These figures are repeated on the state level as well.

Moreover, as Judge Norris describes in his *Watkins* concurrence, the prejudice that gays and lesbians suffer itself creates a "structural barrier" that "make[s] effective political participation unlikely if not impossible." Thus:

> First, the social, economic, and political pressures to conceal one's homosexuality operate to discourage gays from openly protesting anti-homosexual governmental action. Ironically, by "coming out of the closet" to protest against discriminatory legislation and practices, homosexuals expose themselves to the very discrimination they seek to eliminate. As a result, the voices of many homosexuals are not even heard, let alone counted. . . .
>
> Even when gays do come out of the closet to participate openly in politics, the general animus towards homosexuality may render this participation ineffective. Many heterosexuals, including elected officials, find it difficult to empathize with and take seriously the arguments advanced by homosexuals, in large part because of the lack of meaningful interaction between the heterosexual majority and the homosexual minority. Most people have little exposure to gays, both because they rarely encounter gays and because—as I noted above—homosexuals are often pressured into concealing their sexual identity. Thus, elected officials sensitive to public prejudice and ignorance, and insensitive to the needs of the homosexual constituency, may refuse to even consider legislation that even appears to be pro-homosexual. Indeed, the Army itself argues that its regulations are justified by the need to "maintain the public acceptability of military service," because "toleration of homosexual conduct . . . might be understood as tacit approval" and "the existence of homosexual units might well be a source of ridicule and notoriety." These barriers to the exercise of political power both reinforce and are reinforced by the underrepresentation of avowed homosexuals in the decisionmaking bodies of government and the inability of homosexuals to prevent legislation hostile to their group interests.

Judge Norris's commonsense conclusions are fully supported by the expert testimony of Kenneth S. Sherrill in this case. As Professor Sherrill explains, political scientists typically examine a number of factors in assessing the political power of and political resources available to any particular group, including numerosity, deference, affection, group identity and cohesion, safety, and access to allies. Gays as a group come up short on *every single one* of these relevant measures. See Affidavit of Sherrill, par. 16–24, 102.

Gays are not only a small minority, but the influence that their limited numbers could wield is substantially diminished by the fact that only a small percentage of gays will publicly identify themselves as such because of the stigma that certain segments of society attach to homosexual orientation. Ibid., par. 26–30. This same opprobrium diminishes group cohesion and identity and makes it difficult for gays and lesbians to obtain the political allies necessary to overcome their overwhelming numerical disadvantages. Ibid., par. 81–100. In political science terms, all of these factors contribute to a "spiral of silence" that further diminishes the potential political influence of gays. Ibid., par. 31–34.

Moreover, as Professor Sherrill details—and, indeed, as defendants themselves have contended in defending the policy banning gays—while there is some support for civil rights for gays, "Americans do not like homosexuals and do not feel close to homosexuals." Ibid., par. 39, 51. The data show that "Americans were more than five times as likely to have negative feelings toward gay people . . . than toward black people" and that gays are far more unpopular than other disfavored groups such as Palestinians and illegal aliens. Ibid., par. 46–49. Slurs against gays are endemic in the media. As Professor Sherrill concludes, "The success of entertainers, athletes, and politicians who spew hatred of gay people is testimony to the breadth and depth of anti-gay sentiment in the American public." Ibid., par. 55.

Professor Sherrill also discusses the fact that bias-related violence against gays tends to disempower homosexuals as a group:

> [G]roups of powerless people are often targeted for violence because they are not respected and because members of a dominant group wish to keep them in subservient positions in society. Racial lynchings in the United States, concentration camps and systematic murder of Jews, homosexuals, and gypsies in Nazi Germany, and other holocausts are classic examples of [the] nexus among safety, deference, and power. Thus, a lynching is more than the murder of an individual person; it is a threat to

an entire group of people. It is an act of terrorism, designed to strike fear into the hearts of members of the group in the expectation that it will motivate compliant behavior (i.e., powerlessness) and paralyze the instincts to seek to achieve one's own goals and preferences (i.e., bring about powerlessness).

In the United States today gay people as a group are subject to a constant threat, and the all too frequent reality, of violence. This factor tends to diminish the relative political power of homosexuals both because it creates disincentives for gay people to identify themselves as such and because it creates disincentives for members of other groups to associate themselves with gays. [Affidavit of Sherrill, par. 59–60].

Upon reviewing these facts, Professor Sherrill comes to the conclusion that gays and lesbians are precisely the type of "'politically powerless' minority" that the Supreme Court identified in *Carolene Products*. On this record, this Court can come to no other conclusion.

In sum, the factors that argue in favor of heightened judicial scrutiny of particular legislative classifications are all present in this case. It is not surprising, then, that classifications drawn to discriminate against gay persons have been held to require either the strictest judicial scrutiny or an intermediate level of judicial scrutiny. Such scrutiny requires that the state justify a classification that burdens gay persons by showing that the classification bears at least a substantial relationship to an important governmental interest.

B. EVEN IF A HEIGHTENED STANDARD IS NOT APPLIED, THE
   CONSTITUTION PRECLUDES THE GOVERNMENT FROM
   DISCRIMINATING AGAINST ONE GROUP IN ORDER TO CATER TO
   THE PRIVATE PREJUDICES OF ANOTHER.

Even if heightened judicial scrutiny is not invoked, the courts must "reach and determine" whether the classifications drawn are "reasonable" in light of the asserted purposes of the laws. In order to withstand judicial scrutiny under this "rational basis" standard of review, a legal classification must at least be "rationally related to a legitimate state interest." *City of Cleburne*. See also *Pruitt* v. *Cheney* (Army must show that the "reasons put forth on the record for the Army's discrimination . . . are rationally related to any of the Army's permissible goals").

The rational basis equal protection test "'is not a toothless one.'" *Mathews* v. *de Castro* (1976). In a number of cases applying the rational basis test, both the Supreme Court and district courts in this circuit have struck down challenged legal classifications, finding that the state's asserted interests were not legitimate, or not rationally related to the classification, or both.

From these cases emerge a number of important principles underlying the rational basis standard of review. First, it is well settled that the mere desire to discriminate against a particular class of persons is not a legitimate governmental objective. "[I]f the constitutional conception of 'equal protection of the laws' means anything, it must at the very least mean that a bare . . . desire to harm a politically unpopular group cannot constitute a *legitimate* governmental interest." *United States Dep't of Agriculture* v. *Moreno* (1973). "The State must do more than justify its classification with a concise expression of an intention to discriminate." *Plyler* v. *Doe* (1982).

Nor can the government justify unequal treatment of different groups of people merely on the basis of the negative attitudes and prejudices of others in society. In *City of Cleburne*, the Supreme Court applied the rational basis test to hold that a city could not require a special use permit for a home for the mentally retarded. In doing so, the Court carefully scrutinized and rejected the city's claim that it needed to regulate the size, location, and population density of homes for the mentally retarded, reasoning that the same state concerns would apply equally to many other kinds of facilities, such as nursing homes, all of which were not subject to the ordinance.

Most important for purposes presented here, the Court also rejected the city's argument that requiring a special use permit was justified by the "negative attitudes" and fears of local property owners and elderly residents because this did not serve a *legitimate* state interest. The Court concluded: "'Private biases may be outside the reach of the law, but the law cannot, directly or indirectly, give them effect.'" It went on to hold that "requiring the permit in this case appears to us to rest on an irrational prejudice against the mentally retarded."

Chief Justice Burger in *Palmore* v. *Sidoti* was equally clear on this subject. He acknowledged "the reality of private biases and the possible injury they might inflict." He concluded that however real those potential injuries may be, the Constitution does not permit the state to dignify them. In *Pruitt* v. *Cheney*, the Ninth Circuit held that this principle of *Cleburne* and *Palmore* was directly applicable to an equal protection challenge to military regulations that discriminate on the basis of homosexual orientation and that the military could *not* blithely rely on the "prejudice of others against homosexuals" to defend the rationality of those regulations.

In a related vein, the Supreme Court has also rejected attempts to justify discrimination on the basis of "archaic and overbroad" assumptions that rest on "old notions" and stereotypes. See, e.g., *Califano* v. *Goldfarb* (1977); *Heckler* v. *Mathews* (1984). So, for example, in *Frontiero* v. *Richardson*, the Supreme Court invalidated a military compensation scheme that relied on the outdated stereotype of males being "breadwinners" and females being "homemaker dependents." Following these authorities, the Second Circuit in *Crawford* v. *Cushman* (1976) held that a Marine Corps regulation that required the discharge of female servicemembers who become pregnant was violative of equal protection. See also *Owens* v. *Brown* (1978) (invalidating statute that precluded women from serving on Navy vessels because its purpose "was more related to the traditional way of thinking about women than to the demands of military preparedness").

Perhaps the most significant principle to emerge from rational basis precedents is that the courts must in all cases engage in a genuine inquiry into the relevance of a legal classification to the asserted purposes of the laws. The Ninth Circuit in *Pruitt*, citing *Cleburne*, called this an "active rational basis review" in which a court must probe the validity of the justifications offered in defense of "rigid discrimination against" the disfavored group. Thus, the Supreme Court has invalidated classifications under the rational basis test only after engaging in careful analysis of the logical relationship between the challenged classification and the asserted governmental objectives. In other words, the Constitution does not permit the judiciary, in the guise of giving deference to military expertise, to abdicate to "judgments" based on no firmer foundation than irrational prejudice.

C. The Military's Discrimination on the Basis of Homosexual Orientation Unlawfully Caters to Private Biases and Irrationally Concludes That Gays Are Security Risks.

The D.C. Circuit observed over twenty years ago, in *Norton* v. *Macy* (1969), that courts examining regulations discriminating against homosexuals must look behind the stated rationale of such policies to determine whether they are serving as "a smokescreen hiding personal antipathies or moral judgments." An examination of the defendants' own justification for their ban on gays shows, however, that there is little if any pretense as to the basis for its regulations. Defendants themselves have argued that discrimination on the basis of homosexual orientation is justified because "heterosexual soldiers despise and detest homosexuality." With the exception of national security, the same "reasoning"—indeed, the same words—used to justify discrimination against blacks is used to justify discrimination on the basis of sexual orientation. And the national security argument itself is an "old chestnut" that even defendant Cheney himself admits is no longer valid (if it ever was).

The stated rationale for the military's discrimination on the basis of homosexual orientation is set out in DOD Directives 1332.14 and 1332.30. The regulations provide:

> Homosexuality is incompatible with military service. The presence in the military environment of persons who engage in homosexual conduct or who, by their statements, demonstrate a propensity to engage in homosexual conduct, seriously impairs the accomplishment of the military mission. The presence of such members adversely affects the ability of the Military Services to maintain discipline, good order, and morale; to foster mutual trust and confidence among servicemembers; to ensure the integrity of the system of rank and command; to facilitate assignment and worldwide deployment of servicemembers who frequently must live and work under close conditions affording minimal privacy; to recruit and retain members of the Military Services; to maintain the public acceptability of military service; and to prevent breaches of security.

Before discussing each of the particular rationales offered by the defendants, it is worth considering the validity of the blanket assertion that "homosexuality is incompatible with military service." Defendant Cheney himself has admitted that "many gays" are currently serving in the military. Defendant Cheney's admission comports with the findings of every researcher who has studied the issue. Those studies have uniformly concluded that gays serve in the military in numbers proportional to their representation in society at large and that the overwhelming majority of homosexuals who serve in the military do so without incident and are honorably discharged at the normal conclusion of their service. Affidavit of Rankin, par. 9–13. A 1988 study sponsored by the military itself reached the same conclusion.

Indeed, as Dr. Rankin (a retired navy captain) explains in his declaration, "[T]he likelihood that a servicemember will be discharged is a direct function of the attitudes of the servicemember's commanding officer—the individual who has the authority and responsibility to initiate discharge proceedings under military regulations. Most officers do not concern themselves at all with the sexual orientation of their subordinates and do so only if it creates a problem within their chain of command. In my experience, high achievers whose homosexual orientation became known were usually protected by their commanding officers." Ibid., par. 5. Indeed, in 1977, the air force admitted that it "does not have an active program to identify and discharge homosexuals." *Matlovich* v. *Secretary of the Air Force* (1978). Presumably, that remains true today for the Air Force and other branches of the armed forces.

The notion that "homosexuality is incompatible with military service" is also belied by the experience of any number of our allies—including France, Israel, Spain, Sweden, the Netherlands, Denmark, Finland, Norway, and Japan—which permit gays to serve in their armed forces. Affidavit of Dyer. The fact that these allies permit gays to serve in their armed forces means that American servicemembers have served and are serving with gay servicemembers in the Persian Gulf and elsewhere with no apparent deleterious effect.

Perhaps the ultimate irony is that in periods of national crisis, the military itself has altered or suspended its policies concerning gays. During World War II, selective service boards and commanding officers took widely varying approaches to the level of enforcement of the then existing policies with respect to the service of gays and lesbians in order to accommodate the need for the military to obtain sufficient troop levels. The same thing happened during the Vietnam buildup. Most recently, in connection with the Persian Gulf buildup, the military implemented standing orders concerning the callup of reserves that suspended the authority of commanding officers to initiate discharge proceedings against gay reservists.

1. "Discipline, Good Order, and Morale" and "Mutual Trust and Confidence"

The military currently explains that excluding gays is necessary to preserve "discipline, good order, and morale" and "to foster mutual trust and confidence among servicemembers." Defendants themselves have explained that homosexuals pose a threat to morale, discipline, and mutual trust because of the "'tensions'" that will result "'between known homosexuals and other [service]members . . . who despise/detest homosexuality.'"

In 1941, the Navy offered the same rationale for excluding blacks:

> The close and intimate conditions of life aboard ship, the necessity for the highest possible degree of unity and espirit-de-corps; the requirement of morale—all these demand that nothing be done which may adversely affect the situation. Past experience has shown irrefutably that the enlistment of Negroes (other than for mess attendants) leads to disruptive and undermining conditions.

Thus, it is simply not open to debate that promoting "good order and morale" and "mutual trust and confidence" are mere euphemisms for avoiding the perceived difficulties that may arise when bigotry prevails over reason. Compare "Rationale for Exclusion of Homosexuals from Military Service" (Sept. 29, 1980) ("The inclusion into units of a group [homosexuals] whose behavior is viewed as distasteful, deviant and improper by the majority of unit members would frustrate the formation of unit cohesiveness and fragment the unit"), and "Hearings Before the General Board of the Navy" (Jan. 23, 1942) ("an infantry battalion is the very last place [Negroes] would be put. There is no branch of the service that requires more character and a higher degree of morale than the infantry").

2. The "Integrity of Command"

Next, the military claims that excluding gays is necessary "to ensure the integrity of the system of rank and command." Homosexuals supposedly pose a threat to the integrity of command because heterosexual servicemembers will not follow orders from homosexual superiors. "Known homosexuals would also compromise effective command were they permitted to serve and advance in rank to occupy leadership positions. Homosexual leaders are unlikely to command necessary respect and obedience from subordinates."

These same justifications were offered (earnestly, if erroneously) in 1942 hearings in support of the exclusion of blacks from the Navy:

> 16. The Navy system of advancement is one which, like all democratic customs, permits every man an equal chance. This system of equal opportunity greatly helps maintain the extremely high efficiency and morale now obtained in the Navy.

17. Formerly, when a Negro had successfully passed his tests and had become a petty officer, he usually obtained a position of military authority and increased responsibility.

18. As a result of conditions which actually exist now, *he would find himself unable properly to perform his duty of exercising military authority and control of those under him. Such being the case, discipline, harmony, co-operation, team work, and fighting efficiency would be lowered and morale would disappear.* [Emphasis added.]

3. "Worldwide Deployment" and "Privacy"

The military goes on to claim that excluding gays is necessary "to facilitate assignment and worldwide deployment of servicemembers who frequently must live and work under conditions affording minimal privacy." There are two components to this claim: first, that the prejudices of foreign countries may and should dictate American military personnel policies and, second, that privacy interests require the exclusion of gays. Neither can withstand scrutiny.

As an initial matter, the legal status of gays in many foreign jurisdictions is more favorable than in the United States. That is particularly true with respect to the NATO countries. Under Article 8, Sections 1 and 2 of the European Convention for the Protection of Human Rights and Fundamental Freedoms, *no* member of the European Community may criminalize private homosexual conduct.

In any event, foreign prejudices and legal and moral traditions do not shape military personnel policies in any other respect. If that were the case, Jews and women would be excluded from the military in order to cater to the prejudices and beliefs of the Arab world, as would any soldier who has a "propensity" to drink alcoholic beverages. *Guide for Servicemembers Stationed in Saudi Arabia* (advising female servicemembers stationed in Saudi Arabia to ride in the back of public buses and not to "kiss, touch or show affection toward any man ... in public" and advising Jewish and Christian servicemembers to conceal religious symbols).

Again, there is nothing new in the military citing the prejudices and customs of foreign countries and the need to facilitate worldwide deployment as grounds for justifying discrimination against a disfavored minority. In 1941, the Navy claimed that:

The very nature of the many and diversified duties required of the Marines preclude the enlistment of any but those civilians who can be employed at any place at any time. The Marine Corps has a special task in connection with landing forces in foreign countries and this is generally done on the briefest notice. *There are a number of countries where the landing of Negro Marines would create an extremely difficult situation and would go far to prevent such use of Marines in the future.* [Emphasis added.]

In 1942, the General Board of the Navy conducted hearings on the question and again concluded that the need for worldwide deployability justified the exclusion of blacks:

ADMIRAL SNYDER: . . . When it comes to the Marines, they might consider it to be feasible or possible to have a separate battalion. *Of course, there are a great many places in the world where men of this color could not be used, but on the other hand, there are other places where they could be used, as in the West Indies waters.* I am just suggesting these things to help you in your thoughts when you give us information and ideas of your own. . . .

GENERAL HOLCOMB: . . . *Admiral Snyder referred to one possibility of using negro troops in the West Indies.* I know that was just a thought that came into his mind and wasn't intended to be taken too literally. But in answer to that *I would like to say that that is definitely one place where negroes could not be used, as we who have served a long time among those people know. They simply will not have negroes there.* If you want to sabotage the good-will program, that is the way to do it. Down among the Latins so many of them are white men only by their own rules. [Emphasis added.]

Defendants' resort to privacy concerns similarly rings of prejudice. These same privacy concerns justified excluding blacks from "white only" toilets and from "white only" military units. Hearings before the General Board of the Navy, 1942 ("The close and intimate conditions of life aboard ship" precludes blacks from serving in the Navy; blacks should not be admitted to the Marine Corps because it would require that "[s]eparate housing must be provided").

The military's concern over privacy rests on the "archaic" stereotype that homosexuals are hypersexuals who are incapable of controlling their sexual urges and who will exploit their positions of authority to sexually harass their subordinates. Affidavit of Herek, par. 21–24. A July 1990 Navy administrative message from the commander of the Atlantic Naval Surface Fleet expressly adopts this stereotype, positing that "young, often vulnerable, female sailors" will be subjected to "subtle coercion or outright sexual advances by more senior and aggressive female sailors."

There is nothing new in military "experts" resting their "judgments" on erroneous stereotypes. In 1942 hearings on integrating the Navy, Admiral Charles Philip Snyder, a member of the General Board of the Navy who went on to become Naval Inspector General, identified one branch in which blacks *might* be permitted to serve: "It has been suggested that possibly we might open up the musician branch. The colored race is very musical and they are versed in all forms of rhythm. Possibly that would be an avenue."[4]

Like the stereotype that blacks are "very musical," the stereotype that gays are predators who are incapable of controlling their sexual conduct is without any foundation in fact. To the contrary, Dr. Rankin concludes that gay servicemembers are *more* likely than their heterosexual counterparts to conduct themselves in a professional manner in their interpersonal relationships. Affidavit of Rankin, par. 8. Dr. Herek similarly concludes:

> There is no evidence to support the notion that lesbians and gay men are more likely than heterosexuals to engage in sexual harassment or open sexual activity or that gays are less able to control their sexual impulses than straights. Nor is there any basis to the belief that gays are sexually predatory or that they will try to convert or recruit heterosexuals. To the contrary, because many lesbians and gay men must exercise great discretion in order to protect themselves from the negative consequences of societal stigma, they often find it necessary to be more circumspect than heterosexuals and to have a higher degree of self-control. [Affidavit of Herek, par. 23.]

Moreover, it is simply irrational to exclude gays on the basis of these privacy concerns given the prevalence of women in the service in recent times. The same privacy concerns that purportedly provide a justification for discriminating on the basis of sexual orientation do not prevent men and women from sharing tents in army field exercises or in the Saudi Arabian desert. Nor do they prevent men and women from serving together in missile silos during twenty-four-hour tours of duty or on noncombatant Navy ships. See *Cleburne* (rejecting arguments that concerns that apply equally to many groups can be relied on to justify discrimination against one specific group); *Crawford* v. *Cushman* (1976) (invalidating military discrimination against pregnant servicemembers as "irrational" because it was both "underinclusive," since it permitted the retention of ser-vicemembers temporarily disabled for other reasons, and "patently overinclusive" in excluding *all* pregnant servicemembers because *some* might be disabled by pregnancy).

4. "Recruitment" and the "Public Acceptability of Military Service"

The prospect that permitting gays to serve will make it difficult "to recruit and retain members of the Military Service" and to maintain the "public acceptability of military service" similarly rests on preju-dice. As a threshold matter, the factual premise of defendants' ra-tionale is in error. An April 1991 poll shows that an 81 percent major-ity of adult Americans believe that gays should not be discharged from the military solely on the basis of their sexual orientation and that a 65 percent majority favor admitting homosexuals to the armed services. Most significantly in terms of recruitment, younger adults are more likely to support homosexuals in the armed services than older adults; the better educated are also more supportive of homo-sexuals than those with less than a high school education.

In any event, concerns over "recruitment" and "public acceptabil-ity" are simply code words for catering to bigotry. The defendants' own document, "Rationale for Exclusion of Homosexuals from Mili-tary Service," concedes that these concerns arise "[b]ecause of the prevailing homophobia in society."

> A policy permitting known homosexuals to serve in the Armed Forces would drive away many more potential recruits than it would attract and could necessitate a return to the draft. This is supported by surveys which show that *the vast majority of Americans in general and servicemembers in particular strongly disapprove of homosexuals. . . .* Because of the prevail-ing homophobia in society and because homosexual conduct continues to be criminal in many places, the military would suffer in esteem if known homosexuals were allowed to serve. The impact on the military's public image would also endanger recruitment and retention, causing po-tential servicemembers to hesitate to enlist, parents to recommend or ap-prove of their sons and daughters joining an organization in which they would be forced to live and work close to known homosexuals, and serv-ing members to hesitate to reenlist. [Emphasis added.]

As with defendants' other "justifications," the proof that defen-dants' discrimination on the basis of homosexual orientation derives from private prejudices also comes from the fact that the same resort to society's bigotry informed military discrimination against blacks. Thus, during the 1942 Navy hearings on whether blacks should be admitted at all, the General Board of the Navy was told:

> The parents of these boys have been thoroughly propagandized that they were going to associate with men of their own caliber, and the Recruiting Service has endeavored to raise both the intelligence and physical standards. . . . *The minute the negro is introduced into general service*, and we should not consider anything else because it is going to be forced upon us if we accept anything, *the high type of man that we have been getting for the last twenty years will go elsewhere and we will get the type of man who will lie in bed with a negro. . . .*
>
> In this hour of national crisis, it is much more important that we have the full-hearted cooperation of the thirty million white southern Americans than that we satisfy the National Association for the Advancement of Colored People. I realize that you have never lived in the South. I have lived there all my life. You know that our people have volunteered for military service more readily than the people of any other section of the Nation. *If they be forced to serve with Negroes, they will cease to volunteer; and when drafted, they will not serve with that enthusiasm and high morale that has always characterized the soldiers and sailors of the southern states.* [Emphasis added.]

5. "National Security"

As shown above, virtually every rationale that the military relies on in discriminating on the basis of sexual orientation was relied on in excluding blacks from the Navy and segregating the balance of the armed forces. The sole exception is the military's claim that excluding gays is necessary to preserve national security. This rationale was born in the post–World War II cold war hysteria that fomented a search for Communists, homosexuals, and other "subversives" in the federal government. "Employment of Homosexuals and Other Sex Perverts in Government," Doc. No. 241, Interim Report, Senate Subcommittee of Investigations, 81st Cong., 2d Sess. (1950).

The principal defendant in this action, Secretary of Defense Cheney, has admitted that this justification for the military's policy is an "old chestnut" that has no validity. Indeed, the Navy admitted twelve years ago in *Berg* v. *Claytor* (1977) that its regulations were not and could not be justified on this ground. There is nothing remarkable about these admissions given that no branch of the federal government (apart from the armed services) precludes homosexuals from obtaining security clearances and that the Department of Defense itself permits gays to serve in civilian capacities in even the most senior positions.

Secretary Cheney's admission recognizes that there is no basis for concluding that homosexuals pose a special security risk. Gays as a group are not "unstable" and there has not been a single reported instance in American history in which a homosexual betrayed his country under threat of blackmail. Affidavit of Herek, par. 35–58. The military's own 1989 study concludes that gays as a group are *superior* security risks than heterosexuals.

Indeed, the irony is that the military's policy itself *creates* a security risk by introducing a significant incentive for gays to conceal their orientation and for heterosexuals to conceal any homosexual conduct in which they might have engaged. See ibid., par. 58; *Watkins* (Judge Norris's concurrence) ("The Army's concern about security risks among gays could be addressed in a more sensible and less restrictive manner by adopting a regulation banning only those gays who had lied about or failed to admit their sexual orientation. In that way, the Army would *encourage*, rather than discourage, declarations of homosexuality, thereby reducing the number of closet homosexuals who might indeed pose a security risk").

D. There Is No Basis for This Court to Defer to Military Judgments Designed to Cater to Private Prejudice.

Defendants have already argued and will no doubt continue to argue that this court should defer to their expert military judgment in deciding this case. Deference, however, has little, if any, place here.

The doctrine of deference that defendants rely on has two sources. The first is that the regulation of military matters is, as an initial matter, committed to the Congress. The second is that military officers have unique expertise.

The first consideration has no place here, however. DOD Directives 1332.14 and 1332.30 were not adopted by Congress but, rather, by administrative action. Indeed, no act of Congress regulates homosexuality per se in any context. To the extent that the Congress has legislated in this area, it has criminalized sodomy by military personnel whether committed "with another person of the same or opposite sex." Thus, as Judge Norris notes in his *Watkins* concurrence, "[I]f anything, section 925 reflects an absence of congressional intent to discriminate on the basis of sexual orientation."

Deference to the unique expertise of military officers likewise has no place here for several reasons. First, this case involves an equal protection challenge. In *Rostker*, the Supreme Court noted that "a different equal protection test" does *not* apply simply because a case arises in "the military context." Indeed, one of the seminal decisions of equal protection jurisprudence, *Frontiero* v. *Richardson*, arose in the military context. Nowhere in that decision does the Supreme Court even hint that any special deference was due to judgments made in military matters when equal protection concerns are raised.

The Second Circuit in *Crawford* v. *Cushman* expressly rejected the notion that courts should presume that military judgments are entitled to any presumption of rationality:

> These considerations of judicial restraint are relevant to the decision to review, but once review commences the "intrusion" into military concerns has in a sense already occurred. To allow this reluctance to review to spill over into the decision on the merits is *to presume that the military qua military is endowed with a gift of superior rationality regarding its concededly "valid military concerns."* As the Supreme Court demonstrated in *Schlesinger* v. *Ballard* and *Frontiero* v. *Richardson*, military treatment of personnel in allowing benefits for "dependents" and in discharging officers for failure to achieve promotion is subject to judicial review and to constitutional requirements even though such treatment may equally be a "valid military concern."
>
> In the light of *Levy*, *Ballard*, and *Frontiero* we find there to be no basis for a judicial deference to the military here which precludes review of appellant's substantive constitutional claims. . . . [A]ppellant's claims must be evaluated in relation to the specific military justifications alleged here—the demands of readiness, mobility and administrative convenience—*without unjustified presumptions of validity*. [Emphasis added.]

The principal case that defendants rely upon, *Goldman* v. *Weinberger* (1986), involved a First Amendment claim, and the Supreme Court limited its holding to that context. Indeed, the concurrence in *Goldman* makes clear that the regulation at issue there—which barred servicemembers from wearing headgear that was not in conformity with prescribed uniform—was constitutional *because* it treated all religious garb *alike* and that equal protection and First Amendment issues would be raised if the military permitted Jews to wear yarmulkes but prohibited Sikhs from wearing turbans.

More important, no case that defendants can cite holds that it is permissible for the military to abandon the fundamental principles of our Constitution and discriminate against one group in order to cater to the private prejudices of another. *Palmore* v. *Sidoti* suggests that the contrary is true. In that case, Chief Justice Burger acknowledged "the reality of private biases" and that these biases could inflict "real" injury. Notwithstanding that fact, however, the Court held that "the Constitution does not permit the state to dignify" . . . "private biases." Indeed, the very authorities that defendants rely on also hold that "'our citizens in uniform may not be stripped of basic rights simply because they have doffed their civilian clothes.'" *Chappell* v. *Wallace.*

In sum, the regulations at issue cannot withstand constitutional analysis. Defendants can justify Department of Defense Directives 1332.14 and 1332.30 only by arguing (erroneously) that they promote a goal that the Constitution does not countenance or by clinging to "archaic" and irrational concerns over a nonexistent security threat. Whatever level of scrutiny is applied, the regulations cannot pass muster. Plaintiff is therefore entitled to summary judgment declaring the regulations unconstitutional.

Point 3. The Academy's Refusal to Allow Steffan to Graduate, Even Though It Allows Others Similarly Situated to Do So, Was Unlawful.

Quite apart from the unconstitutionality of DOD Directives 1332.14 and 1332.30, the Academy's refusal to permit Steffan to graduate violates applicable principles of equal protection as well as the standards of the Administrative Procedure Act (APA). As the record demonstrates, when midshipmen are deemed to be uncommissionable during their final year for some reason unrelated to their performance, the Academy regularly permits them to complete their degrees before discharging them. The Academy has applied this policy to midshipmen with a wide range of conditions, both medical and psychological.

Despite Steffan's outstanding record at the Academy, and without any showing that he had engaged in any prohibited conduct, the Academy discharged Steffan immediately, refusing his plea to be allowed to graduate. By refusing Steffan the treatment it accords other uncommissionable midshipmen, the Academy deprived him of the fruits of almost four years of study. It also violated the equal protection component of the Fifth Amendment.

When the government treats one group differently from another group, or distributes benefits unequally among groups, it "establishes a classification subject to scrutiny under the equal protection clause." *Frontiero* v. *Richardson* (1973). Because the Academy can offer no constitutionally permissible justification for imposing upon Steffan a burden not imposed on others similarly situated, its discharge policy cannot stand under any level of equal protection scrutiny. Moreover, because the Academy's action in changing Steffan's grade in Military Performance from "A minus" to "F" and in refusing to permit Steffan to graduate was arbitrary and capricious, it must be held violative of section 706(2)(A) of the APA.

A. THE ACADEMY'S DISCHARGE POLICY CANNOT WITHSTAND HEIGHTENED SCRUTINY.

As shown in Point 2.A, sexual orientation clearly fulfills the requirements for treatment as a suspect or quasi-suspect classification and, consequently, merits at least heightened judicial scrutiny. The Academy's uniquely harsh treatment of certain uncommissionable fourth-year students based solely on their sexual orientation is obviously not "suitably tailored" and necessary to serve a "compelling" governmental interest. Nor is this Academy policy "substantially related" to an "important governmental objective" as it must to withstand heightened scrutiny in cases involving quasi-suspect classes.

The Academy simply cannot point to a strong military or academic interest in dismissing students like Steffan without allowing them to continue the few weeks or months until graduation. There are clearly less restrictive alternatives to the Academy's policy, such as evaluating each commissionable student's ability to remain at the Academy based on his or her own prior record.

B. THE ACADEMY'S DISCHARGE POLICY IS NOT RATIONALLY RELATED TO A LEGITIMATE GOVERNMENT PURPOSE.

Even if the court were to conclude that individuals with a homosexual orientation do not constitute a suspect or quasi-suspect class, defendants' refusal to permit Steffan to graduate must still be held to be unconstitutional. As shown above, in this circumstance defendants would have to show "on the record" that their regulations are "rationally related to a legitimate government purpose."

Equal protection requires that "all persons similarly circumstanced shall be treated alike." *Plyler* v. *Doe*. Accordingly, when a burdened group and an unburdened group are similarly situated in relation to the purposes of a statute or regulation, discrimination among them is not permitted.

In this case, the Academy drew a sharp distinction between two groups: fourth-year midshipmen who are determined to be uncommissionable due to poor health or other reasons beyond their control and unrelated to their conduct and those deemed uncommissionable solely because, like Steffan, they admit that they are of homosexual orientation. These classes are similarly situated for all relevant purposes. Both would have been refused admission to the Academy if their conditions had been known at the time; both became ineligible for active duty while in attendance at the Academy through no fault of their own; and both invested more than three years of hard work toward the completion of their degrees. Concededly, the Academy could deny *all* midshipmen the opportunity to graduate. But having decided generally to permit uncommissionable midshipmen to graduate, it cannot deny this opportunity to one group without a valid reason.

In order to justify its policy of discrimination, the Academy must establish that Steffan is different in some way relevant to the purposes of the discharge and temporary retention policies in question. However, the only differences that defendants can point to are factually erroneous and constitutionally infirm.

The Academy will likely try to justify its singling out of gays on the familiar grounds that their immediate discharge is necessary to preserve order, discipline, and morale. Even if the argument can be accepted as a matter of law, it cannot be accepted as a matter of fact. When military officers choose to enforce the ban on gays—which they often do not of their own accord—they exercise broad discretion in the timing of the initiation of proceedings. Affidavit of Rankin, par. 5. Once initiated, it is *impossible* for the discharge proceedings of a Navy, Army, or Air Force officer to be concluded in one week, as was the case here. Rather, the Navy itself has a "goal" of discharging an officer on the basis of homosexuality within four months from the date that the officer is notified of the commencement of proceedings.

Given the relatively leisurely time frame that the Navy itself imposes for the initiation and conclusion of discharge proceedings against gay officers, it simply cannot be argued that the good order, discipline, and morale of the Academy would have been jeopardized by permitting Steffan to complete his studies. Simply put, the fact that the Navy permits gay officers to remain in service for four months or longer once discharge proceedings are initiated puts the lie to any claim that there was a rational basis for concluding that Steffan had to be separated from the Academy in the space of one week and could not be permitted to graduate.

C. The Academy's Refusal to Permit Steffan to Complete His Degree Was Arbitrary and Capricious.

The Academy's refusal to defer Steffan's discharge until after his graduation is unlawful on the additional ground that it violates the constraints placed on federal agency action by the provisions of the APA, 5 U.S.C. §§ 701 *et seq*. The Academy's unexplained refusal to permit Steffan to graduate before being discharged was "arbitrary and capricious" and an "abuse of discretion" within the meaning of 5 U.S.C. § 706(2)(A).

The APA's "arbitrary and capricious" standard requires courts to conduct a "thorough, probing, in-depth review" of the challenged agency action. *Citizens to Preserve Overton Park, Inc. v. Volpe* (1971). Under arbitrary and capricious review, courts inquire into whether there is a "rational connection between the facts found and the choice made" by the agency, and whether there exists in the record a "rational basis" for the agency's action. In order to allow the reviewing court to assess action in question, the agency must supply a "reasoned explanation" of its action. Furthermore, when an agency is "departing from prior norms," it is "incumbent on the agency carefully to spell out the bases of its decision."

The Academy did not have a rational basis for its refusal to permit Steffan to graduate. Its own policy of letting other noncommissionable students remain enrolled until graduation underscores the need for the Academy to explain why it required that Steffan be immediately discharged. That is particularly true given that Navy regulations permit commissioned officers who are to be discharged on grounds of homosexuality to remain in service for four months or more pending disposition of their cases. The peculiarly arbitrary and capricious nature of defendants' actions is demonstrated by the fact that the Brigade Military Performance Board voted to change Steffan's Military Performance grade from "A minus" to "F" solely on the basis of Steffan's admission and without any indication that Steffan's exemplary military performance had changed in any respect.

Even if the Academy has some discretion to determine when discharges will take effect, it has plainly abused its discretion in the case of Joseph Steffan. Defendants' action should therefore be set aside under 5 U.S.C. § 706(2)(A).

John Boswell

On the History of Social Attitudes toward Homosexuality from Ancient Greece to the Present

JOHN BOSWELL, chairman of the Department of History at Yale University and a recognized authority on the foundations of Western moral traditions, provides the initial argument for the plaintiff. Boswell points out that no society except the present has so clearly segregated and condemned homosexual acts or "orientation." Using his own original research and writings, he places this modern treatment of homosexuality in a historical context. Boswell tracks Greek and Roman social and moral treatment of homosexual acts and actors. He follows with a discussion of early Christian response to the behaviors and indicates the differences with modern Christian treatment and morality. Boswell finds wide disparity between ancient and current tolerance and attitudes. He concludes that while certain sexual *practices* have been condemned, no religious or moral code has ever made judgments of an individual on the basis of sexual *orientation*. Boswell's affidavit also addresses the question of whether gay people have suffered a history of purposeful discrimination—the first of the five key questions in deciding whether a group constitutes a suspect class.

1. As discussed in greater detail below, no Western legal or moral tradition—civil or ecclesiastical, European, English, or Anglo-American—has ever attempted to penalize or stigmatize a "homosexual person" apart from the commission of external acts. The terms "sodomy" and "sodomite," the most common rubrics for behavior that would today be called "homosexual," are always and everywhere dependent on the commission of verifiable physical acts. Indeed, until

the very end of the nineteenth century, scientists did not recognize the concept of a "homosexual person." Accordingly, no ancient, medieval, or early modern systems, legal or theological, even used this concept. Given the relatively recent development of the concept of homosexual orientation, it would not have been possible for any of the traditions on which the moral values and public ethos of the United States have been constructed—i.e., either Judeo-Christian ethics or English common law—to penalize what is currently understood as sexual "orientation." Given this moral tradition, it is no surprise then that no twentieth-century religious tradition stigmatizes or makes moral judgments on the basis of homosexual orientation as opposed to conduct and that, to the contrary, a distinction is universally recognized between the two.

The Traditions of Ancient Greece and Rome

2. In the Mediterranean city-states of the ancient world (ca. 400 B.C. to A.D. 400) both public and private "norms" for human conduct were social and behavioral (as opposed, for example, to intentional, psychological, or spiritual), and based on codes of public conduct and behavior anyone could follow, regardless of (what modern writers would call) "sexual orientation." Ideals of human action focused on the fulfillment of social roles and expectations: being a good citizen by serving in the army or civil service or donating resources or labor to the state; being a responsible family member by treating one's spouse properly and caring well for children; being a dutiful child by obeying father and mother, bringing honor to the family through achievement, caring for aged parents; being a faithful friend in joy and sorrow, good fortune and bad. "Sexual identity" had little to do with any of these—including the roles of spouse and parent, since marriage and parenthood were not thought to depend on erotic attachment.

3. Opportunities for sexual expression also tended to obviate questions of orientation. Marriage was a duty for all Roman citizens, in the eyes of the family and the state, but was not generally supposed to fulfill erotic needs. Every male was expected to marry, as were most females, regardless of whether or not conjugal relations afforded an opportunity for erotic satisfaction. In the case of males, extramarital sexuality was normal and accepted; in the case of married females, it was not, but for the latter erotic fulfillment was not a public issue—fair treatment, affection, and respect were the expected rewards of being a good wife and mother.

4. Ethical ideals (as opposed to ordinary behavior) were slightly more complicated and can be distinguished according to three general approaches, depending on whether they emphasized (a) the responsibilities, (b) dangers, or (c) religious significance of human sexuality.

5. The moral views on human sexuality of the "average Greco-Roman" were rarely articulated and are difficult to reconstruct with precision. They seem to have presupposed that sexuality is good or neutral as long as it is responsible—i.e., does not interfere with duties to the state or family, and does not involve the abuse of freeborn children or married women. This loose code is implicit in much of Greek and Roman literature, art, mythology, and law, and it is against it that a second, more ascetic approach urged that sexuality was an inherently dangerous force and should be avoided as much as possible. Some adherents of this view would call their followers to celibacy, some would limit sexual expression to marriage, others to procreative acts within marriage. Although the latter two prescriptions would apply to homosexual and heterosexual acts differentially (since the former would be categorically precluded, while the latter would only be circumscribed), they were not aimed at homosexuality or predicated on any invidious distinction between homosexual or heterosexual. Rather, their objective was primarily to curtail promiscuous or pleasure-centered heterosexual activity. They excluded homosexual acts incidentally or along with activities—such as masturbation—which were not special to any group.

6. A few specific religions attached theological or ceremonial significance to particular aspects of sexuality: traditional Romans idealized the sacrifice of sexual pleasure made by Vestal Virgins, while others embraced mystery cults that incorporated sexual acts into religious observance. Jews had very detailed rules about sexual conduct. Such practices and proscriptions had little impact on popular views: both Jews and Vestal Virgins were considered distinctive precisely because the standards they followed were exceptional. Apart from Judaism, no religion of the ancient world categorically prohibited homosexual relations, although some preached celibacy.

7. There was thus relatively little reason for Romans to confront or pose questions of sexual orientation. Opportunities for erotic ex-

pression were organized around issues of class and age or marital status rather than gender; personal worth was measured in terms of public contributions and family responsibility, neither essentially related to personal erotic interest; private sexual behavior was not an arena of judgment or concern; and even ethical systems did not make the gender of sexual object choice a criterion of moral action.

8. This does not mean that everyone was at liberty to perform any sort of sexual act with anyone of either gender. One's own gender, age, class, and social standing set limitations on the range of acceptable forms of sexual expression for each individual. With a few exceptions, the higher one's social status, the more restrictions would apply to sexual acts, and the fewer to sexual partners. A wealthy and powerful adult male citizen, for example, at the top of the status hierarchy, could penetrate any other person without loss of social status (although a dispute might arise if the other party was the wife or child of another citizen). "What does it matter," Antony wrote to Augustus, "where or in whom you stick it?"* But for the same male to be penetrated—by anyone—would incur disrespect if it were known, and might even subject him to loss of civil privilege. By contrast, although a slave (or even a freed man) would lose no status for performing any particular sexual act, including being penetrated, he might suffer greatly (a slave could forfeit his life) if he had intercourse with anyone other than a partner allowed him by his owner or an adult male citizen.

9. The restrictions on the sexual behavior of adult male citizens were not the result of prejudice against homosexuality: the same man could penetrate as many other men as he wished without incurring any stigma. The code of propriety was related to gender—penetration and power were associated with the prerogatives of the ruling male elite; surrendering to penetration was a symbolic abrogation of power and authority—but in a way that posed a polarity of domination-subjection rather than of homosexual-heterosexual.† It was generally acceptable for a member of a less powerful group to

---

* "An refert, ubi ei in qua arrigas?" Suetonius, *Augustus* 69. *Qua* may be feminine because Antony is thinking primarily of females, but it could also refer to *parte* for parts of the body, male or female.

† "For a man to be penetrated by a richer and older man is good: for it is customary to receive from such men. To be penetrated by a younger and poorer is bad: for it is the custom to give to such persons. It is also bad if the penetrator is older and poorer." Artemidorus Daldianus [A.D. second century], *Onirocriticon libri quinque*, ed. R. Park (Leipzig, 1963), 1.78, pp. 88–89.

submit to penetration by a member of a more powerful one; this was not thought to characterize any defect of personality or to indicate any special psychological constitution or status.

10. The urgent personal question in Augustan Rome was not the gender with which one did "it" but what one did. Martial titillated his audience by speculating on the possibility of "passive" sexual behavior on the part of well-known Roman citizens, and a number of prominent Athenians and Romans were the butt of humor because they had performed an activity inappropriate to their status; conversely, Juvenal composed a long satire on the several inversions of the prevailing ethic involved in a male prostitute's taking the active role with male citizen clients. The issue in all such cases was behavior, not gender preference: no citizen was ridiculed for having recourse to passive partners of either sex, nor were prostitutes or slaves—male or female—mocked for receptivity.

The Early Christian Tradition

11. Beginning around A.D. 400, Christianity began to introduce a new sexual code focused on religious concepts of "holiness" and "purity." The origins and sources of its norms—the New Testament, Alexandrian Judaism, popular taboos, neo-Platonic philosophy, Roman legal principles—are imperfectly understood and too complex to enter into here. For the most part its regulations, like their Greco-Roman predecessors, were conceptually unrelated to sexual "identity" or "orientation."

12. Two general approaches to Christian sexuality can be discerned in the early church, distinct in their relation to "orientation." The earliest, evident in the New Testament, is similar to the "sex is dangerous" approach of pagan ethics: eroticism is a troublesome aspect of a fallen world; Christians should attempt to control it through responsible use. This approach would not, in itself, create distinctions based on gender object choice, because it focuses on the permanence and fidelity of erotic relationships, qualities that could be and were present in both heterosexual and homosexual relationships in the ancient world. Longlasting homosexual unions and even official marriages were known in Greece and Rome, and Christian ceremonies of union for males closely resembling, if not actually constituting, marriage were also common in parts of the Christian world throughout the early Middle Ages; they invoked well-known pairs of saints as models for permanent, erotic, same-sex relationships. Even in areas where such relationships were not recognized, there was through the end of the twelfth century a strong tradition in Christian thought that regarded homosexuality and heterosexuality as two sides of the same coin—either could be put to good or bad use, depending on the extent to which it was directed toward godly or ungodly ends. Any faithful and selfless passion subordinated to God's love, in this tradition, might be holy and sanctifying, just as any selfish lust, homosexual or heterosexual, was sinful.

13. An opposing school of thought held that to be sinless a sexual act must be procreative. Even nonprocreative sexual activity between husband and wife was sinful, since procreative purpose was the sole justification for any sexual act. This idea was almost certainly borrowed from strands of late antique pagan ethics and was at first limited to ascetic Christian writers deeply imbued with Hellenistic philosophy, especially in Alexandria. But it gradually spread throughout the Christian world and became the favored position of ascetics in the West, since it both limited sexuality to the smallest possible arena and appealed to an easily articulated and understood principle. Ultimately it became the standard of Catholic orthodoxy, although hardly inevitably: not for a millennium after it first appeared did it sweep all other approaches before it.

14. By the end of the Middle Ages, although in parts of the Catholic world the "separate but equal" tradition survived, the majority of Catholic churchmen and states had accepted the principle of procreative justification and, as a result, nonprocreative sexual behavior was considered a serious sin everywhere in Western Europe. Most civil law codes included penalties for "unnatural acts," which were, theologically, the discharge of semen in any nonprocreative context: nonprocreative heterosexual activity (i.e., oral or anal), masturbation, homosexual acts involving discharge of semen,* bestiality.† At least from the time of Augustine influential theologians had argued that nonprocreative acts within marriage were even more sinful than those outside because they defiled the marriage bed, which was

---

* It is not at all clear that a scholastic would regard homosexual hugging, kissing, or rubbing body parts as any more sinful than their heterosexual equivalents: doubtless both, as nonprocreative sources of sexual pleasure, would fall under the same mild censure.

† The *locus classicus* for this is Thomas Aquinas, *Summa theologiae* 2a.2ae.154.11–12, but Thomas stands in the middle of a long, relatively consistent tradition.

much worse than defiling a prostitute or brothel, or, presumably, another person of one's own gender. But public legal systems found nonprocreative acts difficult to detect and punish, and civil codes and popular attitudes often reduced the distinction to extramarital versus marital sexuality, or heterosexual versus homosexual acts.

15. This created a kind of dichotomy related to sexual object choice: although much heterosexual activity (even in marriage) and masturbation suffered the same moral sanctions as homosexual acts, only the latter two were categorically prohibited, while forms of the first could be entirely moral. It is essential to note, nonetheless, that whereas this late medieval system placed homosexual activity generically in an inferior category, it did not create a concept of sexual dimorphism in which a homosexual "orientation" or erotic preference was stigmatized as characterizing a special category of person. Those who engaged in forbidden sexual activity—homosexual or heterosexual—were sinners. But *everyone* in Catholic Europe was a sinner. All humans in all times (except Adam and Eve before the fall and the Virgin Mary after) were sinners. The rationale that made homosexual acts morally reprehensible also condemned contraception, masturbation, sexual expression between husband and wife undertaken for reasons of affection or pleasure, divorce, lending at interest, and a host of other common, everyday activities, familiar to (if not practiced by) most Europeans. "Sinner" was a universal, not a special, category, and if the particular vice that included someone in this category was unusual, the category itself was thoroughly familiar to his neighbors.

16. Moreover, being "sinful" was a temporary state, no matter how often or for how long one found oneself in it. Anyone could cease being "sinful" at any moment, through repentance and contrition, ideally but not necessarily solemnized in the sacrament of penance. In this regard the public discourse of Catholic Europe regarding sexual ethics was much like the public ethos of ancient city-states, despite the change from secular to religious justification. Both were predicated on norms of external, modifiable behavior rather than on internal disposition or inclination; and the ethical codes of both either treated homosexuality and heterosexuality as morally indistinguishable or focused on elements of sexual behavior that usually affected all varieties of sexual expression.

17. Not surprisingly given these moral traditions, all European legal structures, from Roman law to French and Spanish adaptations

of it, to Germanic laws, to English common law, evince the same concern for sexual acts as did contemporary theology. Those most influenced by the church's teaching penalized all nonprocreative sexuality under the heading "sodomy" or "unnatural acts," which was either defined as "nonprocreative emission of semen," and thus included masturbation, or as "the use of an improper vessel," and was limited to oral and anal intercourse (heterosexual or homosexual) and bestiality. It is precisely this concept that has been embodied in article 25 of the Uniform Code of Military Justice.[1]

The Modern Tradition

18. In the twentieth century, religious traditions have wrestled with the moral questions posed by homosexuality under multiple headings. Three are particularly prominent: (a) whether the orientation itself—as modern people tend to think of it—could be considered morally wrong; (b) whether homosexual acts are intrinsically evil; and (c) whether "homosexual persons" are suitable candidates for the clergy (Jewish or Christian).

19. As to the first, all official theological statements by organized religious bodies in the second half of the twentieth century have found the orientation itself to be sinless, beginning with a statement by British Quakers in 1956 that homosexuality "is no more to be deplored than left-handedness," and concluding most recently with a Vatican declaration (authored by Joseph Cardinal Ratzinger) that while homosexual acts are morally wrong, the inclination to perform them is at most "disordered"—i.e., as opposed to morally wrong. The word "disordered" has evoked lively controversy in many quarters, theological as well as political, because, as many have noted, the condition so characterized had been accepted by the previous moral tradition as God-given,[2] but no one has argued that this means that "homosexual persons" are generically sinful, a position that would violate basic Christian ethical principles; it is the intention to sin, not the desire to do so, that is the basis of sin and guilt in Christian theology.

20. This is why even the most conservative Christian ethicists continue to maintain the distinction between "sin" and "sinner" in this context. A number of Christian bodies (Quakers, Unitarians, Disciples of Christ) have decided that homosexual acts are in them-

selves neutral and depend for their moral value—like heterosexual acts—on the human context of the actions; while others continue to maintain that homosexual acts are in and of themselves wrong, either because (in their view) they are prohibited by scripture or tradition, or because they fail to meet some ethical test (usually procreative purpose, although this same test is rarely applied to heterosexual behavior, which is why more liberal traditions have rejected this line of argument).

21. Depending on their stand on this point, Jewish and Christian bodies fall into two camps on the question of ordination. Both camps agree that "being homosexual" is not a suitable category of discrimination for candidates for the clergy. The more liberal denominations (Christians as noted above and Reform Jews) allow ordination of openly homosexual persons, as long as their lifestyle accords with the general ethical principles of the group, which usually means limiting sexual expression to a monogamous, nonpromiscuous, and nonexploitative relationship. The more conservative approach allows ordination of homosexuals only if they agree to remain celibate or undertake a heterosexual marriage. Even the most conservative voices have not approved testing for or attempting to ferret out persons whose "orientation" would not pass some psychological test of heterosexuality, because no moral tradition provides grounds for this. All insist, at most, on standards of behavior: the idea that the condition of homosexuality is damaging or dangerous is an outdated medical idea, not a moral one, and cannot be sustained in a moral context.

John Boswell

AFFIDAVIT II

On the Use of the Term "Homo" as a Derogatory Epithet

I N HIS second affidavit, John Boswell responded to the trial judge's repeated use of the term "homo" to indicate the plaintiff. The plaintiff's lawyer immediately moved to have the case assigned to a different judge, arguing that the judge's use of the term "homo" was as an epithet that demonstrated an anti-gay predisposition of the court and seriously jeopardized the plaintiff's right to a fair hearing.

This affidavit traces the development of the term "homo," showing that the term is not classical in origin and is instead a diminutive of a longer modern label with negative connotations. Boswell explains the use of this shortened term by showing its similarity to other diminutive labels used to indicate hostility or as insults.

Further, Boswell uses empirical evidence to illustrate the derogatory nature of the term. Citing media accounts of the judge's language and use of the term, Boswell concludes that there can be no mistake as to the cultural understanding and use of this term. Finally, he effectively uses the defendants' own sources to show that the proffered defense of the term and its use is incomplete.

1. The purpose of this affidavit is to explain the derivation of the word "homo" and to dispel the misconceived notion advanced by the defendants in their memorandum of points and authorities that "homo" is not a derogatory term and that its use does not reflect bias against gays on the part of the speaker. In my opinion, the use of the word "homo" to describe a homosexual male *is* derogatory and evinces a view of homosexuality and homosexual persons influenced by the profound prejudices against them characteristic of English-speaking culture in the twentieth century prior to the 1980s. Indeed, I do not believe that there is any room for debate on the question.

Pre-Nineteenth-Century Usage

2. In Latin, the language of legal and moral institutions in Europe prior to the sixteenth century, there was no word corresponding precisely to "homosexual." *Sodomia* was the general category to which homosexual acts belonged; those who engaged in it were designated *sodomitae*. *Sodomia* was technically any deliberately nonprocreative sexual act and was not therefore invidious or prejudicial in regard to sexual orientation: a man or woman who masturbated alone or a married couple practicing contraception were legally and morally as guilty of *sodomia* as two men or two women who engaged in a sexual act. Moreover, an erotic interaction that did not involve exchange of semen (e.g., kissing) was probably not *sodomia* in the eyes of lawyers (canon or civil). Under modern categories, an erotic interaction between members of the same sex that does not involve the exchange of semen would be a "homosexual" act. (Kissing might constitute a homosexual act in modern terms, though it would not have before the eighteenth century.)

3. Vulgar prejudice and the common languages of Europe, including English, applied the vernacular derivatives of *sodomita* (e.g., *sodomite* in English and French, *sodomita* in Spanish, *sodoma* in Italian) specifically to homosexual males. It was the term most generally used to describe them and very rarely, in everyday speech, to describe the many other actions to which it technically applied. This was clearly the result of popular animus against a suspect minority.

The Derivation of "Homo"

4. In the second half of the nineteenth century, the words "homosexual" and "homosexuality" were coined by Karl Maria Kertbeny, a Hungarian writing in German, and entered the English language chiefly through the psychological and historical studies of Krafft-Ebing and Havelock Ellis.[1] The terms "homosexual" and "homosexuality" rapidly displaced legalistic phrases such as "sodomite" and more polite, neutral terms such as "invert" or "urning" in most of the English-speaking world. Hostile but educated writers used phrases such as "the unspeakable vice of the Greeks";[2] the young and uneducated called gay people "queer," "queen," or "faggot."

5. By the 1950s in the United States and throughout the English-speaking world, the words "homosexual" and "homosexuality" were universally accepted as the correct, scientific, and polite terms for these categories. In a few very sophisticated circles (principally the New York arts community and the theater), an even more polite term was known: "gay," a password homosexuals themselves often employed and that was first publicly used in the film *Bringing up Baby* (1939).

6. As a result of the popularization of the term and concept "homosexual" through the 1947 publication of the Kinsey study of male sexuality, "homo" became a widespread obloquy, especially among adolescents and those openly hostile to homosexuals. It is an almost exact lexical equivalent of the anti-Semitic "Hebe": both are abbreviations of terms applied by a suspicious majority to the minority in question ("homo" from "homosexual"; "Hebe" from "Hebrew"), as opposed to the terms used by the groups themselves ("gay" and "Jewish," respectively) and by those who are not hostile to them. Apocopation of names is a common English mode of intensification: personal names are shortened as expressions of affection ("Bob" for "Robert"; "Liz" for "Elizabeth"); for groups, especially suspect groups, the foreshortening usually betrays intensified hostility.

7. Thus, the distinctly hostile "spic" is shortened from "Hispanic," which is neutral; "kraut" is abbreviated as a hostile denomination from the valueless noun "sauerkraut"; "commie" is unambiguously negative, while "communist" might be neutral or even positive. "Fag" is an uglier insult derived from the word "faggot," which is itself hostile. In Great Britain, "sod" is an abbreviated insult from "sodomite." "Homo" carries a further negative connotation by ending in "-o," like "pinko," "wino," "weirdo," "fatso," and other slang English insults ending in "-o" derived from less demeaning adjectives.

Usage of "Homo"

8. "Homo" has never been employed by the scientific community, which continues to use "homosexual." Legislators have only sporadically recognized the psychological questions posed by the term "homosexual" and have generally relied on the older—but not precisely equivalent—terms "sodomy" or "unnatural acts" to discuss issues of same-gender sexuality. They have never employed "homo." Even there, however, "sodomy" and "unnatural acts" are frequently used to describe nonprocreative sexual acts performed between members of both the opposite and same sexes.[3] When "homo" has appeared in literature, it has been as an expression of antipathy or deep suspicion. For example, C. S. Lewis, the otherwise charitable English writer and expert on the English language, referred in a notorious letter on the subject to "the widespread free-masonry of highbrow homos."[4]

9. Until late in the 1980s, the *New York Times* and other American dailies and journals always used "homosexual," not "homo." (One notable exception is the infamous headline run by the *Daily News* when it reported the 1969 Stonewall riot, which is generally acknowledged as the beginning of the modern gay rights movement: "Homo Nest Raided, Queen Bees Are Stinging Mad.") In the last five years many newspapers—including the *Times*—have begun using the word "gay." When the press has used the word "homo," it has typically done so in quoting individuals who are expressing their bias and hostility against gays.

10. For example, *Newsday* recently reported that when Mayor David Dinkins marched with a gay group in New York's St. Patrick's Day Parade, Mayor Dinkins and other marchers were subjected to the catcall "Go back in the closet, you homos" from a decidedly hostile crowd. *Time* magazine reported that when he appeared on radio phone-in shows, callers labeled Ryan White, a hemophiliac who died of AIDS at age sixteen, "'faggot,' 'homo' and 'queer,'" and [that] more graphic obscenities were scribbled on his locker at school." And the *Independent*, a British daily newspaper, reported that rock singer Bon Jovi could be subject to criminal prosecution under an act proscribing incitement to hatred when he referred to the New York Giants football team as "a bunch of homos" and "a bunch of suntanned faggots" during a concert in Ireland.

11. "Homo" is also frequently used in the press in connection with reports on anti-gay violence as an epithet used by the assailants along with their fists, knives, and baseball bats.

—The *Los Angeles Times* reported on June 22, 1986, that a West Hollywood man was beaten by a group of six men who drove past him shouting "fag, homo and punk" and then parked their car and attacked the victim.

—The *Chicago Tribune* reported on May 11, 1987, that a Chicago man was attacked by a perpetrator who screamed "You faggot, you homo. I'm going to bash your face in. I'm going to break your jaw."

—The *New York Times* reported on August 24, 1988, that two Manhattan men were attacked by a group of teenagers armed with knives and bats shouting "Homos!" and "Fags!"—terms that the *Times* called "anti-homosexual epithets."

The Press Reaction to the Court's Comments

12. The press reaction to the court's statements in this case further evidences the fact that an objective listener would reasonably conclude that the repeated use of the word "homo"— particularly by a judge in a court proceeding—reflects bias on the part of the speaker. The *Washington Post* on Saturday, March 9, 1991, reported the court's comments under the headline "Judge Uses Epithet for Gay Man." The next day, the *Los Angeles Times* characterized the court's comments (properly) as a "sexual slur" and quoted Judge Gasch as stating that he "had no regrets about his remarks." The Associated Press carried a story on the court's comments on March 11 under the headline "Judge Challenged over Use of Epithet for Homosexuals." Thus, the press has had no problem in recognizing the word "homo" for what it is: a "slur" and an "epithet" that manifests bias and prejudice on the part of the speaker.

13. What is equally notable as the headlines themselves is the fact that the national press quickly and widely reported the court's comments. Thus, in addition to the Associated Press (which is distributed nationally), *Washington Post* and *Los Angeles Times* reports referred to previously, stories were also carried in the *New York Times*, the *Wall Street Journal*, the *San Francisco Chronicle*, and *Newsday*. The court's comments were also featured in the "Overheard" column of *Newsweek*, a column that typically features outrageous or startling quotes on events of the prior week. (Notably, *Newsweek* described the plaintiff here as "gay," not as a "homo.") The extent of the press coverage reflects the extreme nature of the court's remarks and the fact that the average person does not expect a federal judge to use a derogatory term like "homo" to describe a litigant, whatever the sexual orientation of that litigant may be.

Defendants' Authorities Do Not Support Their Position

14. The only authorities that defendants rely upon to support their claim that "homo" does not necessarily have "negative connotation[s]" are three dictionaries and a thesaurus.[5] Those authorities do not support their claim. The only current authority defendants rely on is the *Oxford English Dictionary* (1989), which labels not only "homo," but "faggot" and "queer" as well, as colloquial or slang expressions. In accordance with its practice, the *OED* goes on to give examples of usage of "homo," "faggot," and "queer." Those examples make it clear that each of the terms is derogatory. Thus, defendants' own survey indicates that current reference works *all* recognize that "homo" is an "abusive," "derogatory," and "vulgar" term. Defendants' reliance on the 1962 edition of *Roget's International Thesaurus* is also misplaced. For while it does list "homo" as a "slang term," it also lists the synonyms "queer, fairy, pansy, queen, nance, Nancy . . . betty, painted Willie, [and] fag" as "slang terms" as well. When read in context, there is no question that *Roget's* in 1962 implicitly acknowledges what the 1977 edition explicitly acknowledges: that "homo" is a derogatory term.

15. Defendants' remaining citations are no more helpful to their position. Lexicographers themselves are influenced by the prejudices that inform the usages they seek to describe. As a result, the fact that these dated reference works label "homo" as slang but do not go on to say that it is a vulgar, abusive, or derogatory term (as current reference works do) is in no way probative of defendants' point. For example, the 1966 edition of *The Random House Dictionary of the English Language*, cited by defendants, labeled "homo," "fag," "faggot," and "queer" as slang terms. The 1987 edition revised its definition of each word to indicate that they are "disparaging and offensive." The 1976 edition of the *American Heritage Dictionary of the English Language*, which defendants cite, is similarly indiscriminate in labeling "fag," "faggot," "queer," and "homo" as slang without going on to say that they are offensive terms. Thus, as the public's consciousness of anti-gay discrimination has increased, lexicographers have adapted their definitions of words that were implicitly understood to be derisive to explicitly recognize this fact.

Conclusion

16. In sum, I can affirm with absolute assurance that "homo" is and has always been a derogatory term that is usually employed by adolescents or acknowledged opponents of civil rights for gay people. It may be slightly less vulgar than "queer," "fag," or "faggot," but is equally a sign of antipathy. No objective person could reasonably conclude that an adult who repeatedly employs the term "homo" in a public forum, particularly in a courtroom, is open-minded or fair on the subject of homosexual orientation.

Richard Green

AFFIDAVIT I

On Homosexual Orientation as an
Immutable Characteristic

RICHARD GREEN, a professor of psychiatry at the University of California at Los Angeles and a graduate of the Johns Hopkins School of Medicine and Yale Law School, submitted the following affidavit arguing that extensive scientific research demonstrates that homosexual orientation is an innate feature of the human character and is not a consciously chosen behavior. He provides the evidence that is the basis for the scientific community's widely shared belief that sexual orientation is an immutable characteristic—in other words, a trait that may be viewed as a product of an accident of birth. This is one of the key issues in equal protection law as it applies to gays.

Further, Green posits that reorientation or reconditioning homosexuals has not been established as sufficiently reliable to meet the criteria of scientific method. He demonstrates that claims of reconditioning through behavioralist or psychiatric methods are of questionable validity and reliability.

Green's arguments gain authority and strength from his credentials as a leading expert in the study of sex and sexual orientation, and from the broad range and depth of materials presented and analyzed. Using historical as well as contemporary data, Green provides a broad foundation for his conclusions.

1. The purpose of this declaration is to provide the basis for my opinion—which is widely shared in the scientific community—that homosexual orientation is an "immutable characteristic," i.e., that homosexual orientation is not consciously chosen but, rather, that sexual and affectional feelings are a basic part of an individual's psyche and are established by early childhood. The basis for my

opinion derives from a wide range of scientific studies that consider (a) genetic influences; (b) hormonal influences, including the influence of prenatal hormones and possibly prenatal stress; (c) brain differences; and (d) the development of "prehomosexual" children. This research supports the position that sexual orientation is largely determined by genetic, neurological, hormonal, and other factors prior to birth. Clinical research has similarly shown that, whatever the origins of homosexuality may be, "reorientation" of individuals with a homosexual orientation has yielded exceedingly poor results.

The Definition and Scope of Homosexual Orientation

2. It is important to note at the outset that homosexual orientation is separate and distinct from homosexual conduct and that a person's sexual behavior does not necessarily define his or her orientation. Indeed, the military regulations in issue in this litigation distinguish between "homosexuals" and individuals who engage in or have engaged in "homosexual conduct" and do not require the discharge of individuals whose homosexual conduct was a departure from the servicemember's "usual and customary behavior."

3. Heterosexual conduct is common among individuals who identify themselves as lesbian or gay. One study of male homosexuals in the United States, Holland, and Denmark found that from 36 to 59 percent of homosexual individuals studied had had heterosexual intercourse.[1] The sexual experience of lesbians is at least if not more diverse, with estimates of 74 and 81 percent of lesbian women having engaged in heterosexual intercourse.[2]

4. The flip side of the same coin is the incidence of homosexual conduct by individuals who identify themselves as heterosexual. While a considerable range exists among various studies, all find that a relatively small minority of males (less than 10 or 12 percent) and a smaller minority of females (less than 7 percent) in the United States identify themselves as gay or lesbian or principally engage in same-sex behavior.[3] In contrast, Kinsey in his seminal study found that "at least 37 percent of the male population has some homosexual experience [to orgasm] between the beginning of adolescence and old age" and that "[a]mong males who remain unmarried until the age of

35, almost exactly 50 percent have homosexual experience." Indeed, Kinsey concludes that "the actual figures may be as much as 5 percent higher, or still higher."[4]

5. While sexual activity among heterosexuals and homosexuals is common and diverse, significant portions of both populations engage in little or no interactive sexual conduct, both temporarily and for long periods of time, for various reasons. Indeed, there is substantial anecdotal evidence that during World War II, gays in the military simply refrained from engaging in homosexual conduct in order to avoid the harsh penalties that could be imposed.[5] The fact that an individual is celibate for some short or long period of time does not mean that they do not have a sexual orientation, however. Celibacy, like any other sexual choice involving consenting behavior by a partner, is a healthy one when it is freely chosen.

Genetic Influences behind Sexual Orientation

Studies of Twins

6. Studies of twins hold a venerable place in psychiatric research attempting to dissect the relative influences of nature and of nurture. With monozygotic (identical) twins, the pair has a genetic composition as close as can be found for human beings. Therefore, the extent to which the twins differ in their attributes may be ascribed to environmental influences. In the case of dyzygotic (fraternal) twins, the individuals are genetically no more similar than any pair of siblings born of different pregnancies.

7. Earlier categorical theorizing behind the etiology of a range of psychiatric conditions was ascribed simplistically to either nature or nurture. However, the hope of finding a single gene or set of genes to explain fully the development of any syndrome has met with failure except in the case of some chromosomal disorders (such as Down syndrome). With other behaviors for which there had been great hope that a genetic etiology would be demonstrated, such as schizophrenia, research has found that while there may be some contribution from genetics, this is far from being the entire story. Much of the contribution appears to be either environmental or some complex interaction between nurture and nature.[6]

8. Nevertheless, provocative findings relating genetics to homosexual orientation have been reported. The first, in 1934, described six pairs of monozygotic twins concordant for homosexuality. Only two pairs were discordant.[7] The most provocative report was by Kallman, published in 1952.[8]

9. Kallman studied thirty-seven male monozygotic twins, each of whom was bisexual or homosexual (rated 3 to 6 on the Kinsey scale, where 0 is exclusive heterosexuality and 6 is exclusive homosexuality). When Kallman interviewed the co-twin, all thirty-seven were also found to be bisexual or homosexual. For the twenty Kinsey 6 (homosexual) twins, sixteen co-twins were also rated 6 and three were rated 5. For the nine Kinsey 5 twins, three co-twins were rated 6 and three were rated 5. Kallman noted:

> The majority of one egg pairs not only are fully concordant as to the overt practice and quantitative rating of their aberrant sex pattern, but they even tend to be very similar in both the parts taken in their individual sex activities and the visible extent of feminized appearance and behavior displayed by some of them. It also seems significant that most of these index pairs assert to have developed their sexual tendencies independently and often far apart from each other.[9]

10. By contrast, with the dyzygotic twin pairs over half of the co-twins of the bisexual or homosexual males reported no history of homosexuality. For those index twins with a Kinsey rating of 5 to 6, only 11.5 percent of the co-twins were comparably rated, a rate similar to the rate of homosexual orientation within the general male population.[10]

11. Since this astounding study, there have been a few small series or individual case reports of monozygotic twins discordant for sexual orientation. Indeed, a year after Kallman published his report, he also described a pair of monozygotic twins in which one was schizophrenic and homosexual and the other was neither schizophrenic nor homosexual.[11]

12. Not all newer, briefer reports refuted the strong influence of genetics, however. A 1968 study from England used the twin registry of a major psychiatric hospital; while not finding a 100 percent concordance rate among monozygotic twins, it did report one family with three sets of monozygotic twins, two of which were concordant for homosexuality and one for heterosexuality. The authors here too

pointed out that "the striking similar pattern of homosexual behavior developed in these twins entirely independently."[12] All told,
those investigators found five monozygotic male twin pairs, two of
which were concordant for homosexuality. In a third pair, while one
twin was homosexual, the co-twin developed psychotic delusions
of changing sex.[13] During the next years, seemingly every investiga-
tor who could find a pair of monozygotic twins discordant for homosexuality published his findings.[14] On the other hand, papers have
also appeared reporting monozygotic twins concordant for homosexuality.[15]

13. A major methodologic hurdle in dissecting the nature/nurture
mix in monozygotic twin pairs is the confounding variable of the
twins having been raised together. Thus, their environment may also
be nearly identical. However, when monozygotic twins are separated
near birth and raised in different families, there is great interest in
comparing their later behaviors. A recent report is of special interest.
It described a set of male monozygotic twins separated in infancy
who accidentally found each other in their early twenties. Both were
exclusively homosexual.[16]

Family Studies

14. An alternative strategy for uncovering evidence of a
genetic contribution to homosexual orientation is the study of the
relatives of homosexuals. Fifty-one predominantly homosexual men
and 50 predominantly heterosexual men served as index subjects.
The sexual orientation of siblings, which included 115 sisters and 123
brothers, was ascertained by interviews with the index subjects and
by interviews with or questionnaires mailed to the siblings. Homosexual index men had about four times as many homosexual brothers as did the heterosexual index men. Nearly 20 percent of the
brothers of homosexual or bisexual index men were bisexual or homosexual. By contrast, only 4 percent of the index heterosexual
males had homosexual or bisexual brothers. No higher incidence
was found of female bisexuality or homosexuality among the sisters
of the homosexual men. The findings could, however, suggest a
common environmental, rather than genetic, influence on the development of sexual orientation.[17]

15. Other hints of family "predispositions" to homosexual orientation derive from the classic Henry data of 1941. There, family tree information was collected on forty male and forty female "sex variants." In some cases, more than one hundred persons, over four generations, were included. Of particular interest is the finding on parents, aunts, and uncles of the homosexual index persons: of twelve homosexual and bisexual aunts and uncles, eleven derived from the maternal side.[18] A recent family study of homosexuality similarly found that ten of the twelve male relatives of index male homosexual subjects who also were considered homosexual were related through the mother's or sister's side.[19]

16. Although these findings do not prove a genetic etiology of homosexual orientation, they cannot be casually dismissed as irrelevant. That not every monozygotic twin pair is concordant for sexual orientation is not surprising, for few, if any, traits are fully concordant between twins. But the data of Kallman and of Heston and Shields, and the recent report on the separately raised twin pair, argue for a genetic contribution to sexual orientation.

Hormonal Influences on Sexual Orientation

Background

17. At the turn of the century, German sex researchers, of whom Krafft-Ebing was the most noted, postulated a central nervous system (brain) locus of sexual orientation. Simply stated, male homosexuals had a predominantly female sex center in the brain.[20]

18. This thesis fell into disrepute during the advent and heyday of the psychological schools—first, the psychoanalytic, and second, the behaviorist. Then a brief revival for the biological (now hormonal) basis of sexual orientation occurred in the two decades following World War II. The postwar scientists developed primitive tools for measuring sex hormones or their end products. These were usually nonspecific urine assays. Thus, tests gave nonspecific results, and soon this avenue of research drifted into a period of quiescence. In recent decades, however, new techniques have permitted sensitive, specific assays from blood. A wide range of chemicals, including the relevant "sex hormones" and their related compounds, can now be

measured. Consequently, there has been a surge of activity in which male and female homosexuals have been tested for their levels of "male" and "female" hormones, particularly testosterone and "his" relatives and estradiol and "her" relatives.

Blood Levels in Adulthood

19. Blood androgen (male hormone) levels for male homosexuals have been reported in over two dozen studies. In the majority, homosexual males apparently had testosterone levels within the range of male heterosexuals. Only three studies reported significantly lower levels in homosexuals.[21] However, two of these studies lacked adequate control groups, and the third may have been confounded by the high number of drug users in the homosexual group. By contrast, twenty studies reported no differences between homosexuals and controls or among homosexuals with varying degrees of homosexual commitment, and two studies showed elevated levels of testosterone in homosexuals.[22]

20. Because it is the free (not bound to a protein) plasma testosterone that is believed to be the active constituent of plasma testosterone, and not the total level, this vital fraction has been measured in more recent studies. Two compared heterosexual and homosexual males and found that whereas total testosterone levels did not differ, free testosterone was lower in the homosexuals (but within the typical male range).[23]

21. As for estrogen (female hormone) levels in homosexual men, one study reported elevated plasma estradiol and estrone,[24] whereas another showed elevated estradiol but normal estrone.[25] Others found either no group differences in plasma estradiol and estrone or normal estradiol levels.[26]

22. Studies of female homosexuals, too, have failed to show consistent differences for testosterone and estrogen levels compared with those of heterosexual women. However, there may be a subgroup of homosexual women with elevated testosterone levels, although these levels are far below those found in normal males.[27]

23. It is not surprising that the studies of sex hormone levels in blood have been inconsistent in results and generally unrewarding. There are many obstacles in the way of understanding correlates or causes of sexual orientation from this research strategy. The "normal" range—that is, levels found in most "normal" people—of these

hormones is wide. Thus, a statistically significant difference may be found between two groups, but the average of both groups may be within the "normal" range. Furthermore, an individual's measured hormone level may be irrelevant. Tissue needs of the hormone may vary from person to person. Thus, a level within the "normal" range for one person may represent a deficiency for another. The signifi- cance of the findings is compromised further by the fact that hormone levels fluctuate throughout the day, and blood samples stop the action at only one point in time. And if these stumbling blocks were insufficient to dissuade the most intrepid of researchers, consider too the nearly unmeasurable environmental factors that af- fect hormone levels. "Stress" is but one.

Prenatal Influences

24. The quest did not stop with these less than clear-cut results. Increasing understanding of chemical mediators in the body, beginning with secretions from the hypothalmic portion of the brain, with its influence on secretions from the pituitary gland, and their subsequent influence on the gonads led to more sophisticated assessments. Concurrently, there evolved greater understanding from nonhuman research on the effect of hormonal manipulations before birth. These were found to lead not only to modification of the external genitalia, but also to modification in sex-typed behav- iors. An important fundamental finding here was that the basic mammalian state is female. Thus, if you remove the evolving gonad (on its way to either a testicular or an ovarian destiny) from the de- veloping fetus, the fetus progresses along female-appearing lines.[28] Similarly, in the absence of sex hormones in the developing fetus, the body evolves as female.

25. Extension of these findings to the behavioral system was the next research step. It was found, first with rodents, that depriving the developing male of sex hormone at critical early periods of develop- ment, or exposing the developing female to excessive male hormone, would reverse aspects of sex-typed mating behavior. This work was next extended to the nonhuman primate. Investigators injected pregnant rhesus monkeys with testosterone. The rhesus was a good research model because rhesus juvenile behaviors are "sex dimor- phic" in a manner comparable to that found in the human—i.e., the young male rhesus is more often involved in rough-and-tumble and

aggressive play than is the female rhesus. When the fetal female was exposed to elevated levels of male hormone, in consequence of the injections to her pregnant mother, she behaved more like a male (the "tomboy" monkey).[29] This suggested the existence at the primate level of a behavioral phenomenon parallel to the morphological phenomenon. That is, in the absence of sex hormone, femaleness or "femininity" evolves, whereas with male hormone, maleness or "masculinity" evolves. Follow-up of these "tomboy" females revealed that as adults they responded in the typical female manner when sexually paired with males, although there were some minor differences from normal females.[30]

Inherited Defects

A. Congenital Adrenal Hyperplasia

26. Looking for a comparable human model was the next research strategy. One was found in the medical condition known as congenital adrenal hyperplasia (CAH). In this inherited disorder, beginning prenatally, the adrenal gland secretes an excess of masculinizing hormone. Thus, a female fetus, because of exposure to these high levels of male hormone, has masculinized genitalia at birth.

27. A provocative study compared the social play of CAH girls correctively treated at birth, or soon after, with that of their sisters who did not have this syndrome and thus had normal prenatal hormones. The masculine-hormone-exposed girls were more involved in rough-and-tumble play and less involved in play with newborn babies or its surrogate activity, doll-play. They were "tomboys." Thus, the human parallel to the rhesus monkey study was reported.[31]

28. CAH females have also been studied in adulthood. One report was of the most extreme patient group; that is, those whose medical treatment to suppress male hormone did not start until adolescence or adulthood (pre-1950 patients). Thus, they experienced both pre- and postnatal excessive male hormone exposure. Homosexuality was found to be more common among these women than in the typical female population. However, homosexuality did not predominate.[32]

29. Even more provocative findings, this time with females who were treated shortly after birth to suppress male hormone production, have been reported. Thirty patients were studied in whom surgical reduction of the clitoris was performed neonatally, or up to age three in twenty-one cases, between ages four and six years in eight cases, and at age nine in one (mild) case. The onset of hormonal therapy to suppress excessive androgen production was within the first year in over two-thirds. Seventeen percent described themselves as either exclusively or predominantly homosexual, 20 percent as bisexual, 40 percent as heterosexual, and 23 percent were "noncommittal." When rated by the investigators from their impressions derived from the subjects, 37 percent were judged bisexual, 40 percent heterosexual, and 23 percent unratable because they had been noncommittal.[33]

30. Congenital adrenal hyperplasia is also found in males, who are thus exposed to excessive male hormone prenatally. Theory would predict, and the findings confirm, that nearly all who have been studied have grown up to be heterosexual.[34]

B. ANDROGEN-INSENSITIVITY SYNDROME

31. In the androgen-insensitivity syndrome, the individual has the XY male chromosomal pattern, testes (intra-abdominal), and normal levels of testosterone. However, the person's tissue cells are unable to utilize testosterone. Therefore, the child appears to be female at birth and is raised as a girl. (The anomaly is typically discovered in adolescence, when the child does not menstruate and/or the intra-abdominal testes descend, presenting as hernia.) These persons evolve sexual attractions for males (and thus are "homosexual" in the chromosomal or gonadal sense but not the psychological sense). However, it is difficult to separate the socialization influence of having been raised as a female from the lack of androgenic influence on the brain.[35]

C. FIVE-ALPHA-REDUCTASE

32. The five-alpha-reductase deficiency syndrome is a notable contribution to understanding the importance of prenatal hormones for later sexual behavior. In this genetically inherited defect, testosterone is not converted into its androgenizing metabolite, dihydrotestosterone. Individuals with this disorder appear female at birth, although, upon closer examination, some anomalies can be detected. However, in the earliest generations with this disorder, the children were considered to be normal females and were raised as girls. With adolescence, substantial masculinization takes place: what has been an essentially normal-appearing clitoris greatly enlarges to phallic proportions, female breast development does not occur, the voice deepens, and malelike muscular development evolves. During adolescence, these persons assume societal roles as males and sexually pursue females. The investigators concluded that the availability of testosterone prenatally, while insufficient for organizing the genitalia to appear malelike, was sufficient to organize the brain to mediate later sexual responsivity to females.[36]

A Medically Induced Anomaly

33. Recent research on prenatal diethylstilbestrol (DES) exposure has also resulted in provocative findings regarding sexual orientation in the female. DES is a synthetic estrogen that was administered decades ago to pregnant women with a history of difficulty in maintaining pregnancies. Although DES is a synthetic estrogen, it should be a masculinizing drug. This is because one of the masculinizing pathways in the brain is believed to be via the conversion of testosterone, the "male" hormone, into estradiol, the "female" hormone. The "female" hormone masculinizes when in the brain. Naturally produced estradiol does not reach the developing fetal brain, however, because it is inactivated in the fetal blood. By contrast, the synthetic estrogen, DES, does get into the brain.[37]

34. Thirty DES-exposed women were compared with thirty unrelated women without DES exposure and with twelve of their DES-unexposed sisters. The percentages of DES women rated bisexual to homosexual on the Kinsey scale (rated 2–6) were 21 percent for the twelve months prior to the study and 24 percent for their full life, compared with only 3 percent among the nonrelated control group for the preceding twelve months and 0 percent lifelong. Five women had a Kinsey score of at least 3 (bisexual) during the preceding twelve months, compared with none in the nonrelated control group. Six of the seven DES women with a Kinsey score of 2 or higher had had romantic relationships with other women, and five had had experiences involving genital contact. During the twelve months preceding the study, two were living with a homosexual partner.

35. The DES women also had higher homosexual scores than did their non-DES-exposed sisters. Five DES women had ratings of Kinsey 2 or higher for the preceding twelve months and lifelong, compared with one of their twelve unexposed sisters (a comparison percentage of 42 versus 8). Three DES-exposed women (25 percent) had scores of 3 or higher for the previous twelve months and two (17 percent) lifelong, compared with none of their nonexposed sisters. These differences are of borderline statistical significance.[38]

36. Data from these naturally occurring and medically induced abnormal hormonal states suggest that some contribution to sexual orientation derives from prenatal sex hormone levels. That not all persons so exposed show an atypical orientation may reflect not only the existence of other contributors, but also that these hormonal contributions have acted with insufficient dosages and/or at less than optimal developmental periods.

Indirect Measures

37. Increasing evidence has thus been gathered pointing to the importance of prenatal hormonal influences on postnatal sexual behavior. Assessing these prenatal influences directly is, of course, highly problematic. The next research step was a search for endocrine influences that operate before birth in a sex-dimorphic way that could be measured postnatally. In the mid-1960s a German researcher, Dorner, developed a strategy that would, in his view, assess the enduring influences of prenatal levels of androgen on sexual behavior. The system studied was the difference in adult men and women in the luteinizing hormone (LH) response to levels of estrogen in the blood. In the typical female, rising levels of estradiol lead to a drop in LH, followed by a marked rebound above baseline (this is the hormonal basis of ovulation). By contrast, in the typical male, rising levels of estradiol, though also followed by a reduction in LH, do not result in the later marked rebound. The basis of this sex difference is believed to be prenatal levels of male hormone that organize the developing brain.

38. Speculating that homosexual males have an insufficiently "masculinized" central nervous system, Dorner studied the LH feedback response in heterosexual and homosexual males. He found that when subjects were given a single injection of estrogen, the LH response, as a group, differed between homosexual and heterosexual men. More homosexual than heterosexual men showed a more female-type positive rebound effect. (In homosexuals, the response

was weaker and was delayed for twenty-four hours compared with that of women, but nevertheless it was present).[39]

39. For many years these provocative findings lay dormant. In 1984, I sought to replicate the study in collaboration with Gladue and Hellman. We included a heterosexual female control group as well as male heterosexual and homosexual groups, and we studied fourteen male homosexuals, seventeen male heterosexuals, and twelve female heterosexuals. We found that men declaring a lifelong homosexual orientation had a pattern of LH secretion in response to an intravenous pulse of estrogen that was intermediate between those of men and of women declaring lifelong heterosexual orientation. Examination of individual response patterns showed a greater variability among the homosexual men. Nine out of the fourteen homosexuals demonstrated the positive estrogen feedback phenomenon, compared with none of the seventeen heterosexual men and eleven of the twelve heterosexual women. Furthermore, testosterone concentrations in the men that decreased after estrogen administration were slower in returning to baseline in the homosexuals than in the heterosexuals.[40]

40. However, Gooren, in the Netherlands, has failed to replicate fully either the Dorner study or the study that I conducted with Gladue and Hellman. Gooren utilized a somewhat modified design: another substance, luteinizing hormone releasing hormone (LHRH), was administered before estrogen. After estrogen administration, the fall in testosterone was not greater among the male homosexuals than in the heterosexuals. The fall in LH was also not greater in the homosexuals as a group. However, at day four, the LH levels of the male homosexuals had returned to or were slightly above baseline, whereas this was not true for the heterosexuals. Thus, a difference was found in a direction consistent with that of Gladue and Dorner, although the marked rebound phenomenon was not observed. However, Gooren did observe some elevation of LH levels on day four after estrogen in eleven of twenty-three homosexuals, compared with only five of fifteen heterosexuals. Thus, the direction of these findings is consistent with the previous reports. Males with a higher LH level on day four after estrogen had a greater fall in testosterone, again consistent with the earlier relationship. Gooren then assessed testicular function by stimulation with another hormone, human chorionicgonadotropin (hCG). The five heterosexual and six homo-

sexual men with a positive LH feedback effect showed less testosterone response to hCG. Gooren concluded that the quality of testicular steroid production, not sexual orientation, caused this "female-type" estrogen response in the male. However, he also noted, "It is not immediately clear why some heterosexual men, a third, and some homosexual men, about half, had a greater fall of serum testosterone levels in response to the administration of conjugate estrogens."[41] The explanation may rest with a prenatal influence organizing male structures, whether it is the gonad or the neuroendocrine system.

Prenatal Stress

41. The theory of prenatal stress behind a homosexual orientation is derived from evidence that stress causes depressed testosterone production prenatally. This effect is triggered by elevated levels of stress hormones from the adrenal gland, which, carried in the blood, cross the placenta and antagonize fetal testosterone. Investigators working with the rodent have induced lower fetal levels of testosterone and later femalelike behavior in male offspring whose pregnant mothers were severely stressed (for example, by hours of confinement in an intensely lighted enclosure).[42]

42. Studies of stress during pregnancy and resulting human sexual orientation have yielded intriguing findings. Dorner found that among males born in Germany between 1934 and 1953, an unusually high number of homosexuals were born during and immediately after World War II—that is, between 1941 and 1946. He hypothesized that the extraordinary stress of pregnant women during these years resulted in a greater proportion of homosexual sons.

43. Dorner's second study involved questioning a group of mothers of male homosexuals, bisexuals, and heterosexuals about stressful episodes during pregnancy.[43] Nearly two-thirds of the mothers of the male homosexuals, compared with one-third of the mothers of the bisexuals and fewer than 10 percent of the mothers of the heterosexuals, recalled such episodes. Only six of the one hundred heterosexual men were found to have mothers who experienced moderate prenatal stress, such as an undesired pregnancy or anxiety during the pregnancy because the father was at war. However, such prenatal stress was found among ten of forty bisexual men. For the sixty homosexual men, moderate prenatal stress was found in twenty, and

severe prenatal stress was found in another twenty-one. Severe stress was rated when the father had died during the mother's pregnancy, the mother was raped during pregnancy, or there were repeated military bombardments.

Other Biological Influences

A. MALE-FEMALE BRAIN DIFFERENCES

44. Earlier documented sex differences in brain morphology in the nonhuman have recently been extended to findings in the human. In the rodent, the preoptic area is related to sex-typed behaviors. Autopsies on humans reveal that, on average, the preoptic area of the brain is over twice as large in men as in women.[44]

45. The finding of discrete brain differences between human males and females complements the findings of other sex differences, particularly cognitive differences, which are believed related to brain morphology. For example, studies of cerebral asymmetry indicate that whereas both men's and women's left hemisphere is specialized for language functions, women alone tend to have additional language abilities in the predominantly visuospatial right hemisphere.[45] Developmental studies demonstrate that the basic differences in hemispheric specialization may be present in the newborn.[46]

46. Thus, a recent study of homosexual and heterosexual subjects is of particular interest. Investigators studied cognitive differences found between males and females and included for study a sample of homosexual males. They reasoned that if the same prenatal events organize the central nervous system to mediate cognitive sex differences as well as sexual orientation, then cross-sex cognitive findings should emerge in conjunction with homosexuality.

47. Two types of tests employing visuospatial abilities were utilized. Both discriminate between unselected males and females. One requires subjects to indicate the level that water will take in a tilted bottle. Here, performances by heterosexual females and homosexual males were very similar, but both were ten times less accurate than those of heterosexual males. In a subsequent procedure, subjects were required to select a mechanism composed of levers, cogs, or pulleys that would produce a movement demonstrated in test diagrams. They were also required to complete a modified version of the water-level task. On the mechanical diagram test, the homosexual males had a level of performance intermediate between that of heterosexual males and heterosexual females. The scores of the heterosexual females and the homosexual males were significantly different from those of the heterosexual males, but not from each other. On the water-level task, as in the earlier experiment, the performance of the heterosexual females and the homosexual males were significantly different from those of heterosexual males, but not from each other. The authors note, "If we accept that men and women, of whatever sexual orientation, are likely to have equal experience of liquids in containers, the marked differences recorded on the water-level task are intuitively the most surprising."[47]

48. These investigators also found that heterosexual males showed a marked left-visual-field superiority in a dot-detection task, with homosexual males and heterosexual females showing no significant field advantages.[48] They note, "Taken together these findings establish a link among three phenomena, the etiology of sexual orientation, sex differences in cognitive ability, and sex differences in cerebral asymmetry. In each of these areas there is a growing support for some form of biological determination."[49]

B. Immunologic Maternal "Rejection" of the Male Fetus

49. A recent method for modifying sexual orientation in laboratory animals involves the induction of an immune response to one or more of the biochemicals necessary for sexual differentiation of the brain. Immune antibodies exist for nearly all the androgens and estrogens.[50] The more foreign the fetal tissue cells, the more likely there is to be a maternal antibody reaction to them. Thus, males are more vulnerable (most spontaneously aborted fetuses are male).[51]

50. The mother may also produce antibodies that compromise the mechanisms responsible for the hormonal organization of the brain in a male-type direction. These maternal immune responses to a fetus may not be developed fully until a second or third pregnancy (see, for example, the Rh incompatibility phenomenon, where the firstborn is spared, but subsequent births are afflicted).[52] This finding is compatible with reports that male homosexuals are more often found to be later-born siblings.[53]

51. These indirect measures of a physiological influence on both sex-typed brain organization and postnatal sex-typed behaviors are relatively new but provocative. Although the jury is still out on the widely publicized LH feedback studies, the findings suggest that there is a subgroup of homosexual males who show a "female-type" hormonal pattern. This could reflect one developmental route to a homosexual orientation, as could the findings related to stress during pregnancy. And now that the foray has been joined by cognitive psychologists and immunochemists, the promise of additional insights is even greater.

"Insight" Therapy

52. These sobering words of Sigmund Freud did little to dissuade his psychoanalytic followers from attempting to reorient homosexual patients: "In actual numbers the successes achieved by psychoanalytic treatment of the various forms of homosexuality . . . are not very striking. As a rule, the homosexual is not able to give up the object of his pleasure. . . . If he comes to be treated at all, it is mostly through the pressure of external motives, such as the social disadvantages and dangers."[54]

53. The most detailed research report of the psychoanalytic "insight" treatment of male homosexuality appeared in 1962 from Bieber and his colleagues.[55] One hundred six men were studied and treated. Seventy-two were exclusively homosexual prior to therapy. Fourteen of them (19 percent) were reported to be exclusively heterosexual at the end of therapy. Of thirty men who had been bisexual prior to therapy, fifteen were reported to become exclusively heterosexual. Of twenty-nine males who were reported to be exclusively heterosexual after therapy, only two had less than 150 hours of therapy, nine had between 150 and 349 hours, and eighteen had at least 350 hours. Additional prognostic factors beyond length of treatment were: males who had "effeminate voice or gestures during childhood" were more likely to remain exclusively homosexual; most men who reoriented began their analysis at age thirty-five or younger; and most who reoriented had made some attempts at heterosexual intercourse prior to treatment and had had manifest heterosexual content in their dreams prior to treatment. Surveying the treatment results, the authors concluded, "The shift from homosexuality to exclusive heterosexuality for 27 percent of the patients is of out-

standing importance since *these are the most optimistic and promising results thus far reported.*"[56]

54. During recent decades, there have been a few follow-up reports of apparently successful heterosexual reorientation in other, smaller series of male patients. One study reported on fourteen male homosexuals treated in the early 1950s. Seven patients were exclusively homosexual prior to treatment, four predominantly homosexual, and three bisexual. An average interval of four and a half years had elapsed since the end of therapy. Of the seven exclusively homosexual men, two were predominantly heterosexual after therapy. Of the four who were primarily homosexual prior to therapy, two were now primarily heterosexual. The three who were bisexual prior to therapy were now predominantly heterosexual. The level of heterosexuality considered to be a successful adjustment was the ability to derive pleasure and satisfaction in sexual intercourse most of the time, or the ability to enjoy "mature, consistently satisfactory heterosexual adjustment without significant conflicts." However, consistent with other reports of a questionable total heterosexual orientation of treatment "successes," the investigators noted that one patient who married and who was the father of three children, and who had had no homosexual experiences since therapy, still had "occasional homosexual fantasies and dreams related to his dependency needs which treatment had modified only slightly." The authors observed, "On a descriptive behavioral basis, he would be described as 'exclusively heterosexual' but on a purely dynamic basis as 'bisexual.'"[57]

55. Moreover, as one critic of this study has pointed out, "The criteria for 'success' in this report are highly questionable. . . . [T]he self reports of the patients were interpreted by the authors without external validation. This method is insufficient in terms of objective data collection."[58]

56. A more sobering report was published in England in 1956. There, only seven of eighty-one cases referred by courts and other agencies achieved "satisfactory results" of "no homosexual impulses, (or) increased heterosexual interest" through psychotherapy. Furthermore, none of these "successful" patients had been initially exclusively homosexual.[59]

57. Another sobering English study, published in 1957, evaluated one hundred males. Twenty-three had been treated by psychother-

apy, including psychoanalysis. Inpatient care, generally for an associated problem, such as alcoholism, was provided in eleven cases. With sixty-six men, treatment consisted of supportive counseling and medication. On average, only one in six reported less intense homosexual feelings at follow-up. Three men became more homosexual. Of those twenty-four who had been exclusively homosexual, there was no change in twenty-three. Furthermore, there was no difference in sexual reorientation in the men who had received psychotherapy compared with those who had not.[60]

"Behavior" Therapy

58. Psychoanalytic treatment results with homosexuality were disappointing for at least two reasons. First, it was extremely long. Classic treatment involved fifty minutes per day, five days per week, with the weeks extending into years. Aside from the extraordinary expense, the results, as noted above, were less than overwhelming. The majority of previously exclusively homosexual males remained primarily homosexual, and the rates of those previously bisexual males reorienting to exclusive heterosexuality were no better than 50 percent. Considering that those homosexual males who entered such expensive, long-term therapy were the most highly motivated toward change, and that therapists are more likely to report successes than failures, these "gains" are even more modest.

59. With the gradual disillusionment with psychoanalytic therapy in the early 1960s, "behavior therapy" enjoyed a surge in research and clinical application. In contrast to the psychoanalytic approach of uncovering previously unconscious conflicts through a process of verbal "free" associations, and "working through" early-life psychological trauma, the behaviorist approach treated the unwanted behavior not as a symptom of some long-repressed conflict, but rather as a learned behavior that could be unlearned. Sexual arousal by a male to another male was a learned phenomenon, reinforced by the pleasure of the sexual response, that could be changed by substituting pain for pleasure. Later, treatment modifications were introduced that were also aimed at interrupting posited psychologically painful responses associated with heterosexuality.

60. For about fifteen years individual case studies and group reports flooded the treatment literature. Now it is extremely difficult to find new reports. While this dearth is partially due to the falling from grace generally of treating a homosexual orientation, a review of the results of treatment suggests that the less than spectacular outcomes also provide a reason.

61. The first group study, published in 1960, paired painful electrical shock with projected slides of nude males. As treatment progressed, increasing numbers of female-depicting slides were also shown, which were not paired with shock. These latter slides were used to elicit "anxiety relief" and thus were associated with a positive experience. Treatment outcome was measured by reports of heterosexual intercourse. Of nine males who had not experienced heterosexual intercourse prior to therapy, six later "demonstrated decreased homosexual arousal and engaged in heterosexual coitus" at three-year follow-up.[61]

62. Later, a series of forty-three homosexual males were treated with an anticipatory avoidance procedure. Here, the subject viewed a slide of a male nude projected onto a screen. He could remove the image from the screen. If, however, he viewed the slide for too long (eight seconds), he would be shocked. A slide of a female was shown after either the homosexual slide was removed or the shock was given. Of forty-one male patients, twenty-four had been practicing homosexuality for more than a decade, and twenty-five had displayed no heterosexual practice or had experienced no heterosexual fantasy. Nine bisexuals were heterosexually active at the initiation of treatment and, in heterosexual activity, were utilizing homosexual fantasy. On the Kinsey scale of sexual orientation, where 0 is exclusive heterosexuality and 6 is exclusive homosexuality, nineteen men had a rating of 6, twelve a rating of 5, and twelve a 3 or a 4.

63. After treatment, twenty-five "improved to a sufficient degree for their treatment to be described as successful." At one-year follow-up, only thirteen out of the original group of forty-three were engaging in heterosexual intercourse unaccompanied by homosexual fantasy. They were not engaging in homosexual acts. Only fourteen patients, as compared with twenty-five before treatment, had no heterosexual fantasy or practice. With respect to homosexual fantasy or practice, twenty had neither fantasy nor behavior at follow-up, fourteen were still engaging in homosexual practice, and nine had homosexual fantasies. Kinsey ratings after treatment were 0 for fourteen men, 1 for nine, and 2 for two. These constituted the twenty-five "improved" patients. The remainder were rated as Kinsey 3 through 6. Although twenty patients were displaying no homosexual practice, only fourteen could be rated as Kinsey 0, since six were still finding males sexually interesting. (In one especially "unsuccessful" outcome with a female patient, a (bisexual) lesbian who had been practicing heterosexual intercourse before therapy was no longer doing so after therapy.)

64. Prognostic factors were also identified. There was a tendency for those who began treatment with a Kinsey rating of 6 (exclusively homosexual) during the preceding few years to be less likely to become heterosexually reoriented. Only nine of nineteen Kinsey 6 patients (recent pretreatment ratings) had a "satisfactory response to the treatment." However, of the nine, six had displayed some earlier heterosexual interest and practice. Also, for the other three with a "satisfactory" outcome, none had yet commenced heterosexual interaction. By contrast, only two of the ten with a recent Kinsey rating of 6 who failed to improve had had heterosexual practice or arousal before treatment. This study remains the most positive of any large-series behavior therapy report.[62]

65. Later studies employed physiological measures of sexual arousal. One employed electric shock that was contingent upon penile arousal in response to homosexual fantasies and slides. There, five of ten patients showed a reduction of homosexual interest, and four demonstrated reduction of homosexual behavior. This was followed by increases in heterosexual behavior and interest in seven and four individuals, respectively. Three showed significant and lasting improvements at one-year follow-up, and six exhibited a diminished interest in homosexual activity.[63]

66. In another large study of forty-six patients, at one-year follow-up, half reported a decrease in homosexual feelings, and half reported an increase in heterosexual feelings. Only a quarter reported an increase in the frequency of heterosexual intercourse, and 25 percent also reported a cessation of homosexual relations.[64] Later, one of the authors examined both aversive and positive conditioning paradigms. Here, in addition to electric shock paired with homosexual slides, there was pairing of heterosexual stimuli with homosexual slides (positive conditioning of heterosexuality). This innovation was a response to the criticism that aversive therapy was only punishing homosexual arousal and not rewarding heterosexual arousal. At one-year follow-up, about half the patients reported an increase in heterosexual activity and feeling and a decrease in homosexual interests and activities. Another outcome measure was penile responsivity to erotic stimuli. There was no evidence that the positive conditioning produced a greater increase in heterosexual response than did the aversive technique.[65]

67. Probably the most positive outcome with at least a one-year follow-up of any of the behavior therapy studies utilized laboratory conditioning with the pairing of heterosexual slides with previously arousing homosexual slides. The subject viewed a series of heterosexual slides followed by a slide of a nude male. During the sequence, the subject was masturbating. Over the course of weeks, the number of male slides was reduced and then eliminated. After ejaculation, the subject was shown slides of nude males only and received electric shocks.

68. There were three married and six single male subjects, all of whom were more homosexual than heterosexual at the onset of treatment. Four had been exclusively homosexual. Penile erection patterns to the heterosexual and homosexual stimuli were reversed during the course of treatment, so that by the end of treatment all subjects showed more responsivity to female than to male slides. Nine subjects were free of homosexual behavior one year after treatment. However, at eighteen-month follow-up, two were living in homosexual unions, while seven "continued their heterosexual adjustment." The authors also reported that subsequent to the completion of the study, two additional subjects, both previously exclusively homosexual, went through the treatment program and were heterosexual at eighteen-month follow-up.[66]

69. On the other hand, a more sobering study of the effectiveness of an aversive shock treatment procedure in sixteen males found that only five demonstrated any change and that only two demonstrated decreased homosexual arousal accompanied by an increase in heterosexual behavior. Therapy gains were maintained after two-year follow-up in only two of the sixteen patients.[67]

70. There have also been many single-case or small-series reports. In one, masturbation training in response to heterosexual stimuli was used in conjunction with electrical aversion in response to homosexual stimuli. At eight-month follow-up, subjects showed increased heterosexual and decreased homosexual arousal.[68] A combined systematic desensitization procedure (where a patient practices relaxation procedures in conjunction with exposure to previously anxiety-provoking stimuli) was also reported. At eighteen-

month follow-up, verbal reports indicated that homosexual urges were minimal, homosexual behavior was nonexistent, and the client was functioning in a heterosexual relationship. This man had been bisexual before treatment.[69]

71. Another procedure used "orgasmic reconditioning" (masturbation training) to alter sexual preference. Here, the patient began masturbation to homosexual stimuli and gradually faded in heterosexual stimuli when he was aroused. Short-term follow-up revealed that two previously exclusively homosexual males were now engaging in heterosexual intercourse and that a bisexual patient was more heterosexual.[70]

72. A biofeedback procedure has also been employed. Here, the individual was given "social and monetary reinforcement" for penile responsivity to heterosexual stimuli. The treatment was not effective.[71]

73. Most of these follow-up results have been based on patients' reports. A drawback to this outcome measure is evident in another study. There, an orgasmic reconditioning procedure was used with four homosexual males. All subjects reported improvement. However, the physiological and behavioral measures of their sexual arousal pattern remained unchanged.[72]

74. In summary, a review paper reporting the status of behavior therapy, published in 1977, noted that thirty-seven studies had offered "reorientation services" to a total of 350 homosexuals (346 males) whose history of homosexual preference ranged from six months to thirty-eight years. The authors concluded, "[T]here is no evidence that aversion relief is a direct and potentially effective procedure for increasing heterosexual arousal itself." Furthermore, they concluded that "[t]he reduction of homosexual arousal and behavior is now being viewed as only one component of an effective treatment program. If treatment gains are to be maintained, other sexual and social behaviors must be instituted to replace the previously reinforcing homosexual patterns."[73]

75. Candid reports by two clinicians, very experienced in the behavioral treatment of homosexual orientation, provide sobering views of purported treatment "successes." These investigators are Kurt Freund, a professor at the Clarke Institute of Psychiatry in Toronto, and Neil McConaghy, a professor at the University of New South Wales, Sydney, Australia. Both reveal that the "heterosexual-

ity" reported for many "successfully treated" patients is not genuine heterosexual orientation.

76. Freund reported on forty-seven patients treated with a chemical aversion procedure (nausea paired with homosexual stimuli) in Czechoslovakia. Twelve were considered at follow-up to have, generally, a heterosexual adaptation. Freund then reports on these men in detail. After the initial brief follow-up period, one of the twelve reverted to his previous homosexual orientation and another could not be traced. For the remaining ten, follow-up periods ranged from two to seven years. One patient, four years later, requested further treatment because of renewed homosexual drives. Another, married for six years, then fell in love with a male and became impotent with his wife. He underwent hypnotic therapy and then renewed heterosexual intercourse. Another entered the military four years later and claimed, in contradiction to previous statements alleging heterosexuality, to have always been oriented in a purely homosexual way. Another divorced his wife and remarried, but during the last year of evaluation he fell in love with a male. Another, who claimed to be happily married for six years, was having homosexual intercourse about once every ten days. Another, married and the father of two children, claimed to be happily married but would not let the researchers interview his wife. Another, married for seven years and the father of one child, had homosexual intercourse on three occasions over the follow-up period. Another, married for five years and with two children, had homosexual intercourse only once during that time. But another, married for nine years, had homosexual intercourse as frequently as heterosexual intercourse, and another, married for three years, had homosexual intercourse once every ten days and intercourse with his wife about once a week. These ten patients "have heterosexual intercourse exclusively or predominantly, [but] all claim that their motivation is still almost exclusively homosexual."[74]

77. The report by McConaghy also challenges sexual "reorientation" in "successfully" treated patients.[75] After treating 157 male homosexuals with various forms of behavior therapy in four studies, he states first that with all forms of treatment, only about 25 percent of patients reported a definite increase in heterosexual feelings at short-term follow-up of less than one year. Further, somewhat fewer than a sixth of the patients reported an increase in the frequency of

heterosexual intercourse up to four weeks after treatment, and only about a quarter reported such an increase at the six- or twelve-month follow-up. Most of these patients with increased heterosexuality had experienced heterosexual intercourse before treatment. After treatment applying aversive stimuli, about half the patients reported a reduction in homosexual feeling at the three- or four-week follow-up interview, and after positive conditioning toward heterosexuality, about a quarter reported a reduction in homosexual feelings. At the six- or twelve-month interview with aversion therapy patients, half reported a reduced number of homosexual encounters, and a quarter reported no homosexual encounters.

78. McConaghy also assessed penile responsivity to pictures of nude women and men at follow-up. As measured by penile reactions, these patients' sexual orientation changed in the heterosexual direction to a significant extent after treatment. When he evaluated the four studies separately, he noted that in the first two there was a significant relationship between the change in penile responsivity and the reported reduction in homosexual feelings. From this he initially concluded that the change in penile responsivity indicated a shift in sexual orientation. However, in the third and fourth studies, the relationship between the penile responsivity changes and the reduction in homosexual feelings was either insignificant or absent. McConaghy concluded, "[T]he most likely explanation is that the significant relationship in studies one and two was a false positive."[76]

79. McConaghy then went on to conclude that "it would therefore appear that the significant change in reduction in homosexual feelings and behavior after aversive therapy, as compared with positive conditioning, is not accompanied by change in the sexual orientation of the patients."[77] McConaghy then asks, "What significance can be attached to the change in penile responsivity scores that followed treatment?" and answers, "It is not great. In all studies, over half the patients continued to obtain a score indicating a homosexual orientation after treatment." He then asks, "Can treatment alter homosexual orientation?" and concludes, "The aversive therapies investigated in the four studies reported would appear not to have altered the patient's sexual orientation. . . . [I]t must be assumed that present treatments may reduce or eliminate homosexual behavior and awareness of homosexual feelings *without altering the sexual orientation*" (emphasis added).[78] The American Psychological Association's "Fact Sheet on Reparative Therapy" succinctly

concludes that "[n]o scientific evidence exists to support the effectiveness of any of the conversion therapies that try to change sexual orientation."

Religion Therapy

80. One report of heterosexual reorientation claims a religiously mediated influence.[79] Changes occurred in the context of a crisis service provided by a Pentecostal church to its homosexual members. The investigators located thirty men who claimed to have changed from homosexuality to heterosexuality out of a group of three hundred "dissatisfied" homosexuals who had initially requested treatment. Only eleven of the thirty would cooperate in the study by submitting to interviews. When interviewed, one man acknowledged homosexual dreams, three acknowledged homosexual fantasies, and five acknowledged homosexual impulses. The homosexual impulses of three subjects were "a source of neurotic conflict."[80] The subjects who married reported that initially their homosexual dreams, fantasies, and impulses had not vanished. However, "as they progressed in a satisfactory marital relationship, their homosexual dreams, fantasies, and impulses gradually diminished over time."[81] None of the unmarried men was engaging in heterosexual intercourse "because of religious prohibitions."[82]

81. The Pattisons' study has been subjected to substantial criticism. One researcher, after reviewing the study, concluded that the "Pattison data present an unconvincing picture of heterosexual conversion following a treatment program that is poorly described to begin with, and founded upon ill-defined constructs."[83]

"Homosexual" or "Prehomosexual" Children

82. A fifteen-year longitudinal study that I conducted also points to the very early and essentially irreversible establishment of sexual orientation in the male. In that research there was identified a series of sixty-six boys, ages four through twelve, who displayed extensive cross-gender behaviors. This included statements of wishing to be a girl, preferential cross-dressing in women's or girls' clothes, preferential play with stereotypically female-type toys (dress-up dolls), preferential role playing as a female in fantasy games, a female peer group, and avoidance of rough-and-tumble play and sports. These boys and their parents were matched demographically with families in which the boys showed conventionally masculine behaviors. Two-thirds of both groups were followed for fifteen years.

83. Of the previously cross-gender or feminine boys, three-quarters are currently homosexually or bisexually oriented. By contrast, all but one of the previously conventionally masculine group are heterosexual.

84. The irreversibility of the prehomosexual behavioral pattern, even when "treated" early, was demonstrated. Approximately one-third of the cross-gendered boys were involved in psychotherapy with treatment directed at changing sexual identity. Yet the rate of homosexual or bisexual behavior in the treated group is no different from that in the untreated group.[84] Thus, not only is treatment during adulthood aimed at reorienting homosexual orientation generally unrewarding, but so is treatment during boyhood aimed at preventing the development of homosexual orientation.

85. On the basis of my research and the research of other investigators, most experts in the area have concluded that sexual orientation is set by early childhood.[85] The fact that sexual orientation is "predetermined" at an early age, however, does not mean that all (or even most) gays identify themselves as such at an early age. Rather, the evidence shows self-identification of individuals as homosexuals frequently occurs substantially after, often in young adulthood. Harry concluded that "[t]he median age for 'coming out' or fully realizing one's homosexuality . . . is approximately 19 or 20."[86]

Conclusion

86. The poor results of treatment directed at homosexual orientation and the evidence for a genetic or hormonal basis of homosexual orientation are not reverse sides of the same coin. Learned phenomena may be extremely resistant to change, particularly those learned early in life. The paradigm of the first language is an example. Conversely, a behavior may be inborn and related to brain functioning but still amenable to change. The paradigm of left-handedness is an example.

87. The research reviewed above does not prove that sexual orientation, or at least homosexual orientation, is entirely genetically determined or entirely hormonally induced. The data do point, however, to some degree of contribution from these sources. An objective comparison of the evidence behind genetic and/or hormonal influences reveals it to be at least as strong as the posited Freudian concepts or the behaviorist idea of "mislearning" homosexual arousal. Indeed, the very disappointing outcome of psychotherapy based on these theoretical constructs casts doubt on these theories.

88. Nor does the finding that one can with great effort graft apparently heterosexual behavior over an earlier homosexual orientation mean that sexual orientation is mutable. The arduous process of "reorientation" is psychologically wrenching and has been sometimes physically painful. Therapy may not be much more effective than what would be expected from attempts to reorient heterosexuals.

Kenneth Sherrill

AFFIDAVIT

On Gay People as a Politically Powerless Group

KENNETH SHERRILL is a professor of political science at Hunter College, City University of New York, and at the Graduate School and University Center, City University of New York. A recognized expert in the field of American politics, he specializes in the study of public opinion, political participation, political movements, voting, and other forms of political behavior.

His affidavit develops a theoretical model for measuring the relative political power of a given group. Sherrill then applies this model to the characteristics of the gay community in the United States today and identifies the factors that have led gays to be disadvantaged politically. He combines original data and secondary analysis to demonstrate the lack of political power by the lesbian and gay community. Sherrill provides a framework in which to argue that a lack of sufficient levels of cohesive community and collective identity forestall most efforts at the effective exercise of political power by lesbians and gays.

Using data from national surveys as well as evidence from congressional debates and from popular culture, Sherrill demonstrates that lesbians and gays are disadvantaged as individuals and as a group by the overwhelmingly negative stereotypes and by prejudice. This further weakens the political impact gay people might reasonably expect to have and creates disincentives for collective activity to advance the cause of equal rights for gay people.

Thus, Sherrill concludes, gay people—as a result of being burdened by discrimination—lack the political power necessary to obtain redress for their grievances through normal majoritarian mechanisms of the national political process.

The Political Theory of Pluralist Democracy

1. Political scientists generally agree that "pure" democracy, a system of government in which all citizens participate in both ruling and being ruled, in which all citizens participate fully in the process of making decisions that are then binding on the entire political community, is neither practical nor possible when the population of the community exceeds that of a small city-state, such as Aristotle's Athens. Nevertheless, most political scientists operate on the assumption that some form of democracy, or rule by the people, is a desirable characteristic of a political system.

2. One distinguishing characteristic of realistic systems of popular sovereignty (i.e., rule by the people) is a system of representative government in which the citizens choose people from among themselves who are entrusted with the day-to-day responsibilities of governing, but who remain, in some fashion, responsible and accountable to the people. Thus, direct democracy is replaced with indirect democracy. For the average citizen, then, participation in political life moves from fully sharing in the decision-making process to participating in the choice of decision makers and to articulating one's political interests, needs, and wants.

3. Once again, however, the sheer size of the population of a modern political system precludes all but a few of the citizenry from communicating directly with decision makers. In fact, in modern complex societies, only a few can participate fully in framing the choices placed before the citizens—that is, in determining from among which relatively small set of candidates the citizens may choose their representatives and in determining the specific issues and policy alternatives that are debated publicly.

4. In such a political system, it is unreasonable to participate as individuals. Even those with immense personal wealth and personal fame must acquire the support of others in the process of choosing among competing candidates and policy options if they are to have any legitimate hope of prevailing in the political struggle. Thus, the political struggle becomes transformed from one in which individual citizens participate fully in the process of governing to one in which *groups* of people choose sides over candidates and policies in the hope of prevailing.

5. The transition to group-based politics raises vexing questions of equality of political opportunity and of equal rights. How are competing groups to be treated when it comes to articulating their policy preferences and participating fully in debate and other aspects of the political process? James Madison, in *Federalist No. 10*, provided one of the most compelling theories of a political process seeking to maximize popular sovereignty and political equality while also seeking to prevent tyranny and the severe deprivation of natural rights (e.g., life, liberty, and property). In many ways, the Madisonian system provides the basis for modern theories of pluralist democracy.

6. To prevent tyranny, it is essential to prevent the concentration of power in a few hands. Political power must be dispersed widely, so that the tyrannical impulses of some might be checked by the power of others. There are three major mechanisms for achieving the dispersion of power. One is a written constitution, establishing rules for the political process that are placed beyond the realm of normal political action. This written constitution would disperse political power into an elaborate clockwork mechanism of checks and balances, separation of powers, and federalism. Essential to the success of such a system would be an independent judiciary, insulated from the tyrannical passions of the moment. In such a system of countervailing powers in which virtually all groups would be guaranteed access to the decision-making process at some crucial point, virtually all groups could articulate their preferences. As important, given the complex and cumbersome processes of assembling majorities with different bases in each formal institution of government, virtually any significant group would have access to veto points, to times and places in the decision-making process at which a threatened group might stop a potentially tyrannical action. The sheer difficulty of making and implementing policies for the nation, Madison expected, would prevent tyranny and abuse of power.

7. Structural dispersion of the power to make decisions, however, would not be sufficient to prevent tyranny. The tyranny that Madison most feared was *tyranny of the majority*—the severe deprivation of the rights of the minority. Many, such as Charles Beard,[1] contend that the particular minority the Framers were concerned with protecting was the propertied. Pluralist democracy in general, and the American constitutional system in particular, are devoted to protecting the rights of those who are hopelessly outnumbered and despised. It matters not, however, with *which* minority we are con-

cerned. Certainly, in a system of one person, one vote, those without property were likely to outnumber those with property, and they were highly likely to covet and seek to obtain that property for themselves. Indeed, it was not difficult to imagine a situation in which those without property might seek to acquire property for themselves by force and violence.

8. Thus, Madisonian democracy—and pluralist democracy by extension—looks to the structure of society as a source of guarantees against tyranny. To the degree that the citizenry is extended and diverse, Madison argued, the very nature of the population would frustrate the formation of a tyrannical majority. This means that there would have to be widespread participation in the political process (an extended citizenry) and there would have to be a wide range of competing interests (a diverse citizenry). The more diverse the citizenry, the harder it would be to form a permanent and tyrannical majority. The simple fact is that the wider the range of political interests that must be satisfied, the harder it is to hold a majority political coalition together.

9. Modern-day pluralists such as Robert A. Dahl[2] contend that American politics is best characterized as *minorities rule*, a political system in which diverse and amorphous coalitions of minorities constantly re-form and coalesce, in which different groups and interests coalesce to form majorities in different policy domains so that there is no permanent majority. Since there is no majority, there is no tyranny of the majority—at least not in the ideal case. Indeed, in demographic terms, there are very few groups capable of being permanent majorities in the United States and thus capable of being tyrannical over minorities. One such group is women, making up about 53 percent of the population. Rarely, if ever, in American history have women coalesced as a political group to deprive men of natural rights. In fact, men deprived women of the right to vote for a majority of the life of our constitutional system.

10. The other nationwide demographic majorities in the United States have had an easier time depriving minorities of their rights. These groups are: whites, who systematically tyrannized nonwhites, including through a system of slavery; Christians, who constantly must be restrained in their efforts to impose their religious preferences on Jews, Moslems, agnostics, and atheists; and heterosexuals, who through control of the apparatus of the state and of virtually all social institutions tyrannize homosexuals.

11. Finally, in the pluralist system, there would be psychological constraints against tyranny. People would believe in the constitutional system and support the rules of the game. Of course, if people were angels, there would be no need for a written constitution or to rely on ambition to countervail ambition. Over time, however, it might be reasonable to expect that people would discover the joys of living in a nontyrannical republic and would develop a vested interest in protecting a system that guarantees the rights of all. To the degree that outcroppings of tyranny such as racism, religious bigotry, and heterosexism persist, we must rely on constitutional guarantees.

Pluralism and Power Resources

12. To assess a group's political power, a political scientist will look at the net balance of all "power resources" available to the group and at its use over a wide range of situations, including varying venues and policy domains. Power resources are those things that people may use in order to acquire or exercise political power. In many cases, these resources are acquired as a result of being powerful and are then reinvested in the quest for additional power. Political skill is the knowledge of how to use power resources wisely; it is the knowledge of how to achieve political ends without expending power resources, of how to use existing resources to gain power and to develop new resources.

13. Political power is understood to be the ability to get others to act in accordance with your preferences, without regard to their preferences.[3] The powerful are understood to be those with the ability to get the most of what there is to get of the available values in society (those things that society highly values): deference, safety, and wealth.[4] Political power is not an absolute quality, nor is it a tangible substance to be "poured into a keg, stored, and then drawn upon as the need arises."[5] Rather, political power is best conceived as a relational concept. One group has power over another on a certain issue, but not necessarily on other issues. As Key writes, "Politics as power consists fundamentally of relationships of superordination and subordination, of dominance and submission, of the governors and the governed."[6]

14. Since power is a relational concept, it makes little sense to speak of being powerful or of being powerless in absolute terms.

Rarely, if at all, does a group prevail on all issues in all jurisdictions. Similarly, the fact that a group prevails on occasional issues in certain jurisdictions does not mean that the group has meaningful political power on a national scale. Rather, in assessing the relative power and/or powerlessness of a group, one must examine the group's access to available political resources and values and the relative frequency of the group's effective use of those values and resources in its quest for political power.

15. One must not confuse the political power and effectiveness of individuals who are members of a particular political group with the group's power. In a modern, complex, pluralistic society, individual persons are members of many overlapping groups: groups that often compete with one another for the loyalty of individual members and for dominance in various policy arenas. Indeed, this was one of the reasons why Madison valued a diverse and extended electorate. Today, overlapping membership in groups is a fundamental tenet of theorists of group-based politics.[7] The fact that individuals who are members of a group are powerful does not mean that the group is powerful. It is possible that some individuals are powerful in spite of their having certain group memberships.

16. Thus, it is inaccurate to argue, for example, that because certain homosexuals are in positions of power, gay people are a powerful political group. It is also inaccurate to argue that because gay people may be powerful in certain jurisdictions or with regard to certain policy domains, gay people as a group have meaningful national political power. To make such an argument, substantially more—and better—evidence must be adduced.

17. The available values for which people compete in political life have been identified by Harold D. Lasswell as deference, safety, and income or wealth. Deference values include respect, affection, and being perceived as holding power itself, as well as rectitude or moral righteousness. Income values include wealth, well-being, skill, and enlightenment. While safety is a value in and of itself, it is best understood as meaning that members of a particular group have a low probability of meeting a violent death or of being the object of violence.

18. Other scholars have identified additional power resources that political groups might use in their quest for power. A list would include, but not be limited to, numbers, the sheer number of people who may be in a particular group, as well as the group's size in relation to that of other groups; and cohesion and shared identity—the propensity of people to think of themselves primarily as members of a particular group and to act in accordance with that identity. In a modern, complex, pluralistic society, a group must be cohesive to compete effectively for available values and resources. The group's members must place a priority on identifying with that group, as opposed to the other groups with which the person might identify. The group's members must have a sense of solidarity and of sharing common values, conditions, and/or grievances. The more strongly people feel about a group, the more likely they are to take action on matters affecting the group. Indeed, the more strongly people feel, the greater the number of ways in which they are likely to take action: getting into discussions with other people about these issues, voting, using group-related issues as standards for determining how to vote, contributing money, volunteering time, writing letters, joining organizations, attending rallies.

19. Finally, particularly for groups that are low on these resources, allies are a critical resource. In majoritarian politics, any minority must obtain the support of other groups who are willing to enter the political fray in their support. Media attention, or news coverage, is often essential to gaining allies.[8] Access, the ability to get the attention of those people who are in positions to make decisions affecting a group and the causes that matter to it, is also central to the effective use of other resources.

20. Thus, modern political theory teaches that in assessing the political power of gays as a minority group, one would assess the extent to which gays as a group have the resources necessary to achieve their goals through the political process. An examination of these factors shows that gays are relatively politically powerless.

A Consideration of Political Resources Available to Gay People: Numerosity

21. In majoritarian politics, those who accumulate more than half of the votes cast are the winners. As noted earlier, in complex modern societies with diverse and extended electorates, there are few "natural" majorities. Groups must combine into coalitions in order to assemble enough votes to form a majority. Groups that are numerous need to find fewer allies in order to enter into a winning majority coalition, while groups with few members must find many

allies. Groups that are easily outnumbered are relatively powerless. Accordingly, the natural starting point in assessing the political power of gays and lesbians is estimating their numbers.

22. The time-honored Kinsey estimate of the percentage of Americans who are primarily homosexual in orientation is 10 percent.[9] In fact, Kinsey and his colleagues concluded, on the basis of extended interviews with twelve thousand men, that "at least 13 per cent of the male population [are] predominantly homosexual."[10] Thus, it would appear that solely on the basis of the numbers, gays constitute a minority group that is relatively politically powerless. The numbers themselves, however, overstate the extent to which gays can use their votes to exercise political power.

23. The Kinsey researchers noted the sharp disjuncture between their estimate and the estimate that might be arrived at based on evidence that might be derived from data collected by the American military. They report that "over-all figures show that about one-tenth of 1 per cent of all the men were rejected by draft boards ... and about 0.4 per cent were turned down at induction centers ... and about as many more were subsequently discharged for homosexual activity while they were in active service. The total gives about 1 per cent officially identified as 'homosexual'. These figures are so much lower than any which case histories have obtained that they need critical examination."[11] Their critique of the quality of the military's estimate of the percent homosexual continues:

> The most obvious explanation of these very low figures lies in the fact that both the Army and Navy had precluded the possibility of getting accurate data on these matters by announcing at the beginning of the war that they intended to exclude all persons with homosexual histories. . . . While the reasons for elimination of any man were supposed to be kept confidential, they were in actuality not infrequently known to the whole community in which he lived. . . . Consequently few men with any common sense would admit their homosexual experience . . . at induction centers or in the services.[12]

24. Many other estimates of the percent of the population who are gay or lesbian are sharply lower than the Kinsey estimate. Some of these studies asked the respondent directly whether he or she was homosexual, gay, lesbian, or bisexual. Clearly, a respondent fearing the opprobrium showed toward gay people would feel substantial pressure to deny his or her homosexual orientation. Other studies, such as the General Social Survey, conducted by the National Opinion Research Center at the University of Chicago in 1988, asked the respondent whether he or she had had sexual relations with men, women, or both in the past year, and about how many times each had occurred.[13] Again, a respondent fearing opprobrium and loss of anonymity would feel great pressure to give a response conforming to social norms. Consequently, the Kinsey questions may be the most reliable because they encourage the respondent to believe "that we would not be surprised if he had had such experience" because "we always assume that everyone has engaged in every type of activity."[14]

25. It thus appears that estimates of the gay population that fall substantially below 10 percent are, in fact, measures of the pressures not to reveal one's homosexual orientation. To the extent that this is the case, gay people who are unable to run the risk of revealing their gayness are disempowered politically. One of the burdens of anti-gay prejudice and the fear it engenders is that many people will be silent about a crucial aspect of their identity and that others will misperceive their group to be substantially less numerous than it is.

26. Fear of being identified with an unpopular group also diminishes the likelihood that an individual will take any other form of political action that manifests support for a group—actions such as wearing buttons, placing bumper stickers on a car, signing or distributing petitions, or making campaign contributions. Thus, beyond being made less numerous through repressive devices, gay people are further disempowered. This process is known as "the Spiral of Silence," which Elisabeth Noelle-Neumann identifies as "the process by which ideologies and social movements prevail or are swept away." "The fear of isolation seems to be the force that sets the spiral of silence in motion."[15]

27. Noelle-Neumann's research indicates that in a wide range of situations, people who believe that they hold unpopular beliefs or positions fear isolation and retaliation by those in the majority and consequently refuse to reveal their views. In politics, this magnifies the power of the majority and further diminishes that of the minority. Given the public's distaste for homosexuals, and given the extraordinary levels of anti-gay violence and hate crime (discussed in greater detail below), the number of gay people willing to take political action is further diminished, and gay people are rendered even more powerless.

28. Evidence of this "spiral of silence" is provided by a recent survey conducted by Voter Research and Services (VRS) on November 6, 1990. Of 17,768 voters leaving the voting booth, a total of 203 respondents checked a box at the end of the questionnaire that said they were "gay or lesbian." In most ways, the Kinsey data lead one to conclude that homosexual orientation is relatively randomly distributed about the population. The VRS data, based on exit polls, provide a dramatically different picture of the gay voter.* About 90 percent of lesbian and gay voters in this study have completed more than high school, compared to two-thirds of the national sample. In the VRS study, gay and lesbian voters are about twice as likely as the national sample (27 percent versus 14 percent) to be under thirty, while they are over three times less likely to be over sixty years old (6 percent versus 22 percent). Gay and lesbian voters are also found to be more heavily concentrated in the 30–44 age range (48 percent versus 37 percent) and less concentrated in the 45–59 age group (20 percent versus 26 percent).

29. The disparity between the VRS and Kinsey studies, and the two studies' differences in research methods, provide a political scientist with a means of viewing the impact of the spiral of silence on gay people. There is no good reason to believe that there is any relationship between homosexual orientation and higher education. In spite of the impact of AIDS, one ought not expect the relationship between age and homosexual orientation to be as dramatic as that shown by the VRS data. Rather, as many as 90 percent of gay people may not feel free enough to reveal their homosexual orientation on an exit poll. If nine out of ten gay people do not feel safe revealing their homosexual orientation under these conditions, one can hardly expect gay people to feel safe enough in heterosexist society to take the public actions that successful political action requires. Clearly, those gay people who feel least vulnerable—the highly educated and the young—are much more likely than older and less well-educated gay people to be capable of trying to take political action.

30. Thus, the data lead to the conclusion that gay people are a minority—perhaps 10 to 13 percent of the American people, roughly the same percent of the population as is African-American. Unlike African-Americans, however, gay people are invisible. They can be

---

* One might speculate that gay voters differ from gay nonvoters in manners similar to those in which all voters differ from nonvoters. A sample of voters is likely to be older, better educated, and more affluent than the population as a whole.

presumed to be heterosexual and pass for heterosexual. Further, by passing for heterosexual, gay people can try to avoid the opprobrium and violence visited on gay people by heterosexists. Thus, there are substantial personal incentives for individual homosexuals to act in a fashion that encourages straight society to believe that there are many fewer gay people than is the truth. Heterosexual society, intentionally or not, has constructed a system of incentives for gay people to remain invisible. This has the effect of diminishing the perceived number of gay people and also inhibits the capability of gay people to organize for effective political action. That inhibition has its greatest impact on those who are already relatively powerless: those who are older and less well educated. We see a cycle in which the political deprivations of gay people become increasingly cumulative.

31. The other way in which the political power of gay people is artificially deflated beyond their numbers results from the pattern of dispersion of individuals who are willing to disclose their homosexual orientation across the country. Areas of the United States vary in their general political tolerance and in the degree to which they are homophobic or homophilic. There is no good reason to believe that gay people are disproportionately born in one area of the country or another. Some areas of the nation have developed reputations, however, for being oases of tolerance and some of those gay people who are able to migrate leave the more repressive areas of the nation for those areas in which they are relatively free to lead lives as openly gay people.

32. Thus, the VRS data indicate substantial variation in the percent of voters in each state who are willing and able to avow their homosexual orientation. In California, 2.43 percent of all voters said they were gay or lesbian; in Colorado, 2.04 percent did. At the other extreme, only 0.31 percent of voters said they were gay or lesbian in Ohio and in Kentucky. This variation both reflects the political climate in the various states and affects it, serving as a further example of the spiral of silence and its disempowering impact on gay people.

33. Other data from the VRS study confirm the validity of this analysis. Respondents living in communities with populations of 50,000 or higher were twice as likely to say they were gay or lesbian than those living in suburbs, rural areas or towns with populations under 50,000. Respondents in the West were twice as likely as those in other regions of the country to say they were gay or lesbian. Only

11 of 6,422 married respondents said they were gay or lesbian, as did only 6 of 2,295 retired respondents. Finally, there was no difference between those who had a family member in the armed forces on November 6, 1990—during the Persian Gulf buildup—and those who did not to say they were gay or lesbian. One percent of each group responded positively to the item.

34. As a result of this phenomenon, the gay minority is particularly handicapped in exercising political power on the national level. That is because the House of Representatives was designed to represent the population and the Senate was designed to represent states and the political interests concentrated in those states. While gays may be sufficiently concentrated in particular congressional districts to exercise some influence, gays as a group are not numerous enough in any state—let alone a majority of the states—to expect that their interests will be represented in the Senate on a regular (or even irregular) basis.

Deference, Affection, and the Political Powerlessness of Gays

35. Another factor that diminishes the relative political power of gays is the fact that Americans do not like homosexuals and do not feel close to homosexuals. Data collected in the 1988 General Social Survey conducted under the direction of the National Opinion Research Center at the University of Chicago and made available for scholarly analysis under the auspices of the Inter-University Consortium for Social and Political Research reveal that while 59.5 percent of the American people would allow a homosexual to teach in a local college or university, 61.4 percent would not allow someone who favored doing away with elections and allowing the military to run the country to teach in one.[16]

36. The overwhelming fact is that Americans are not positively disposed to homosexuals. Being known as a homosexual is not a political asset. In a nationwide telephone survey of a random sample of 1,424 adults, a CBS News/New York Times Poll asked, "How much sympathy do you have for people who have AIDS—a lot, some, or not much?" Fifty-one percent said "a lot"; 33 percent said "some"; 9 percent said "not much"; and 2 percent volunteered "none." (Five percent did not know or did not answer.) When the question was changed to "How much sympathy do you have for people who get AIDS from homosexual activity—a lot, some, or not much?" the responses changed dramatically. Only 19 percent said "a lot" and 20 percent said "some." Under these conditions, 42 percent said they had "not much" sympathy and 18 percent volunteered "none." Only 1 percent did not know or had no answer. In the abstract, 84 percent had some or a lot of sympathy for a Person with AIDS (PWA), yet only 39 percent—less than half as many—did for a gay PWA. The disease had not changed; only the sexual orientation of the person had. This serves as a classic example of lack of the value or power resource Lasswell terms "rectitude": "The sense of responsibility and the standards of right conduct."[17]

37. A second deference value in Lasswell's conceptualization of power is affection. In a democracy, "the myth emphasizes the desirability of congenial human relationships, and emphasizes the capacity of human beings for entering into such relations."[18] Further, in a democracy, "there needs to be equality of opportunity for the exercise of affection as a means of achieving affection . . . [and] the scope of affection for human beings needs to be as wide as humanity."[19]

38. Since 1964, the National Election Studies conducted by the Center for Political Studies at the University of Michigan have used a technique known as the "feeling thermometer" to measure the feelings Americans have toward various groups in society. The respondent is told: "Here's how it works. If you don't know too much about a group or don't feel particularly warm or cold toward them, then you should place them in the middle, at the fifty degree mark. If you have a warm feeling toward the group, or feel favorably toward it, you would give it a score somewhere between fifty and one hundred degrees depending on how warm your feeling is toward the group. On the other hand, if you don't feel very favorably toward some of these groups—if there are some you don't care for too much—then you would place them somewhere between zero and fifty degrees." The respondents are then handed a list of groups and asked to locate their feelings toward each group on the feeling thermometer.

39. The 1984 Michigan study asked people to place their feelings toward fourteen groups on the thermometer. One of the groups was lesbians and gay men. Fully 61.5 percent of the sample placed their feelings toward gay people *below* 50 degrees, with 30.5 percent at

zero—the coldest and most negative feelings possible. Only 2.3 percent were over 90 degrees, including 1.8 percent at 100 degrees.*

40. These data must be placed into the context of Americans' feelings toward other groups. In the same survey, Americans were asked about thirteen other groups—women, blacks, Hispanics, the middle class, poor people, whites, liberals, conservatives, evangelicals, Catholics, people on welfare, anti-abortionists, and the military. Of all fourteen groups, only lesbians and gay men were placed below 50 degrees by a majority—61.5 percent—of this national sample. The closest that any other group came to evoking such cold feelings from their fellow Americans was evangelicals (40.2 percent—less than two-thirds as much). They were followed by anti-abortionists (35.8 percent), people on welfare (30.1 percent—less than half as much), and liberals (23.1 percent). No other group evoked cold feelings from as much as 20 percent of the American people. In fact, the 30.5 percent who placed their feelings toward gay people at zero degrees exceeded the total percent having cold feelings for all groups other than evangelicals and anti-abortionists. No other group competed with gay people's having virtually half of all people holding cold feelings toward the group placing those feelings at the coldest extreme.

41. These data may be replicated with data collected in the 1988 National Election Study conducted by the Michigan team of scholars. Negative and cold feelings on the part of Americans toward homosexuals actually increased slightly in the intervening years. This time, respondents were asked to evaluate unions, feminists, civil rights leaders, people on welfare, women, conservatives, poor people, Catholics, big business, blacks, evangelical groups active in politics, the federal government in Washington, liberals, Hispanics, the military, the elderly, people seeking to protect the environment, the Supreme Court, illegal aliens, Palestinians, opponents of abortion, whites, Jews, gay men and lesbians (that is, homosexuals), Congress, and Christian fundamentalists.

42. In 1988, 35 percent of the American people placed their feelings toward gay people at zero degrees—the coldest possible extreme. The closest any other groups came to this were illegal aliens at

---

* This leads us to believe that few respondents other than those who might have been openly gay placed their feelings at one hundred degrees. Those people who felt compelled to hide their homosexual orientation may well have manifested self-hate in order to avoid injudicious revelations about themselves.

18 percent and Palestinians at 15 percent. Americans are almost twice as likely to have the coldest possible feelings toward homosexuals as we are to have them toward illegal aliens. In 1988, a total of 63 percent of the American people indicated negative feelings toward homosexuals. No group—not even illegal aliens at 59 percent and Palestinians at 51 percent—exceeded the total percentage of Americans holding cold or negative feelings toward them accorded to gay people. The only other group toward which a majority held negative feelings were evangelical groups active in politics, with a total of 53 percent negative—but only 15 percent were at zero, less than one-quarter the percentage holding the most extreme negative feelings toward gay people.

43. A final way of looking at these distributions is to compare the mean, or arithmetic average, of the groups' ratings on the feeling thermometer. Gay people have the lowest average score: 29 degrees. The only other groups having averages below 50 degrees are illegal aliens at 36, Palestinians at 37 and evangelical groups active in politics at an average of 39 degrees on the feeling thermometer. At the other extreme, the elderly have an average score of 82 degrees, women average 79, and people seeking to protect the environment average 77 degrees on the feeling thermometer.

44. The feeling thermometer data on feelings toward gay people stand in sharp contradistinction to the data on feelings toward other groups. For example, in 1988, the average feeling toward blacks was placed at 62 degrees, with 12 percent saying that they had cold or negative feelings toward black people and only 2 percent placing their feelings at zero degrees, the coldest extreme. Interestingly, in 1964, the year of the passage of the Civil Rights Act of 1964, the average feeling toward blacks was 67 degrees, with 13 percent placing their feelings below 50 degrees and 2 percent at zero. In the intervening years, there has been relatively little change in Americans' feelings toward black people as measured by the feeling thermometer. The average score has ranged from a low of 61 degrees in 1976 to a high of 67 in 1964. The total percent having cold or negative feelings toward blacks has ranged from a low of 10 percent in 1986 and 1968 to a high of 15 percent in 1966. The percent having the coldest feelings toward blacks has varied between 1 percent in 1984 and 3 percent in 1966 and 1970.

45. These data mean that in 1988, Americans were more than five times as likely to have negative feelings toward gay people (63 per-

cent) than toward black people (12 percent) and over seventeen times as likely to hold the coldest possible feelings toward gay people (35 percent) as toward black people (2 percent). Only 7 percent said they had negative feelings toward Jews, and only 1 percent placed their feelings toward Jews at the coldest extreme. Only 2 percent said they had negative feelings toward women and none placed these feelings at the coldest extreme.

46. These data make the magnitude of Americans' hostility toward gay people eminently clear. On the other hand, the low levels of hostility toward women, Jews and blacks seems counterintuitive. We routinely experience manifestations of sexism, anti-Semitism, and racism. One explanation for the difference may well be found in the fact that for over a generation it has been illegal to discriminate on the basis of race, religion, or sex. The existence of laws against discrimination has taught the American people that it is *wrong* to discriminate and that it is not prudent to indicate that one holds hostile attitudes toward protected groups. The existence of antidiscrimination legislation may well have changed attitudes as well as behavior. The absence of such protection for gay people indicates to many Americans that it is still socially acceptable behavior to be a homophobe.

47. Despite their hostility, the American people, however, tend to support many civil liberties for gay people. For example, the 1988 General Social Survey found that 72.6 percent believed that homosexuals should be allowed to give a speech in their home town; 62.7 percent would oppose a proposal to remove a book by a homosexual author from the local library; and 59.5 percent would allow a homosexual to teach in a local college or university. This represents some progress. In 1973, only 60.7 percent of the American people said they would allow gay persons to give a speech in their home town; 53.5 percent would oppose a proposal to remove a book by a gay person from the library; and only 47.3 percent supported the right of a gay person to teach in a college or university. In fifteen years, Americans did not learn to like homosexuals. Rather, with increasing higher education and replacement of a more conservative older generation with a more liberal younger generation, the American people became more aware of civil liberties and more willing to support basic constitutional rights for people whom they did not like.

48. The increasing tendency of Americans to view the rights of gay people as a civil liberties issue distinct from their evaluation of homosexuals is evidenced by data collected by Penn and Schoen for a report to the Human Rights Campaign Fund. They find that 80 percent of Americans said that "homosexuals should ... have equal rights for jobs" and that 65 percent thought "homosexuals should ... be admitted to the armed forces." In addition, 81 percent thought that the government should not discharge a homosexual from the armed forces if the person "is otherwise doing a good job."

49. Nevertheless, the everyday language of American mass culture reveals a litany of slurs against gay people. For example, in speaking in favor of the Hate Crime Act, which merely enabled the government to collect data of crimes motivated by prejudice on the basis of race, religion, ethnicity, or sexual orientation, Senator Bill Bradley felt compelled to point out that the bill "expresses no approval of homosexual behavior. Moreover, this act gives no substantive rights."

50. Two points are immediately clear. First, given the large number of members of both Houses who felt compelled to point out that the bill did not approve of homosexual behavior and did not create a right to an action based on discrimination, a bill that *did* one or both of those things would have no chance of passage and many members feared that merely collecting data on anti-gay crimes might jettison all hope of passing legislation collecting data on *any* sort of hate crimes.*

51. Second, no other type of hate crime required a disclaimer. Try to imagine a member of Congress feeling that he or she had to reassure colleagues and constituents that collecting data on racial violence or anti-Semitic acts in no way condoned being African-American or Jewish. The absurdity of the situation makes the magnitude of anti-gay bias manifest. Why should an effort to count the number of hate crimes committed against various groups in society set off this sort of struggle? The answer is twofold: first, there is substantial opposition to considering gay people a group in society at all—thus confirming the low level of respect and deference accorded gay people; second, some politicians think they can advance their careers by reflecting in their own statements the homophobia they perceive in the mass public.

* Indeed, hate-crime legislation has not passed in the state of New York *because* the Republican-controlled State Senate refuses to pass it as long as it includes anti-gay hate crimes, and the Black and Latino Caucus, following the lead of State Senator David Paterson of Harlem, has refused to support a "compromise" version that excludes anti-gay hate crimes.

52. While Senator Bradley's remarks were probably intended to be helpful to gay people, and while his remarks were probably not intended to be insulting or demeaning, many people in public life seek to profit from debasing gay people. The success of entertainers, athletes, and politicians who spew hatred of gay people is testimony to the breadth and depth of anti-gay sentiment in the American public. Following is only a small sample of examples:

—On February 5, 1986, Bob Grant, the host of a popular call-in show on New York's WABC Radio station, introduced a guest with the following remarks: "There are some individuals who have not been intimidated by the 'gay' community. There are a few stalwart individuals who are still able to call a spade a spade. There are some individuals who are still able to recognize that homosexuality is a craven aberration." One person called in, saying, "I was a schoolteacher. But I was fired because I was gay." Grant responded, "Well, thank God they did! Good for the school that fired you." A second caller said, "There are homosexuals who are decent people, who hold jobs, make a living, pay taxes, and you know, are family oriented." Grant broke in, "Family oriented? That's impossible. That's a contradiction in terms. You can't be a faggala and be family oriented." On March 10, 1986, Grant asked a caller, "Are you a homosexual?" The caller responded, "Yes, I am." Grant responded with salvo that included the following remarks: "You, you're not capable of looking at yourself in the mirror and saying, 'I am a fag. I am a queer. I am a perverted individual.' You can't do that, but you should . . . repeat after me; 'I am a perverted misfit.' . . . Make the trip in. . . . Let me punch your nose right down your throat."

—C. Boyden Gray, the White House counsel, in response to a question at a meeting of the Montgomery County Republican Club in Chevy Chase, Maryland, explained that former House Speaker Jim Wright had spread rumors that a Federal Home Loan Bank Board examiner "was a fag," and according to the *Bethesda Gazette*, Gray repeated the word when he was later questioned about his remark.

—In the lyrics to the song "One in a Million" on the album *Lies*, the heavy metal group Guns N' Roses sings: "Immigrants and faggots / they make no sense to me / They come to our country / And think they'll do as they please / Like start some mini-Iran / Or spread some fucking disease."

—The Associated Press reported that California Assemblyman Gil Ferguson "called a group of gay protesters 'faggots' [and] did not realize that the term was offensive but will not apologize." He is quoted as saying, "I didn't even know that 'faggot' was a derogatory term. That's what I've always heard them called. I know that people don't call them 'queers' any-more," he said.

—A coach at a midwestern college is quoted in the June 4, 1991, issue of *The Advocate* as saying, "As unfortunate as it is that this sort of harass-ment goes on, these girls really bring it on themselves. It just isn't impor-tant to be openly lesbian in college. . . . I don't think it's discrimination if these coaches keep these players off their teams. It's for the good of the team. And frankly, in the long run it can only benefit women's sports."

53. The point of this litany of slurs is to give qualitative evidence of the low levels of respect, deference, and affection for gay people in the United States. People who make such statements do so because they know that among wide segments of the American population, such sentiments are shared and applauded. These slurs encourage and reinforce homophobia. They also serve to remind gay people of their unpopularity and powerless situation. No doubt they serve to discourage gay people from participating in politics and attempting to share in power.

54. The disempowering effects of a rhetoric of slurs may be great-est for young people as they come to realize that they are gay or les-bian. The media present images of reality to people who have not yet directly experienced events. Listening to talk show hosts, popular musicians, comedians, politicians, and coaches such as the ones we have cited must have an extraordinarily negative effect on the self-image of gay people and discourage them from taking effective polit-ical action. Listening to these people teaches Americans that bigotry is acceptable and reduces the probability that gay people will be ac-corded the respect, deference, and affection that characterize the politically powerful.

Safety and the Political Powerlessness of Gays

55. There is a dual nexus among deference, safety, and power. On one hand, highly respected and powerful people are often the targets of violence in wars, assassination plots, and coups, and by deranged persons. Such lack of safety, however, tends to charac-terize individuals as opposed to groups of people. On the other hand, groups of powerless people are often targeted for violence be-cause they are not respected and because members of a dominant group wish to keep them in subservient positions in society. Racial lynchings in the United States; concentration camps and systematic murder of Jews, homosexuals, and gypsies in Nazi Germany; and other holocausts are classic examples of this latter nexus among safety, deference, and power. Thus, a lynching is more than the murder of an individual person; it is a threat to an entire group of people. It is an act of terrorism, designed to strike fear into the hearts of members of the group in the expectation that it will motivate compliant behavior (i.e., powerlessness) and paralyze the instincts to seek to achieve one's own goals and preferences (i.e., bring about powerlessness).

56. In the United States today gay people as a group are subject to a constant threat, and the all too frequent reality, of violence. This factor, too, tends to diminish the relative political power of homosexuals both because it creates disincentives for gay people to identify themselves as such and because it creates disincentives for members of other groups to associate themselves with gays.

57. The evidence for the proposition that gays as a group are disproportionately the targets of violence and that that violence is motivated by bias is overwhelming. On August 9, 1991, the *New York Times* reported that during the first week in August, the Houston police initiated an experiment in which they sent police decoys posing as gay men into the Montrose section of Houston, a gay neighborhood. During that week, two officers posing as a gay couple were sprayed with Chemical Mace and another undercover officer was beaten with a baseball bat. The police arrested thirteen people, and said the attacks were made by "groups of young men from outside the neighborhood who thought their victims were homosexuals." In other words, marauding gangs of heterosexual youth go out for an evening's fun to do some fag bashing. They may well do this because they see nothing wrong with it and because they believe that they will not be punished if they are caught. To get the police in Houston to investigate the earlier anti-gay murder (of a banker), the *Times* reported "more than one thousand neighborhood residents, organized by the group Queer Nation, rallied in Montrose on July 13, blocking traffic for several hours and chanting at the police. On July 27, about 150 protesters marched . . . [in] the suburban community where most of the suspects in the killing live."[20] Only a politically powerless group would have to go to such extremes to get the police to investigate the murder of a banker.

58. Other evidence abounds. Between 1979 and 1988, the number of sixteen- to nineteen-year-olds who were the victims of violent crimes ranged from 70 per thousand (1986) to 79 per thousand (1989).[21] At Yale University in 1986, in a sample of 166 lesbians and gay men, 1 was assaulted or wounded with a weapon, 5 were beaten, punched or kicked, 19 had objects thrown at them, 25 were followed or chased, 10 had property damaged or destroyed, and 25 were threatened with physical violence. The national average for crimes of violence for all people aged sixteen to nineteen that year would lead us to expect that 7 percent, or between 11 and 12 of 166, would have been victims. In fact, only 17 percent of crimes of violence against people of that age occurred at school between 1985 and 1988, so we would only expect 2 of the 166 Yale students to have been victims. Given that crime victims disproportionately come from lower socioeconomic groups and given the social origins of Yale students, we would probably expect fewer than two, as opposed to the numbers found at Yale.

59. Similarly, in a 1987 study of 141 lesbians and gay men at Rutgers University, 2 were assaulted with weapons; 4 were punched, kicked, or beaten; 12 had objects thrown at them; 18 were followed or chased; 6 had property destroyed, and 16 were threatened with physical violence. Given a national rate of about 75 per 1,000 for people between sixteen and nineteen, and a 17 percent incidence rate at school, we would have expected under 2 cases by chance alone—no more than the number of lesbians and gay men in the sample who were assaulted with weapons at Rutgers that year.

60. A 1989 study of 125 lesbians and gay men at Pennsylvania State University found that 1 had been threatened with a weapon; 5 had been punched, kicked, or beaten; 12 had objects thrown at them; 22 were followed or chased; 17 had property damaged or destroyed; and 26 were threatened with physical violence. No national data are available for 1989, but making the generous estimate of an 80 per 1,000 rate, and maintaining the 17 percent who were victimized at school between 1985 and 1988, we would expect fewer than 2 of the members of the Penn State sample to have been victims of violent crimes—again fewer than those assaulted or wounded with a weapon.

61. The lack of safety for gay people and the disproportionate levels of violence against gay people are both a source and a consequence of gay people's powerlessness. Because gay people are powerless, they are easy targets for acts of violence, and the government cannot be relied upon to guarantee their safety as much as it does for

what is euphemistically termed the "general public." Indeed, a 1989 study found that 14 percent of a sample of lesbian and gay crime victims who declined to report the crime to the police did so because they feared abuse from the police.

62. Violence has consequences for people's attitudes and behaviors well beyond the immediate pain visited upon the victim. If it is not safe to be a homosexual, it is not safe to let people know that you are a homosexual. Thus, it is not safe to advocate the rights of gay people to the political process if taking part in public life means encouraging people to think you are a homosexual. As the police in Houston learned, even heterosexuals are not safe from other heterosexuals who mistakenly believe them to be homosexual. Thus, it often is not safe to be an ally of homosexuals. This atmosphere discourages average citizens not given to heroism from becoming allies of gay people in their struggle for equality. Without allies, gay people cannot prevail in a majoritarian political system.

Wealth

63. There is no good reason to assume anything other than that gay people are randomly distributed about the American population. Certainly, there is no reason to think that gay people are any wealthier than average Americans. People who are low in deference, respect, and safety may well be forced to accept jobs at low wages or, at the very least, trade off cash income for job security and freedom from harassment. On the other hand, by virtue of having fewer children as dependents, gay people may have more disposable income than heterosexuals who earn as much money.

64. Making campaign contributions is a traditional mechanism for multiplying the political power of a group. Multimillionaires may be few in number, but by investing funds in candidates for public office and by supporting charities and political causes they may enhance their influence.*

* Of course, not all people with disposable income use it for public purpose. Unless money is extorted, people are free to spend as they please. Many prefer to spend on private pleasures—travel, works of art, clothing, homes, cars, or whatever. Not more than one in five or ten Americans makes political contributions. Making contributions is a function of individual interest in politics, the sense of personal political effectiveness, perceived responsiveness of the political system, receiving appeals for funds, as well as of having the money to donate.

65. Members of minority groups in American politics are often disproportionately likely to make campaign contributions. Matthews and Prothro, in their classic study *Negroes and the New Southern Politics*,[22] report that "[in] giving money, ... Negroes participate more than do whites. Giving money is ordinarily a high-income activity and southern Negroes are one of the lowest-income groups in the country.... [M]onetary contributions are a relatively anonymous form of participation that is possible for a more subordinate minority that cannot participate more openly."[23] In fact, they report that, in the north in 1960, blacks also were almost twice as likely as whites to give money to candidates. About 20 percent of blacks, compared to 10 percent of whites made campaign contributions.[24] High levels of campaign activity and contributions are often a characteristic of religious and ethnic minority groups in "machine-style" urban politics. Certainly, the level of campaign contributions by American Jews is legendary. If the logic of this analysis is correct, then gay people might well be rationally motivated to be more likely to make campaign contributions than might heterosexuals of the same income levels.

66. No systematic data are available to measure the political contributions of gay people. Certainly, the fund raising associated with the AIDS crisis indicates that gay people are developing the habits of charity. There is, however, one political action committee devoted to lesbian and gay civil rights issues, the Human Rights Campaign Fund (the HRCF or the Fund). While there is no way to determine the sexual orientation of contributors to the Fund, one can examine its level of fund raising and the impact of HRCF contributions to candidates for heuristic purposes in order to get a handle on the impact of gay money in national politics.

67. In the 1989–90 election cycle, HRCF ranked twenty-seventh among nonconnected PACs in fund raising, at $560,000. To place this in perspective, the top fifteen nonconnected PACs raised amounts ranging from $1,056,367 (National Abortion Rights Action League PAC) to $5,083,520 (Voter Guide). At twenty-seventh, HRCF ranked just behind the Fund for a Conservative Majority and just ahead of the Keep Hope Alive Political Action Committee. HRCF ranked twenty-ninth among nonconnected PAC spenders, spending $523,496. Again, all of the top fifteen spenders in the nonconnected category spent over a million dollars, ranging from the National Security Political Action Committee (at $1,088,781) to the Voter Guide (at $5,071,119). On the average, about three-eighths of PAC funds end up being contributed to congressional candidates.[25] HRCF contributed $480,621 of its $560,000 in the 1989–90 cycle, ranking fourth in contributions by nonconnected PACs, and contributing roughly six-sevenths of the funds it raised. Among nonconnected PACs, the biggest contributor to congressional candidates was National PAC, contributing $968,500 out of the $2,069,011 it spent and the $2,152,000 it raised. Second was the Auto Dealers and Drivers for Free Trade PAC. The National Committee for an Effective Congress was third. HRCF was followed by the NARAL-PAC on the list of nonconnected contributors to congressional campaigns.

68. There are several categories of PACs. To get some sense of HRCF's power, one must compare it to PACs in these other categories for the 1989–90 election cycle as well. HRCF ranked fourth among nonconnected contributors. Twenty PACs in the Trade/Membership/Health category contributed more money to federal candidates—starting with the Realtors' Political Action Committee at $3,094,228 and the American Medical Association PAC at $2,375,992. Twenty-two Labor PACs contributed more than HRCF in the 1989–90 cycle—starting with the Teamsters' Democratic Republican Independent Voter Education Committee at $2,349,575 and the National Education Association PAC at $2,320,155. Among corporate PAC contributors, HRCF would rank sixth, just behind Philip Morris PAC's $573,410 in contributions, but substantially behind AT&T PAC's $1,457,360. Finally, among PACs for corporations without stock, HRCF would rank third, behind the Aircraft Owners and Pilots Association PAC at $513,900 and the Commodities Futures Political Fund of the Chicago Mercantile Exchange PAC at $459,500. Thus, fifty-two PACs contributed more money to federal candidates than the Human Rights Campaign Fund did in the 1989–90 electoral cycle.

69. Of course, HRCF does not have as easy a time raising money as do labor and corporate PACs. Gay people have no common place of business at which contacts and fund-raising solicitations might take place. Gay people cannot avail themselves of payroll deductions or letters from the boss to overcome any reluctance to contribute funds. The difficulty in locating and organizing gay people, the stigma attached to contributing to the cause of gay rights, the necessity of substantial individual initiatives being required to make a contribution at all combine to explain why HRCF is twenty-seventh among nonconnected PACs in raising funds.

70. HRCF's contributing six-sevenths of the funds it raises also re-flects a choice of political strategies: it does not spend money on in-dependent campaigns, such as those made notorious by the Na-tional Conservative Political Action Committee (NCPAC) in the 1980s or the famous "Willie Horton" independent campaign of 1988. There are times when a PAC is more effective and gets a bigger "bang for its bucks" by bypassing official campaigns and appealing directly to voters. One can assume that HRCF's decision not to engage in inde-pendent campaigns is related to its fear of homophobia in the mass public. Another example of the spiral of silence is apparently evident here: believing that public support for gay rights is low, gay rights campaign funds are not directed into campaign commercials stress-ing gay rights as an issue. Thus, the opportunity to use the campaign to educate the public is lost. The result is that contributions go to support candidates who promise to support gay rights and to those running against opponents of gay rights, that is, rewarding "friends" and punishing "enemies." This is a cautious strategy for proponents of a controversial cause.

71. Another indication of HRCF's political strategy can be seen by analyzing contributions made to supporters of the 1991 Lesbian and Gay Civil Rights Bill, an act that would ban discrimination on the basis of sexual orientation. The bill was first introduced in 1975, six-teen years ago. There are currently 92 members of the House who are sponsors of the bill—less than half the minimum number needed to pass the bill and 198 short of the number required to override a presidential veto. The bill currently has 13 sponsors in the Senate—barely a quarter of the votes needed for passage, just over a fifth of the number required for closure should any senator attempt to fili-buster the bill to death, and less than a fifth of the number needed to override a presidential veto.

72. In the 1989–90 election cycle, HRCF made contributions to eleven Senate candidates. Two were defeated. Of the remaining nine, four (Senators Akaka, Simon, Pell, and Adams) are sponsors of the bill. Five are not sponsors of the bill: Senators Biden, Harkin, Cohen, Bradley, and Spector. In the 1991–92 cycle, contributions were made to six campaigns, including second contributions to Senators Adams and Spector. Of the remaining four, two (Wellstone and Inouye) are sponsors and two (Wirth and Dodd) are not.

73. In the two election cycles (1989–90 and 1991–92), HRCF con-tributed funds to 127 victorious candidates for the House of Repre-sentatives. Of these, 92 became sponsors of the Gay Rights Bill and

35 did not. Twenty-nine of the 35 members of the 1988 House who voted against the 1987 Helms Amendment, which prohibited federal expenditures that promote or encourage "safe sex" practices among homosexuals, and were candidates in the 1988 election received HRCF funds in subsequent campaigns. Thirty-five of the members of the House who voted in favor of the Helms Amendment subsequently received HRCF contributions to their campaigns for re-election.

74. Some data exist to show that in some respects, individuals who identify with gay causes are disproportionately affluent. The Gay Press Association (GPA) represents 127 gay and lesbian publications in 33 states, the District of Columbia, Puerto Rico, and Canada. The GPA conducted a readership survey that found that the median personal income of its readers was three times the median personal income of the readership of the "straight" press.

75. Given that the readers of the gay press have a substantially higher personal income than the public at large, one might assume that a rational strategy for many businesses would be to advertise in the gay press. Yet virtually all advertising in the gay press comes from within the gay and lesbian community. One will not find advertising for clothing, automobiles, electronic equipment, or virtually anything else that the readers of the gay press might buy from mainstream merchants. The apparent explanation for the failure of "straight" businesses to advertise in the gay press is their fear of being associated with homosexuals.

76. If it is the case that businesses make rational, profit-oriented decisions not to market directly to lesbians and gay men because they fear negative public reactions to any association with gay publications, then the low levels of public respect, affection, and deference devalue what wealth gay people have. In the hands of people who are not respected, money has diminished political clout.

Group Identity and Cohesion

77. For gay people to be a politically powerful group, people who are lesbian or gay must think of themselves as members of a group of lesbian and gay people and must place a very high priority on that aspect of their collective identity. There are substantial structural impediments, however, to the formation of group identity among gays and lesbians.

78. Over two generations of studies of American voting behavior have demonstrated that group benefits—asking is X good for people like me—is the most frequently used standard by which people evaluate political objects. Americans are five to ten times more likely to ask "Who benefits?" than to use abstract ideological standards (that is, abstract notions of justice) to evaluate issues, candidates, and political parties. Identity is thus more likely to be the basis of political action than is ideology. Americans are more likely to join religious groups, professional societies, labor unions, veterans' groups, and neighborhood groups than they are to join political and ideological groups.

79. Most significant forms of political identity are transmitted within the family. We know, for example, that party identification— the psychological attachment one feels to a political party, thinking of oneself as a Democrat or a Republican—develops by the time a child is in the fourth grade and is transmitted within the family. If a fourth grader is asked why he or she is a Democrat or a Republican, the child typically responds, "That's what my family is." This identification remains relatively stable for a lifetime and typically forms the single most powerful explanation of a person's voting behavior. Other forms of identity, such as race, gender, religion, and ethnicity, are transmitted within the family even earlier in life and with considerable efficiency.

80. This poses a great barrier to the political empowerment of gay people. First, gay people are overwhelmingly born into heterosexual homes. Rather than being "like" their families, gay people are socialized to be straight. Gay people are a minority in society; gay children are minorities within their own homes. Gay children are deprived of their parents as role models of healthy, happy, successful homosexuals who evaluate the external world by asking whether or not events are "good for the gay people."

81. For gay identity to be a person's prime political identity, it often must supersede political, religious, and social identities transmitted within the home. There is no good reason to believe that gay children are more likely to be born to Democrats than to Republicans, to liberals than to conservatives, to the secular than to the devoutly religious, to the well off than to the not well off, to families in dominant groups in society than to families in subordinate groups in society. Yet we know that those identities formed at an early age and reinforced by family, friends, and other socializing agents of society are the most powerful and the hardest to overcome. Cataclysmic events such as wars and depressions are often required for people to reconsider their political loyalties. Religious conversion is relatively rare. Everyday life does not facilitate meeting other gay people as readily as it facilitates meeting co-religionists. Family, school, and media all reinforce heterosexual images of society. Rather than forming the basis of group identity for effective collective political action, same-sex identity develops in an atmosphere of isolation more conducive to political powerlessness.

82. Gay identity develops relatively late in life. Garnets and Kimmel's recent review of the field identifies many sources of the several year time period it takes lesbians and gay men "to move from their initial awareness of same-gender sexual feelings to self-identification and then to acceptance of and commitment to a positive gay male or lesbian identity."[26]

83. First, it takes some time for gay men and lesbians to learn about homosexuality and then to identify as part of homosexuals as a group, particularly because it is easy to feel that one has little in common with homosexuals as the group is defined by straight society. Second, the less open and tolerant society is, the less available accurate information is, the fewer significant others are available to be positive role models or to share positive views of homosexuals, the longer it takes to identify with gay people as a social and political community. Third, widespread assumptions of universal heterosexuality mean that lesbians and gay men must invent for themselves the sense of self-worth and self-esteem that leads to articulating political grievances. Fourth, the impact of the assumption of universal heterosexuality is that many lesbians and gay men misclassify themselves and make an effort to conform to heterosexist expectations by attempting other-gender sexual behavior, only to discover later in life that their orientation is toward same-gender sexual behavior. Thus, Garnets and Kimmel write, "Lesbians and gay men may misclassify themselves, their behavior, or experiences as heterosexual, which [interferes with the] ... process of homosexual identity development."

84. Another factor inhibiting the development of sufficient gay identity, cohesion, and consciousness is the probability that, at least at birth, gay people are randomly distributed about the population. Not only are gay people a minority, gay people are a dispersed minority. If the rhetorical claim is "We are everywhere," then the political fact may be closer to being that gay people are majorities nowhere. Absent sufficient concentration to affect local political cultural norms and styles, individual gay people are not likely to have sufficient opportunities to learn the desirable and effective modes of collective behavior that are a prerequisite of political and group consciousness.

85. Developing collective identity and a sense of shared values and shared demands for redress of injustices by the political system is the crucial step in a group's developing the capacity for exercising effective political power. The classic example of this comes from the experiences of workers in factories. Out of mutual discussion, they develop a sense that they share one another's conditions and that what had once been perceived as individual personal problems are really shared collective grievances. They learn that the source of their grievances is not in their personal inadequacies but rather in the operation of the larger social and political system. They then learn that they must translate their new understanding of the source of their discontent into demands for change and that they must take collective action to articulate these demands effectively.

86. The question now becomes: Is there an analogous process for gay people? What is the functional equivalent to the factory system for workers and the trade union movement or to the church and the struggle for equal rights for black people? In many ways, the absence of residential segregation on the basis of sexual orientation, with gays randomly distributed about the population, and the scarcity of workplaces in which gay people are concentrated in substantial numbers, all contribute to the disempowerment of gay people by profoundly limiting gay people's capability for developing a sense of collective grievance and the need to take collective action to demand redress of grievances. To the degree that gay people—or at least gay men—have a functional equivalent of the ghetto, the factory, or the church, it is the gay bar. Obviously, it strains credulity to believe that gay people go to gay bars primarily to form political action groups. Nonetheless, gay bars do perform the function of providing a place where individual gays can establish a collective gay identity.

87. Gay bars are not randomly distributed about the nation. According to the authoritative listing on the subject, there are 278 gay bars in California, 139 in the state of New York, 133 in Florida, 120 in Texas, and 84 in Illinois. At the other extreme, there are no gay bars in Wyoming or North Dakota, only two each in Idaho and South Dakota, and three in each of Alaska, Montana, and Vermont. While

there is some tendency for the number of bars to vary with population, other factors enter into the equation. Oases of tolerance and tourist destinations have more gay bars than do other areas. There are many fewer listings of bars in low-income areas and in communities of color. So, for example, there are no gay bars listed in the Bronx.

88. The presence of gay bars also varies with the political culture of an area. (The reverse may also be the case: bars affect political culture.) The only member of the House or the Senate from the six states with the fewest gay bars to be a sponsor of the Gay Rights Bill is Bernie Sanders, the newly elected independent representative from Vermont (and formerly the socialist mayor of Burlington). On the other hand, New York and California account for thirty-eight of the ninety-two House sponsors of the bill and two of the thirteen Senate sponsors.

89. A survey of the seventy-seven localities that have adopted some form of protection for gays in the United States indicates that almost half of them, thirty-eight, have more than one gay bar per hundred thousand population. Another twelve are college towns with populations of under fifty thousand and no gay bars, but with alternate structures for the generation of gay consciousness, community, and identity.

90. The point of this exercise is not to sing paeans to bars, but rather to show that for gay people to be politically powerful, they must have some institutional structures for the generation of shared identity and consciousness. Less than 1 percent of all political jurisdictions in the United States have gay rights legislation (and many of them have only resolutions, policy statements, or declarations as opposed to protections with the full force of law). This fact indicates how far gay people must go to manifest meaningful political power in the United States.

Allies

91. Minority groups must have allies in order to prevail in majoritarian political systems. The low deference and high levels of stigma gay people suffer combine to make it difficult to attract allies in numbers sufficient to advance claims for protection of rights or redress of grievances. The preference of advertisers not to enrich themselves by advertising in gay media is one example of this difficulty in attracting allies. The failure to respond adequately to the AIDS crisis is another. Often both political elites and the mass public can mistake the fear of being associated with homosexuals to be the belief that support for gay rights is wrong. At least anecdotally, lesbian and gay political activists know of many elected officials who say they believe in gay rights but cannot take the political risks of being associated with gay rights. The failure to support gay rights often reflects the stigma attached to associating with gay people.

92. The widespread failure to enact gay rights legislation stands as the hallmark of the inability of gays to obtain allies. At least thirty-two of the seventy-seven jurisdictions that have enacted some form of protection for gays are college towns, generally prestigious college towns such as Cambridge, Massachusetts; Berkeley, California; Chapel Hill, North Carolina; Ithaca, New York; and Yellow Springs, Ohio. These are jurisdictions in which legislators are relatively free from the fear of irrational homophobic backlash; they are not typical of small-town America. These are towns with a political culture of tolerance and places where a higher percentage of the electorate has the cognitive skill and capacity for abstract reasoning to understand the meaning of equal rights. These are localities in which a lower percentage of the electorate is attached to archaic myths and fears.

93. Of the seventy-seven jurisdictions that have any sort of legislation or other governmental action that protects lesbians and gay men, sixteen are merely resolutions, guidelines, or policy statements and are not fully binding. Only four states—Wisconsin (1982), Massachusetts (1989), Connecticut (1991), and Hawaii (1991)—have any statewide legislation protecting these rights; these are states with substantial histories of tolerance. Seven other states have executive orders issued by governors. These orders are necessarily limited by the range of discretionary gubernatorial power and are rescinded more easily than are legislative acts. Thus, not over fifty-four jurisdictions in the entire United States have substantial legislative protections for gay people. In half of the states, no jurisdiction at all has *any* legislation or other governmental action or policy whatsoever protecting the rights of lesbians and gay men.

94. At the national level, a federal gay rights bill was introduced by Bella Abzug and twenty-two co-sponsors in 1975. Today, the bill is sponsored by ninety-two members of the House and thirteen senators. Half the states are represented by someone sponsoring the bill

and half are not, but only ten of the fifty states have a member of the Senate sponsoring the bill. Three states—Massachusetts, Rhode Island, and Hawaii—have both senators supporting it. Two of those states, Massachusetts and Hawaii, are among the four states having statewide gay rights legislation.

95. The original sponsors of the bill were a coalition of minorities: of 23 members, there were seven Jews, six blacks, and one Asian. In the subsequent sixteen years, a grand total of 138 members of Congress have signed onto the bill.* Over the years, congressional support for this legislation has continued to come from a coalition of minorities. Among these 138, there have been 25 Jews, 22 blacks, 5 Latinos, 7 Asians and Pacific Islanders, and 29 Roman Catholics. Both of the openly gay members of the House are among the sponsors, as was the only member of the House to die of AIDS. Over a third of the sponsors have come from two states: California (30) and New York (22).† In a sixteen-year period, 26 states, the District of Columbia, Guam, and American Samoa have been represented by sponsors. Overwhelmingly, the sponsors have been Democrats: 124 Democrats, 13 Republicans, and Bernie Sanders. Further, geographic support is concentrated: 82 of the 138, almost 60 percent, represent states or localities that have passed gay rights laws.

96. We see from these histories of gay rights legislation a pattern of very limited support. The pace of coalition building has been glacial. After sixteen years, the bill has gone from twenty-three to ninety-seven sponsors in the House, an increase of 4.3 members a year. In sixteen years, thirteen members of the Senate have signed onto the bill. Assuming that this rate could be sustained, it will take another twenty-eight years to build a majority in the House and forty-eight years to build a majority in the Senate.

Conclusion

97. A review of the political condition of gay people in the United States leads to the inevitable conclusion that gay people are a politically powerless minority. Lesbians and gay men are peculiarly

---

* In many cases this merely represents replacements of members from the same district.

† There is no statewide legislation in California or New York, the home of over a third of the sponsors.

disadvantaged in gaining access to the political processes to redress their grievances through the national political mechanism.

98. A review of the sources of gay people's being a politically powerless group would include the following:

—Gay people are hopelessly outnumbered.

—Gay people are despised; being gay is a stigmatized condition.

—Gay people are the object of violence.

—Heterosexuals are reluctant to associate themselves with the cause of gay rights for fear of contagion of anti-gay stigma.

—Gay people are deprived of the normal prerequisites of group formation and effective political action, notably in the area of development of collective identity and group cohesion and in the development of political consciousness.

—Gay people are widely distributed about the nation, politically dispersed, and lacking in sufficient numerical concentration to form a majority in any significant political jurisdiction in the nation.

—Gay people cannot develop adequate functional alternatives to the political resources utilized by heterosexuals in the United States.

—Because of prejudice and inaccurate stereotypes, gay people have been the victims of invidious and gross unfairness.

—The majority is unable to empathize with gay people, to put themselves in gay people's shoes, to feel as gay people must feel.

Thus, the majority feels no compunction about depriving gay people of life and liberty.

99. The logic of the American constitutional system is that the judicial branch must intervene to protect the rights of powerless minorities who are being deprived of their rights by tyrannical majorities. Gay people are such a minority.

Dr. Sherrill's affidavit, as submitted to the court, ended at this point. However, the analysis of the Helms Amendment as a paradigm of political powerlessness was prepared in the course of the research for the affidavit. The Steffan case involved neither sexual behavior nor AIDS as issues and, as a result, this analysis was not included in the final version of the affidavit. We include it here in large part because—as the reader will see—Judge Gasch introduced these issues into his decision, without regard to the issues litigated in this case.

THE HELMS AMENDMENT

A PARADIGM OF POLITICAL POWERLESSNESS

100. The 1987 actions of Congress in connection with an amendment offered by Senator Jesse Helms of North Carolina to prohibit the Centers for Disease Control (CDC) from using funds for AIDS education, information, or prevention materials that promote or encourage, directly or indirectly, "homosexual sexual activities," provide a paradigm of the political powerlessness of gays. Acquired Immune Deficiency Syndrome (AIDS) is an overwhelmingly fatal illness that has disproportionately attacked gay men for the past ten years, at the very least. Among the mechanisms for transmitting the Human Immunodeficiency Virus (HIV), believed to cause AIDS, are through the exchange of semen and blood from an HIV+ person to another person.

101. Thus, under the Helms Amendment, CDC funds could not be used to educate or inform gay men about "safer sex" techniques, that is, methods of engaging in homosexual sexual activities without running a substantial risk of transmitting HIV infection. The inevitable result of this legislation has been the spread of HIV infection among gay men, attended by suffering and death. This situation enables us to examine the political power of gay people—without regard to the reasons, whether religious, moral, or partisan, for individual Congress members' votes. The simple point here is that gay people were fighting for their lives and were using every political resource at their command in this struggle—and they failed.

102. The Senate adopted the Helms Amendment overwhelmingly, by a vote of 94–2. On October 20, 1987, by a vote of 368–47, the House of Representatives adopted a motion to instruct House members of the House-Senate Conference Committee to accept the Senate language of the Helms Amendment.[27] Democrats voted for this resolution by a 196–46 margin; Republicans voted for it by a 172–1 margin.*

---

* The lone Republican to vote against this resolution is something of an anomaly in the Republican party. Bill Green represents a district that includes Manhattan's East Side and parts of Greenwich Village, two areas widely believed to have substantial gay populations and that have a relatively high incidence of HIV infection. Further, al-

103. While only one Republican in the House opposed this resolution, 19 percent of the Democrats opposed it. These Democrats,
however, were not a random sample of all Democrats in the House.
To begin with, over one-third of them, sixteen of forty-six, were from
California, and are highly concentrated within that state: seven come
from the Sacramento to San Jose area of Northern California; the remaining nine cluster around Los Angeles in an area stretching from
Beverly Hills through Riverside.

104. Three other states—Massachusetts, Michigan, and New
York—are each represented by five members opposing this resolution. Washington, Texas, Pennsylvania, and Illinois each are the
home of two members opposing the resolution. One representative
from each of the following states opposed the resolution: Connecticut, Florida, Georgia, Indiana, Maryland, Minnesota, Missouri, and
New Jersey. No members of the House from the remaining thirty-
four states opposed the resolution.

105. In the House, support for saving the lives of gay people was
heavily concentrated among representatives who, themselves, are
members of minority groups. Twelve of the forty-seven opponents of
the resolution (over 25 percent) are Jewish; thirteen of the forty-
seven are Roman Catholic (over 27 percent). Eight of the twenty-two
Protestants opposing the resolution (over 36 percent) are African-
American. A total of eleven African-American members of the House
voted against the resolution. Two of the opponents are Latinos.
Thus, not over fourteen of the forty-seven opponents of the resolution (under 30 percent) are white Protestants. The demography of
opposition to tyrannizing gay people is not that of a representative
sample of the American people. Rather, it is the demography of the
traditionally discriminated against—members of minority religions
and people of color.*

106. In political terms, House opponents of the resolution are

---

though Green received 58 percent of the vote in the 1986 congressional election—and
61 percent in 1988—Michael Dukakis defeated George Bush by a 66–33 percent margin
in Green's congressional district in the 1988 presidential election. Bill Green may have
been the only member of Congress to have found it to his substantial electoral benefit
to vote against condemning gay men to death.

* Only four members from states in the Old South, the Confederacy, voted to protect
the lives of gay people. One, Lehman of Florida, is Jewish. Two, Lewis of Georgia and
Leland of Texas, are African-American. The fourth, Gonzalez of Texas, is Latino. Not a
single white Christian Congress member from the South voted against this resolution.
Also, the only Republican to vote against this resolution was Jewish.

also atypical. Not only are they liberal Democrats, but they disproportionately come from safe districts. Only three of the forty-six
Democrats represent a district in which the Democratic candidate
for Congress received under 60 percent of the vote for the House in
1986. Only seven represent districts George Bush carried in 1988.
Thus, most of these votes to protect the lives of gay men can hardly
be taken as profiles in legislative courage. Nevertheless, not all members of Congress who are free to vote their conscience also can be
said to have consciences to vote.

108. These members of the House are also disproportionately
likely to be civil libertarians. Only two of the Democrats and the sole
Republican had ACLU ratings below 90 for the 101st Congress. And
only eleven of the forty-seven had AFL-CIO COPE ratings of under
90—with only three below 85—for 1987.[28]

108. Finally, many of these members of Congress represented districts that are the homes of great universities: Harvard, Yale, Columbia, Hunter College, City University of New York Graduate School,
New York University, University of California at Berkeley, University
of Chicago, University of Minnesota, UCLA, and Stanford, among
others. These districts have a repository of citizens who understand
the abstract concepts of democracy and who are less likely to be victims of appeals to fear and hysteria. (These same types of communities are disproportionately more likely to enact legislation protecting
the rights of gay people; such communities are atypical in the United
States.)

109. Given this extraordinary distribution—and the fact that only
two senators, one each from New York and Connecticut, opposed
the amendment—it is impossible to conclude that, on a matter of life
and death, on the single most salient issue to gay people, gay people
are a politically powerful group. Certainly, in this case, there is no
evidence to conclude anything but that gay people are a politically
powerless group, a minority for whom the political processes ordinarily relied upon to protect minorities fail to do so.

A Note on Sources

For reasons of space, several descriptions of sources were
omitted from the affidavit submitted in the court papers. These
sources are listed below.

The litany of slurs was derived from materials in the files of the Gay and Lesbian Alliance Against Discrimination, 80 Varick Street, New York, N.Y.

The CBS/New York Times Poll data were provided by Kathleen Frankovic, Director of Surveys, CBS. The VRS data were provided by Murray S. Edelman of Voter Research and Surveys.

The data from the General Social Surveys conducted by the National Opinion Research Center at the University of Chicago and the data from the National Election Studies conducted by the Center for Political Studies at the University of Michigan were made available under the auspices of the City University of New York's membership in the Inter-University Consortium for Social and Political Research.

PAC data came from Federal Election Commission records provided at the request of the office of the late Congressman Ted Weiss of New York.

Data on the Gay Press Association were provided by its late president, Joe Sabato, in an interview with the author. Other data on gay markets were provided by Sean Strub of Strub-Dawson, a direct mail firm specializing in gay and lesbian marketing.

The nationally recognized source of listings of gay bars used to develop the measure of bars per capita is *Bob Damron's Address Book '91* (1991) San Francisco, CA, the Damron Company.

Much of the conclusion (paragraphs 97–98) was greatly influenced by a reading of a draft manuscript of H. N. Hirsch, *A Theory of Liberty* (New York: Routledge, 1992). We thank Professor Hirsch for making his draft manuscript available to us in the summer of 1991.

Gregory Herek

AFFIDAVIT

On Prejudice toward Gay People and Gays as Security Risks

$\mathbf{G}$REGORY M. HEREK is an associate research psychologist at the University of California at Davis, from which he received a
Ph.D. in personality and social psychology in 1983. He has also
taught at Yale and at the Graduate School and University Center of
the City University of New York. Herek has written and lectured
widely on the social psychology of societal attitudes toward gays and
lesbians. In 1989, he received an award for Distinguished Scientific
Contributions to Lesbian and Gay Psychology from a division of the
American Psychological Association.

Herek's affidavit addresses several of the key issues in determining
whether a classification is suspect. He demonstrates that gay people
have been saddled with disabilities resulting from prejudice and inaccurate stereotypes. Notably, he discusses the scientific evidence
refuting the notion that homosexuality is an illness—a notion often
derived from prejudice and inaccurate stereotypes. Herek further reviews the scholarly literature demonstrating that homosexuality has
no bearing on an individual's ability to perform or to contribute to
society and that gays do not pose a special security threat.

1. The purpose of this declaration is twofold. The first is to provide
the basis for my opinion—which is widely accepted among social
psychologists—that gay people constitute a minority group comparable to racial, ethnic, and religious minorities and that prejudice
against gays and lesbians, like all prejudice, can be eroded. The second is to provide the basis for my opinion that gays do not pose any
special security risks. It is noteworthy that on July 31, 1991, Secretary
of Defense Richard Cheney, testifying under oath before a House
Budget Committee hearing on defense policy in the post–cold war

era, called the notion that gays pose a security risk an "old chestnut." A few days later, on August 4, Secretary Cheney again disavowed the idea that gays pose a special security risk and affirmed the right of gays and lesbians to work in civilian capacities at the Department of Defense.

Gay People as a Minority Group

2. Although the notion that gay people constitute a minority group comparable to racial, ethnic, and religious minorities was articulated nearly forty years ago,[1] it only recently has begun to enjoy a degree of acceptance in American society. Lesbians and gay men differ from other minorities in important respects. Nevertheless, they can reasonably be viewed as a minority group because they manifest four important characteristics by which minority groups are defined.[2] First, gay people comprise a subordinate segment within a larger complex state society. Second, they manifest characteristics that are held in low esteem by the dominant segments of society.[3] Third, they are self-consciously bound together as a community by virtue of these characteristics.[4] Finally, they receive differential treatment based upon these characteristics, ranging from discrimination[5] to assault and victimization.[6]

3. Although the existence of such differential treatment usually is not disputed, its justification often is.[7] Public figures generally are unwilling to endorse outright violence against gay people. Discrimination in employment, housing, and services, in contrast, frequently is justified on the basis of beliefs that gay people possess various undesirable characteristics, for example, that they are mentally ill and dangerous to children.

4. A principal justification for discrimination and hostility toward gay people appeals to religious morality. Because certain homosexual *conduct* is condemned by several major religions, it is argued, laws prohibiting discrimination would require heterosexual individuals to violate their personal moral standards. In this context, gay people can be viewed as a religious minority group: although they do not manifest a unified religious ideology, they often are persecuted on the basis of the dominant majority's religious beliefs.[8] Opposition to civil rights for gay people is perceived by some Americans as a litmus test of religious commitment. The correlation be-

tween religiosity and anti-gay prejudice is well documented.[9] Many Roman Catholics, fundamentalist Christians, and orthodox Jews have used religious teachings to justify their active opposition to enactment of statutes or policies designed to protect gay people from discrimination.[10]

The Social Psychology of Anti-Gay Prejudice

5. Although each form of bigotry has its own unique history and content, anti-gay prejudice manifests the same general psychological structure and dynamics as racism, anti-Semitism, and other prejudices against stigmatized groups. Each can be understood by the same social scientific theories and measured by the same methodologies.[11]

6. Empirical research has demonstrated that heterosexuals' attitudes toward gay people consistently are correlated with various psychological, social, and demographic variables. In contrast to heterosexuals with favorable attitudes toward gay people, those with negative attitudes are (a) more likely to express traditional, restrictive attitudes about gender roles; (b) less likely to report having themselves engaged in homosexual behaviors or to self-identify as lesbian or gay; (c) more likely to perceive their peers as manifesting negative attitudes; (d) less likely to have had personal contact with gay men or lesbians; (e) likely to be older and less well educated; (f) more likely to have resided in areas where negative attitudes represent the norm (e.g., rural areas, the midwestern and southern United States); and (g) more likely to be strongly religious and to subscribe to a conservative religious ideology.

7. Additionally, heterosexual males tend to manifest higher levels of prejudice than do heterosexual females, especially toward gay men.[12] This sex difference may result from the strong linkage of masculinity with heterosexuality in American culture, which creates considerable pressures (both social and psychological) for males to affirm their masculinity through rejection of that which is not culturally defined as masculine (male homosexuality) and that which is perceived as negating the importance of males (lesbianism). Because heterosexual women are less likely to perceive rejection of homosexuality as integral to their own gender identity, they may experience fewer pressures to be prejudiced and consequently have more op-

portunities for personal contact with gay people, which in turn tends to foster positive attitudes.

8. Some individuals display a personality pattern of general intolerance for stigmatized groups, often subsumed under the label of authoritarianism. A significant correlation consistently has been observed between anti-gay attitudes and high scores on measures of authoritarianism.[13] Given this propensity for some individuals to express intolerant attitudes toward a variety of out-groups, it is not surprising that anti-gay prejudice has been found to correlate with racism.[14] In my research, I have demonstrated that this correlation is affected by religious orientation. White heterosexual college students tended to score high on both anti-black racism and anti-gay prejudice if their religious beliefs were extrinsically motivated (i.e., if their religion functioned primarily as a means for fitting in with a social group). In contrast, those with intrinsically motivated religious beliefs (i.e., beliefs that provide an overarching framework by which all life is understood) tended to score low on racism and high on anti-gay attitudes. My own empirical research has explained this pattern as reflecting the norms and values associated with each orientation: intrinsics conformed to religious ideals (which condemn racism but not anti-gay prejudice), while extrinsics conformed to community norms (which fostered both racism and anti-gay prejudice).

9. Strongly correlated with negative attitudes toward lesbians and gay men is acceptance of negative stereotypes—exaggerated and fixed beliefs—about them.[15] Because stereotypes and prejudice both involve reactions to individuals in terms of their group membership, and because beliefs about the characteristics of a group often include an evaluative component, the two concepts often are equated.[16] Some researchers, however, have found it useful to distinguish between them and have begun to study the cognitive processes through which stereotyping occurs.[17]

10. *Stereotyping.* Individual survival requires that we be able to detect important occurrences in the environment, make reasonably accurate predictions about how they will affect us, and behave accordingly. Consequently, we use a variety of strategies for judging the importance of information and for integrating it with our past experiences. These strategies enable us to perceive the world as reasonably stable, fairly predictable, and generally manageable.[18] One such strategy is categorization, a mental process whereby we associate or "clump" different objects (including people) according to some characteristic that they all share. Once an object is grouped with others, we have available a considerable amount of information about it by simply recalling the defining features of the category. For example, trying to remember the individual characteristics of twenty-five different objects in a room is impossible for most people; but if twenty of those objects fit the category of "chair" and the remaining five fit the category of "table," the memory task suddenly becomes fairly simple.

11. When categorization is applied to people, the consequence often is a stereotype.[19] Stereotypes result when we (a) categorize people into groups on the basis of some characteristic; (b) attribute additional characteristics to that category; (c) then attribute those other characteristics individually to all of the group's members.[20] Whereas a categorization is based on features that actually define the group (e.g., the belief that all gay people have a primary sexual or romantic attraction to others of their own sex), a stereotype involves characteristics that are unrelated to the criteria for group membership (e.g., the belief that all gay men are effeminate or that all lesbians hate men). Heterosexuals often notice only those characteristics that are congruent with their stereotypes about gay people (a phenomenon called "selective perception"), fail to recall incongruent characteristics retrospectively ("selective recall"), and use the content of stereotypes as the basis for "illusory correlations."

12. *Selective Perception.* People often perceive the world selectively, attending to information that supports their stereotypes and ignoring information that contradicts them. This process of selective perception influences heterosexuals' responses to gay men and lesbians. For example, Alan Gross and his colleagues found that students at their university believed gay men generally to be theatrical, gentle, and liberated, whereas heterosexual men were thought to be more aggressive, dominant, competitive, strong, and stable; the same students believed lesbians generally to be dominant, direct, forceful, strong, liberated, and nonconforming, whereas heterosexual women were perceived as more likely to be conservative and stable. The researchers asked a separate sample of students to describe a man or woman in terms of these characteristics after watching a brief videotaped interview with her or him. Students who were told that the person was gay rated her or him higher on "gay traits" and lower on "heterosexual traits" than those who received no informa-

tion about the interviewee's sexual orientation.[21] Using only a gay male stimulus person, Gurwitz and Marcus found the same effect at a different university.[22]

13. *Selective Recall.* Stereotypical beliefs not only distort perceptions of current interactions, but also can affect an individual's memory for past events. Snyder and Uranowitz, for example, provided undergraduates with a 750-word case study of the life history of a woman named "Betty K." After reading the file, some students were told that Betty later became involved in a lesbian relationship and went on to a satisfying career as a physician living with her female lover. Other students learned that Betty married and went on to a satisfying career as a physician living with her (male) husband. On subsequent factual questions, students tended to remember events that fit with their subsequent knowledge about Betty's sexual orientation. Those who learned that Betty became a lesbian tended to remember that she did not have a steady boyfriend in high school, for example, whereas students who learned that she married heterosexually recalled that she dated boys.[23]

14. *Illusory Correlations.* Heterosexuals' observations of gay people as a group are likely to be distorted by illusory correlations, that is, the erroneous perception that a particular characteristic occurs with disproportionate frequency among gay men and lesbians. In their classic studies, Chapman and Chapman found that illusory correlations influenced perceptions of homosexuality among clinicians and lay people alike. In one study, clinicians responding to a survey were asked to describe their own observations of the kinds of responses "prominent in the Rorschach protocols of men with problems concerning homosexual impulses."[24] The responses that the clinicians reported that they had observed more frequently with homosexual respondents (e.g., human/animal anal content, feminine clothing, humans with sex confused) had in fact been found in independent empirical studies *not* to be unusually prevalent among homosexual respondents. The clinicians' associations of certain signs with homosexuality, in other words, were not accurate. The Chapmans found, however, that the signs listed by the clinicians closely matched those associated by members of the lay public with homosexuality. The clinicians' impressions thus appeared to have been shaped by cultural preconceptions about homosexuality rather than by their own unbiased observations.

15. In a subsequent experimental study, the Chapmans presented college students with various types of responses to a series of Rorschach cards, each response attributed to a person manifesting particular "symptoms." For example, the response of "a woman's buttocks" on card 9 might have been attributed to a man who "has sexual feelings toward other men" or, alternatively, to a man who "feels sad and depressed much of the time." Although each kind of response was paired with each symptom exactly the same number of times, the students perceived that particular responses were given more frequently by homosexual men. These were the *same* responses that clinicians in the first study had believed to be associated with homosexuality. The Chapmans concluded that the students' observations, like those of the clinicians, had been influenced by their preexisting ideas about homosexuality; they erroneously remembered "seeing" certain Rorschach preconceptions.

16. Because of illusory correlations, and the selective perception and recall of stereotype-confirming information, anti-gay stereotypes are very resistant to change, even when reality contradicts them. Thus, many heterosexuals erroneously "see" (or remember seeing) a disproportionate number of gay men and women who are maladjusted, obsessed with sex, and incapable of committed relationships. They fail to notice gay people who violate these stereotypes or heterosexuals who fulfill them.

17. *The Content of Anti-Gay Stereotypes.* Negative stereotypes about lesbians and gay men, like those about other minority groups, do not result from cognitive processes that occur in a social vacuum. Rather, they are shaped by historically evolved cultural ideologies that justify the subjugation of minorities. Because these ideologies are ubiquitous in popular discourse, individual stereotypes are continually reinforced. Some stereotypes reflect ideologies that are specific to a particular out-group. Gay men, for example, are presumed to manifest characteristics that are culturally defined as "feminine," and lesbians are widely believed to manifest "masculine" characteristics.[25] This incorrect stereotype is sufficiently strong that men and women who manifest characteristics inconsistent with those culturally prescribed for their gender are more likely than others to be labeled homosexual.[26] Lesbians and gay men who violate stereotypical expectations, as many do, may actually be disliked.[27] And an individual who is perceived as being able to label a nonobvious homosexual may subsequently be better liked by others.[28]

18. The rationale for the military's ban on gays appears to be based in part on incorrect stereotypes of this type. In a July 1990 administrative message from the commander of the Atlantic Naval Surface Fleet to his subordinates, Vice Admiral Donnell stated that "[e]xperience has shown that the stereotypical female homosexual in the Navy is more aggressive than her male counterpart, intimidating those women who might turn her in to the chain of command."

19. Other stereotypes reflect cultural ideologies about out-groups in general, usually portraying out-group members as simultaneously threatening and inferior to members of the dominant in-group. B. D. Adam has documented some themes common to cultural images of gay people, blacks, and Jews alike: all are perceived as animalistic, hypersexual, overvisible, heretical, and conspiratorial.[29]

20. Again, the military's rationale for excluding gays rests on the basis of these stereotypes. The policy is justified on the notion that homosexuals will not be able to control their sexual impulses and will therefore invade the privacy of fellow servicemembers, use their positions of authority to sexually exploit and harass their subordinates, and engage in conduct that will offend the sensibilities of foreign countries where they may be stationed. Vice Admiral Donnell's memo endorses these stereotypical views wholeheartedly, positing that "young, often vulnerable, female sailors" will be subjected to "subtle coercion or outright sexual advances by more senior and aggressive female sailors." Again, these are stereotypes that are not grounded in fact. There is no evidence to support the notion that lesbians and gay men are more likely than heterosexuals to engage in sexual harassment or open sexual activity or that gays are less able to control their sexual impulses than straights. Nor is there any basis for the belief that gays are sexually predatory or that they will try to convert or recruit heterosexuals. To the contrary, because many lesbians and gay men must exercise great discretion in order to protect themselves from the negative consequences of societal stigma, they often find it necessary to be more circumspect than heterosexuals and to have a higher degree of self-control.

21. Vice Admiral Donnell's stereotype of "aggressive" homosexuals and "vulnerable" female sailors fits a classic historic pattern in which disliked minority groups are portrayed as preying upon the vulnerable. Oberman, for example, quoted a sixteenth-century German account of how a group of Jews "purchased seven Christian children" whom they subsequently "pierced with needles and knives, tortured, and finally killed," and then "prepared the blood with pomegranates and served it for dinner."[30] Lynchings of American blacks were traditionally justified with the contention that many

blacks were literally wild beasts with uncontrollable sexual passions; black males were portrayed as a threat to white women.[31] Discrimination against gays has often been justified on the basis of the stereotype that gays are child molesters. However, empirical data indicate that in fact, gay men are no more likely than heterosexual men to molest children.[32]

22. Yet another ideology ascribes disease (physical and mental) to blacks, Jews, and gays. For example, Benjamin Rush (considered by many to be the father of American psychiatry) proposed that being black was itself an illness, a form of congenital leprosy.[33] Being black also was equated by many nineteenth-century white Americans with being insane, and free blacks were alleged to be substantially more prone to mental illness than were black slaves.[34] In 1851, Samuel Cartwright even identified a form of psychopathology unique to blacks: *drapetomania*, a disease that caused black slaves to run away from their owners. Jews also have been regarded as mentally ill[35] and as carriers of disease, for example, plague in the fourteenth century[36] and venereal disease in Nazi Germany.[37]

23. Similarly, homosexuality was officially labeled a mental illness by the American Psychiatric Association in the 1952 and 1968 editions of the Diagnostic and Statistical Manual of Psychiatric Disorders (DSM). This classification originally was urged by mental health professionals who considered it preferable to the then-prevalent view of homosexuality as criminal. Empirical evidence, however, overwhelmingly showed no correlation between sexual orientation and psychopathology. As a result, in 1973, the American Psychiatric Association voted to remove homosexuality from the DSM and to replace it with "ego-dystonic homosexuality." In 1986, even this diagnosis was dropped. Bayer, *Homosexuality and American Psychiatry* (1986). In 1975, the American Psychological Association (APA) passed a resolution strongly supporting the psychiatrists' actions and committed itself to removing the stigma associated with a homosexual orientation. Among its other actions in this regard, the APA passed a resolution on August 18, 1991, condemning the military policy of discriminating on the basis of sexual orientation.

24. *The Psychological Functions of Anti-Gay Prejudice.* National surveys reveal that heterosexual Americans show considerable variability in their attitudes toward lesbians and gay men. This raises the question of why some heterosexuals are strongly hostile toward gay people while others are tolerant or accepting in their attitudes. I have addressed this question in my own empirical research, using a perspective that other social psychologists earlier applied to whites' attitudes toward blacks and Americans' attitudes toward Russians. Known as the "functional approach," this perspective analyzes attitudes according to the psychological needs they meet.

25. From a content analysis of essays about homosexuality written by 205 heterosexual college students, my research has detected three principal functions. Attitudes serving an "experiential-schematic function" assisted the respondent in making sense of her or his previous interactions with gay people and provided a guide for future behavior. Those who had experienced pleasant interactions with a gay man or lesbian, for example, generalized from that experience and accepted gay people in general. A total of 14 percent of the respondents had attitudes serving an exclusively experiential-schematic function; another 9 percent manifested the experiential-schematic function along with one or more others.

26. In contrast to the experiential-schematic function, the other attitude functions were not based on actual experiences with gay people. Rather, they were beneficial to the respondent in that they permitted expression of important aspects of the self. Attitudes serving a "self-expressive function" increased the respondent's feelings of self-esteem in either of two ways: (a) by expressing values of central importance to her or his self-concept (e.g., a fundamentalist Christian condemning homosexuality as a way of affirming her or his religious identity); or (b) by expressing opinions supported by friends or family (e.g., telling a "fag joke" in order to gain others' friendship). A plurality of the respondents (40 percent) had attitudes serving an exclusively self-expressive function; another 43 percent manifested this function along with others.

27. Finally, the attitudes of some respondents served a "defensive function": they reduced anxiety associated with an unconscious psychological conflict, for example, personal conflicts about sexuality or gender. With defensive attitudes, an unacceptable part of the self is projected onto gay people; by rejecting (or even attacking) gay people, individuals are able symbolically to attack that unacceptable aspect of themselves. A total of 11 percent of the respondents manifested a defensive function, and another 24 percent manifested defensive attitudes in conjunction with one or more other functions.

28. The functional approach is important not only because it explains the motivations for anti-gay prejudice in individuals, but also

because it suggests a strategy for changing attitudes. Prejudice can be eradicated most effectively by appealing to the primary psychological functions that it serves. This means that different strategies will be necessary for changing the anti-gay attitudes held by different individuals. For example, creating social norms that support acceptance of gay people will be an effective strategy for reducing prejudice among heterosexuals whose hostile attitudes derive from their need to be accepted by others. Presenting alternative, noncondemnatory religious perspectives on homosexuality[38] will be most likely to have a positive effect on individuals whose prejudice results from their need to perceive themselves as a religious person.

29. *Eliminating Anti-Gay Prejudice.* Because anti-gay attitudes have complex cultural roots, are affected by many other social and psychological variables, and serve a variety of psychological functions, they cannot be eradicated through any one approach. Nevertheless, two clear conclusions can be drawn from empirical research. First, heterosexuals with openly gay friends or acquaintances are more likely than others to hold accepting attitudes toward gay people in general.[39] This pattern may result partly from a preference among gay people for disclosing their sexual orientation to others perceived as likely to be already supportive.[40] Nevertheless, knowing an openly gay person is predictive of supportive attitudes even in demographic groups where hostility is the norm, for example, among the highly religious and the uneducated.[41] Thus, the military's current policy excluding gays, like its discredited policies concerning blacks and women, have the effect of reinforcing prejudice against gays and creating a self-fulfilling prophecy that permitting gays to serve would disrupt good order, discipline, and morale.

30. Second, heterosexuals' attitudes tend to become more favorable after they are exposed to an educational program about gay people and homosexuality.[42] Attitude change has been documented after general human sexuality courses,[43] courses and workshops on homosexuality,[44] lectures about homosexuality,[45] lectures by openly gay people,[46] video presentations featuring gay people,[47] videos ridiculing prejudice against other (nongay) minority groups,[48] and exercises in which participants role-played a gay person coming out to others.[49]

31. Notably, research and experience show that precisely these same types of strategies are effective in combatting prejudice against women, blacks, Jews, and other discriminated against groups.[50] Indeed, it is no doubt precisely for this reason that the United States Naval Academy instructional program includes training specifically designed to break down prejudice.

Homosexuals and National Security

32. Stereotypes about gays and lesbians can also be found as the basis for the conclusion that homosexuals as a group pose special security risks. There are three frequently raised objections to granting security clearances to gay people: (a) that gay people are more likely than heterosexuals to manifest psychological disorders; (b) that gay people are more susceptible than heterosexuals to blackmail; and (c) that gay people are less likely than heterosexuals to be trustworthy and respectful of rules and laws. Empirical research indicates, however, that there is no scientific basis for any of these generalizations.

Homosexuality and Psychological Functioning

33. As noted above, one basis for concluding that gay men and lesbians are poor security risks is the assumption that they are inherently psychologically unstable, personally unreliable, or impaired in perceiving reality. Such suspicions are based on outdated prejudices and unfounded stereotypes. A large body of empirical research now clearly refutes the notion that homosexuality per se is indicative of or correlated with psychopathology.

34. The classic study in this area was conducted by Dr. Evelyn Hooker in 1951.[51] In her study, Dr. Hooker administered the Rorschach, Thematic Apperception Test, and Make-a-Picture-Story Test to thirty homosexual and thirty heterosexual men recruited through community organizations. The two groups were matched for age, IQ, and education; none of the men was in therapy at the time of the study. Outside experts on projective tests, unaware of each subject's sexual orientation, evaluated his overall adjustment using a five-point scale. The experts categorized two-thirds of the heterosexual men and two-thirds of the homosexual men in the three highest categories of adjustment. When asked to assess which protocols were obtained from homosexual respondents, the experts were unable to identify the men's sexual orientation at a level better than chance.

Dr. Hooker concluded from her data that homosexuality as a clinical entity does not exist and that homosexuality is not inherently associated with psychopathology.

35. Since Hooker's pioneering work, dozens of subsequent empirical studies have supported her conclusion that no correlation exists between sexual orientation and psychopathology. J. C. Gonsiorek,[52] for example, reviewed published studies comparing homosexual and heterosexual samples on psychological tests. He found that while differences have been observed in test results between homosexuals and heterosexuals, both groups consistently score within the normal range. Gonsiorek concluded that "[h]omosexuality in and of itself is unrelated to psychological disturbance or maladjustment. Homosexuals as a group are not more psychologically disturbed on account of their homosexuality."[53]

36. One recent study by M. McDaniel specifically focused on the question of whether gays as a group possess the characteristics that the military itself focuses on in determining whether an individual is suitable for positions of trust (such as school problems, drug and alcohol use, adverse job experiences, and felony convictions).[54] McDaniel concluded on the basis of data drawn from the Educational and Biographical Information Survey that "the preponderance of the evidence . . . indicates that homosexuals show preservice suitability-related adjustment that is as good or better than the average heterosexual" and that gays as a group do not possess characteristics that make them unsuitable for positions of trust.

37. As noted earlier, confronted with the overwhelming empirical evidence refuting the linkage of homosexuality with psychopathology, psychiatrists and psychologists have radically altered their views of homosexuality. As a result, the current Diagnostic and Statistical Manual of Mental Disorders of the American Psychiatric Association contains no diagnostic category for homosexuality. The American Psychological Association has endorsed the psychiatrists' actions.

38. Although the position that homosexuality is indicative of psychopathology is now widely considered to be scientifically indefensible, a variation of the argument recently has gained popularity. Gay people are claimed to be more susceptible to psychopathology, not because of their sexual orientation per se, but because of society's negative reaction to them. The roots of this argument can be traced to a 1950 report of the Senate Subcommittee on Investigations entitled "Employment of Homosexuals and Other Sex Perverts in Government."[55] (The committee was generally termed the "McClellan Committee," after its chair, Senator John McClellan. Senator Joseph R. McCarthy of Wisconsin was the ranking Republican member of the committee.) Among other things, the report concluded that homosexuals were dangerous because they were high-strung and neurotic from leading double lives.

39. Members of any stigmatized minority may indeed experience psychological stress because of their hostile treatment by the societal majority.[56] This observation applies to blacks and other people of color, religious and ethnic minorities, people who are physically disfigured or unattractive, and disabled people. Because of continuing patterns of gender discrimination in American society, women also could be considered a group at risk for psychological instability according to this line of reasoning. Unlike gay people, however, blacks, women, physically unattractive people, and other minority group members are not systematically excluded from security clearances. The fears about the deleterious effects of being out of the mainstream are thus selective.

40. Even if the government consistently attempted to screen out members of all stigmatized groups, however, the policy would not be valid because experiencing stigma does not necessarily lead to psychopathology. In the previously cited studies comparing the mental health of heterosexuals and homosexuals, most research subjects, heterosexual and homosexual alike, scored within the normal range on a variety of psychological tests. Like other minority group members, most gay people function effectively in American society. Some lesbians and gay men undoubtedly experience emotional problems adjusting to their sexual orientation, just as some African-Americans undoubtedly experience problems in dealing with racism. Similarly, some heterosexuals experience emotional problems adjusting to their adult sexuality or to their status as wife or husband. Those few cases, however, do not provide a basis for disqualifying all homosexual people, or all blacks, or all heterosexuals from security clearances, or even for subjecting their applications to unusually intensive review.

41. Indeed, the evidence shows that gay men and women have been able to function effectively in the military, an institution that is particularly homophobic. In his book *Coming Out under Fire: The History of Gay Men and Women in World War II*,[57] Allan Bérubé discusses the results of previously unpublished studies conducted by military physicians and researchers during World War II. These stud-

ies challenged the equation of homosexuality with psychopathology, as well as the stereotype that homosexual recruits could not be good soldiers:

> A common conclusion in their wartime studies was that, in the words of Maj. Carl H. Jonas, who studied fifty-three white and seven black men at Camp Haan, California, "overt homosexuality occurs in a heterogeneous group of individuals." Dr. Clements Fry, director of the Yale University student clinic, and Edna Rostow, a social worker, who together studied the service records of 183 servicemen, discovered that there was no evidence to support the common belief that "homosexuality is uniformly correlated with specific personality traits" and concluded that generalizations about the homosexual personality "are not yet reliable."
>
> ... Sometimes to their amazement, [researchers] described what they called the "well-adjusted homosexuals" who, in [William] Menninger's words, "concealed their homosexuality effectively and, at the same time, made creditable records for themselves in the service." Some researchers spoke in glowing terms of these men. "The homosexuals observed in the service," noted Navy doctors Greenspan and Campbell, "have been key men in responsible positions whose loss [by discharge] was acutely felt in their respective departments." They were "conscientious, reliable, well-integrated and abounding in emotional feeling and sincerity." In general, "the homosexual leads a useful productive life, conforming with all dictates of the community, except its sexual requirements" and was "neither a burden nor a detriment to society." Fry and Rostow reported that, based on evidence in service records, homosexuals were no better or worse than other soldiers and that many "performed well in various military jobs" including combat.

Homosexuality and Susceptibility to Blackmail

42. The second major argument supporting the idea that gays pose a special security risk is that homosexuals are at greater risk for blackmail than are heterosexuals. In order to be justified, this concern requires two conditions: the gay person must be hiding her or his own sexual orientation or that of a partner, and the threat of exposure must be so frightening or repellant that the individual is willing to betray her or his country in order to avoid it.

43. Susceptibility to coercion or blackmail is a characteristic of individuals who attempt to conceal their stigma and "pass" as a member of the majority.[58] Gay men and lesbians who pass must be concerned with managing potentially damaging information about themselves (i.e., their sexual orientation). Gay people whose status is known to others, in contrast, need not manage that information. An openly gay person, therefore, cannot be coerced by threats of exposure of her or his sexual orientation. Nor can a gay person be coerced by threats to expose her or his partner's homosexuality if that partner is openly gay.

44. Given the changes in societal attitudes, it is indefensible to assume that most gay people are subject to a meaningful threat of exposure and that all must therefore be excluded from positions of trust. A significant proportion of gay people in the United States have disclosed their sexual orientation to others. In a 1989 national telephone survey of four hundred lesbians and gay men, between 77 percent and 60 percent of the respondents (depending upon geographical region) had told their family of their sexual orientation.

45. The most meaningful data for assessing whether gay Americans are likely to disclose classified information as a result of blackmail are the government's past experiences with security breaches. In the approximately four decades during which the United States has had security clearance programs, no instance has been recorded of successful blackmail of an American for espionage in which homosexuality was involved. Of the forty significant espionage cases documented by the FBI and Defense Intelligence Agency for the Senate Permanent Subcommittee on Investigations, none involved blackmail of a gay person.[59] No evidence exists to suggest that gay Americans have betrayed their country in order to avoid disclosure of their sexual orientation, even in times when public disclosure of homosexuality carried more serious negative consequences than it does today.

46. Perhaps because the data indicate that gay people do not pose a threat to national security, the government has extended its argument to purely hypothetical situations. In a letter denying approval for SCI access to a lesbian applicant, William Kopatish, director of security for the CIA, cited a risk to national security posed by "the clear possibility that any future relationships that you establish may involve a partner who is not an open homosexual, and who fears public exposure." This charge is based on several major assumptions, including: (a) that the applicant will someday establish a relationship with a partner who is passing as a heterosexual; (b) that she will be the target of a blackmail attempt; and (c) that she will reveal

classified information to a foreign government in order to protect her partner from involuntarily coming out as gay.

47. The government is willing to accept all of these hypothetical circumstances in the case of gay applicants for security clearances. Yet they are not equally thorough in considering the possible future vulnerabilities of heterosexual applicants. A spouse or partner (current or future) might wish to conceal many stigmatized conditions other than homosexuality, such as a cancer diagnosis, a history of mental illness, an "illegitimate" birth, or the suicide of a family member. None of these conditions is rare, and all continue to be sufficiently stigmatized in our society that some people try to prevent their public disclosure. But the government does not reject applicants for security clearances on the grounds that a partner or loved one might someday bear such a stigma and wish to conceal it. Once again, the government's criteria for security clearance are suspiciously selective.

48. In summary, although lesbians and gay men with access to sensitive information hypothetically might be susceptible to blackmail if they were attempting to hide their sexual orientation (or that of a partner), no cases of security leaks resulting from such blackmail have been documented. As the American social climate has become more tolerant and gay people feel less pressured to hide their homosexuality, opportunities for such coercion have decreased markedly and will no doubt decrease even further.

Homosexuality, Trustworthiness, and Respect for Laws

49. In addition to specific allegations that they are psychologically impaired or unduly susceptible to coercion, gay women and men have been targeted as security risks because the government alleges that they manifest a variety of character flaws, in particular that they are prone to illegal conduct and to dishonesty. As with the previously stated governmental arguments, no data exist to support these allegations.

50. Convictions for criminal activity clearly are relevant considerations in evaluating applications for security clearances. The government has argued, however, that an applicant's homosexuality in itself can be considered an indicator of criminal conduct or disregard for the law. This argument was based on the existence of sodomy laws in one-half of the states and the District of Columbia and under the Uniform Code of Military Justice (UCMJ).[60] Technically, lesbians and gay men who engage in certain forms of homosexual activity in those jurisdictions are violating statutes, whether or not they are prosecuted.

51. In examining this argument, scrutiny first should be directed to the statutes themselves. As of 1987, all but four outlawed only those acts involving the genitalia of one person and the mouth or anus of another. Without cataloging the entire repertoire of sexual behaviors available to two men or two women, it can be stated simply that many people engage in forms of homosexual conduct that are not prohibited by these statutes. Such noncriminal homosexual activity is especially common among gay men in this era of AIDS and safer sex.[61] Moreover, of the twenty-two jurisdictions (including the District of Columbia) that criminalize sodomy, thirteen make no distinction between the sex of the participants and equally criminalize "homo-" and "hetero-" sexual sodomy. The UCMJ likewise criminalizes all "unnatural carnal copulation," regardless of the gender of the participants.[62]

52. Even if we assume that many gay people (like many heterosexual people) engage in specific illegal sexual acts, however, we must ask whether violation of these obscure and rarely enforced statutes somehow reflects "adversely upon the individual's reliability or trustworthiness." No evidence exists, however, to indicate that violating state sodomy statutes generalizes to an overall disrespect for law or authority. Rather, empirical research dating back to classic studies by H. Hartshorne & M. May, *Studies in the Nature of Character*,[63] suggests that rule violation in one situation is a poor predictor of behavior in other situations.[64] More generally, empirical research has demonstrated repeatedly that possession of a particular disposition or trait poorly predicts an individual's other behaviors in different situations.[65] According to some theorists, a principled choice to violate a law that is perceived as unjust may even indicate an unusually high level of moral development.[66] Thus, knowledge that a gay man or woman (or, for that matter, a heterosexual man or woman) has violated a state sodomy statute does not permit inferences about her or his respect for other laws, general adherence to rules, or overall morality.

53. As noted, a double standard is evident here. The UCMJ and all but nine of the state statutes outlaw heterosexual as well as homosexual sodomy. Consequently, in the military and in most states with sodomy statutes, heterosexuals are lawbreakers to the same extent as

are gay people if they engage in fellatio, cunnilingus, or anal intercourse. These heterosexual practices are quite common, and no evidence indicates that heterosexuals avoid them in states in which
they are prohibited by statute.[67] In contrast to its treatment of gay
applicants for security clearances, however, the government does
not presume heterosexuals who engage in illegal sexual practices to
be unreliable or untrustworthy, nor does it subject them to intensive
investigation; indeed, the government does not collect information
about heterosexual behavior in most cases.

54. A principal flaw in policies surrounding security clearances
for gay applicants is that they themselves create many of the problems that they supposedly are needed to address; if the policies were
changed, many of the arguments for denying security clearance to
gay applicants also would be eliminated. As already detailed, for
example, gay people are susceptible to blackmail only to the extent
that their sexual orientation remains hidden. But much of the motivation for gay people to keep their sexual orientation a secret (and,
therefore, much of the basis for blackmail) derives from existing discriminatory employment policies. Many lesbians and gay men jus-
tifiably fear or have directly experienced employment discrimination
and, consequently, keep their homosexuality hidden or carefully
control disclosures to others.[68] The risks, of course, are particularly
great in the military context. If the opportunities for discrimination were eliminated, gay people would feel encouraged to disclose
their sexual orientation to others, thereby eliminating any basis for
blackmail. Similarly, gay people are considered suspect because
they do not volunteer information about their sexual orientation,
even though to do so would destroy or significantly decrease their
chances for security clearance. If homosexuality were no longer used
as a justification for denying clearance, however, gay applicants
could disclose that information freely during the investigation. Ironi-
cally, such a change in policy also would make knowledge of an em-
ployee's homosexuality largely irrelevant to the entire application
process.

Conclusion

55. Lesbians and gay men constitute a minority group in
American society. In contrast to the situation only twenty years ago,
Americans now appear to think differently about homosexuality de-

pending upon the context in which it is raised: many still consider homosexual behavior to be immoral from a religious perspective yet, within a legal context, they consider gay people to be entitled to freedom from discrimination.

56. Joining the chorus of outcry against this long-entrenched form of bigotry are social and behavioral scientists, who have recognized it as a serious societal problem. They have created an impressive body of scientific theory and empirical research on the social and psychological bases of hostility toward lesbians and gay men. This scientific evidence conclusively establishes that gays and lesbians bear the classic indicia of a discriminated-against minority group and that, like other prejudices, attitudes can be changed and are changing as a result of education and greater interaction between open homosexuals and their heterosexual counterparts in society.

Robert Rankin

AFFIDAVIT

On the Ability of Gay People to Perform Well in the Military

$\mathbf{R}$OBERT RANKIN, an associate professor of psychiatry at the University of California at Davis and the University of California at San Francisco Medical School, submitted an affidavit based on his experiences while in the Navy. Dr. Rankin's military experience overall encompasses twenty-one years of active and reserve duty. His active service included a tour in Vietnam, and he later provided counseling for over three hundred gay and lesbian servicemembers from all branches of the armed forces.

Rankin's affidavit shows that gays have historically served—and are serving—in the military and that many gays in the military are known to their commanding officers and their peers and are tolerated by them. Thus, being gay has no relation to one's ability to perform or contribute to society—another key issue in equal protection law.

This affidavit, based on personal experience, substantiates the conclusions in Gregory Herek's affidavit that gay and lesbian servicemembers experience prejudice and suffer from the unsupported stereotypes assigned them by fellow servicemembers and command personnel.

Rankin's affidavit illustrates a more traditional aspect of the affidavit process: it relies on personal knowledge and experience as a basis for the affidavit's use as evidence. This affidavit also provides a strong factual basis for the plaintiff's claim that lesbian and gay servicemembers are effective and patriotic individuals. Rankin reports that, in his experience, gay and lesbian servicemembers, "even more than their heterosexual counterparts, conduct themselves in a professional manner." His affidavit discredits the government's claim that gay and lesbian servicemembers would lower morale, threaten the effectiveness of the fighting force, or undermine the command structure. Instead, Rankin notes that gays and lesbians in the service are the object of the prejudice characteristic of attitudes toward other minorities in the service. Lesbians and gays are distinguished only by the absence of the protections afforded other minorities.

1. Most often, gay sailors and Marines came to me because they were feeling pressure from shipmates who had guessed their sexual orientation. The gay servicemembers whom I counseled rarely fit the stereotypes assigned them by society. Typically, their sexual orientation would become known from an overheard telephone call, a letter left on a bunk, or a conversational slip. For the most part, when their sexual orientation did become known, friends on the ship remained friends. If the individual was a senior enlisted man or woman, a chief petty officer, or a commissioned officer, those under his or her command continued to follow orders and to perform.

2. Nonetheless, being well aware of the Navy's and Marines' policy on homosexuality, gay sailors and Marines lived in fear of discovery if they wanted to remain in the service, which most of them did. It was this pressure—not conflict with a shipmate and, still less, conflict about their sexuality—which brought them in for counseling. I also counseled African-American, Jewish, and Asian-American sailors who felt the sting of prejudice. The major difference, however, was that the Navy would protect them from discrimination. Gay sailors and Marines would be discharged posthaste if they were discovered by an unsympathetic commanding officer.

3. Based on this professional experience, it is plain to me that there is a wide disparity in the level of enforcement of the military's ban on gays within the Navy. In essence, the likelihood that a servicemember will be discharged is a direct function of the attitudes of the servicemember's commanding officer—the individual who has the authority and responsibility to initiate discharge proceedings under military regulation. Most officers do not concern themselves at all with the sexual orientation of their subordinates and do so only if it creates a problem within their chain of command. In my experience, high achievers whose homosexual orientation became known were usually protected by their commanding officers.

4. Confirmation of this is provided by a July 24, 1990, administrative message issued by Vice Admiral Joseph S. Donnell, the commander of the Navy's surface Atlantic Fleet. In that message, Vice

Admiral Donnell urged his subordinates to increase the level of enforcement of the military's ban against lesbians, tacitly conceding that enforcement is lax. The vice admiral's message itself provides the explanation as to why many commanding officers are reluctant to strictly enforce the military's policy requiring the discharge of gays. He states that "[e]xperience has ... shown that the stereotypical female homosexual in the Navy is hardworking, career-oriented, willing to put in long hours on the job and among the command's top professionals. As such, allegations that this woman is a homosexual, particularly if made by a young and junior female sailor with no track record, may be dismissed out of hand or pursued half-heartedly."

5. In my professional experience, as Vice Admiral Donnell acknowledges, homosexual enlisted men and women and officers were some of the most effective and patriotic I knew. Homosexual sailors did not tend to drink more heavily than their shipmates, or abuse drugs more frequently. If anything, the rate was probably a little less, especially in foreign ports.

6. My professional experience also shows that gay servicemembers conform their sexual conduct to the requirements of military life. During my twenty-one years of Navy service, there were only three occasions on which a sailor was referred to me for discharge on grounds of sexual activity onboard ship. Virtually uniformly, gay servicemembers, even more so than their heterosexual counterparts, conduct themselves in a professional manner in their interpersonal relationships.

7. My professional experience confirms the findings of a major study on this subject conducted by the Kinsey Institute and reported in C. Williams and M. Weinberg, *Homosexuals and the Military*. The Kinsey study focused on 136 homosexuals who had served in the military. Of this group, 76 percent received honorable discharges, i.e., they completed their term of service without incident. The Kinsey study cited other studies that similarly found that the overwhelming majority of homosexuals who serve in the military do so without incident and receive honorable discharges. For example, a 1945 study found that out of a group of 118 homosexuals, only 14 were discharged from the service; 58 percent of the group became officers. Similarly, a 1957 study conducted by the Navy (known as the "Crittenden Report") concluded that "[m]any exclusively homosexual persons have served honorably in all branches of the military

service without detection." A 1967 study by the Institute for Sex Research showed that out of a group of 458 male homosexuals, 214 had served in the military. Some 77 percent of that subgroup received honorable discharges. Another study published in 1967 indicated that only 20 percent of 550 white homosexual males who had served in the military had reported any difficulties.

8. A recent book by Allan Bérubé, *Coming Out under Fire: The History of Gay Men and Women in World War II*, provides exhaustive documentation of the extensive service of lesbian and gay male soldiers and sailors during World War II. As Berube details, many of these servicemen and women were known by their comrades to be gay and were accepted as such. The book also documents the fact that selective service boards and commanding officers took widely varying approaches to the level of enforcement of the then-existing policies with respect to the service of gays and lesbians in order to accommodate the need for the military to obtain sufficient troop levels.

9. More recently, in 1984, a study by Joseph Harry analyzed interview data on 1,456 respondents who had served in the military. The study found that homosexual men and heterosexual men were equally likely to have served, while homosexual women were more likely than heterosexual women to have served. The same study also found that 80 percent of the homosexual servicemembers in these samples received honorable discharges.

10. Another recent study, by Sarbin and Karols, reviews the available data with respect to the incidence of homosexuality in the general population and the declining number of separations from the military on grounds of homosexuality. From this data, among other things, the authors conclude "that a large number of homosexual men and women are performing satisfactorily and that their sexual orientation does not come to the attention of their commanders." Given the fact that psychiatrists long ago abandoned the notion that homosexuality is an illness and all available evidence shows that, sexual orientation aside, gays as a group are indistinguishable from the population at large, there is nothing remarkable about this conclusion. Indeed, the defendants would be hard pressed to dispute it given that Secretary of Defense Richard Cheney has stated that there is no doubt in his mind that "many gays" are currently serving in the military. (A June 27, 1991, *USA Today* article quoted Cheney as say-

ing, "No question in my mind, we've got a large number of gays in military service.")

11. In short, all available research confirms what common sense and my own professional experience indicate: that gay men and women have served in the United States armed services throughout their history and in every armed conflict with distinction and in substantial numbers; that a significant percentage of servicemembers currently serving in the armed forces are gay; and that a meaningful percentage of those currently serving are known to be gay by their commanding officers and peers.

Kate Dyer

AFFIDAVIT

On Other Nations' Policies toward Gays in the Military

KATE DYER is the former executive assistant to Congressman Gerry Studds of the United States House of Representatives. Her affidavit provides evidence that many nations, including several of the United States' military allies, do not discriminate against gay people in the military solely on the basis of orientation. The absence of such policies in the militaries of many of our allies casts severe doubts on the rational basis of the U.S. military's policy of excluding gay people solely on the basis of orientation.

1. In August 1990, while I was employed by Congressman Studds and at the Congressman's direction, I wrote to the embassies of a number of countries to inquire as to their policies concerning the service of homosexuals in their armed forces. A sample of the form of letter I sent is annexed as Exhibit A hereto. True and correct copies of the responses from Denmark, Switzerland, Sweden, the Netherlands, Belgium, Spain, France, Finland, and Norway are annexed as Exhibit B hereto.

Excerpts from Exhibit A

August 9, 1990

Military Attache
Embassy of ———

We are interested in learning what, if any, regulations exist in your military with respect to homosexual men and women.... [W]e would like to know whether [your nation] does or does not permit homosexuals to serve.

Sincerely,
Gerry E. Studds   Ted Weiss
Member of Congress   Member of Congress

Excerpts from Exhibit B

Embassy of Spain   August 24, 1990

The Spanish Constitution recognizes the equality of all individuals before the law without the discrimination of birth, race, sex, religion or any other condition, personal or social circumstances. Therefore, homosexuals are considered in all respects the same way as hetero-sexuals are as far as rights and duties are concerned.

Homosexuals as such are not barred from service.

[French Embassy to the United States]   5 September 1990

There is no written policy concerning the acceptability of gay or lesbian soldiers in the French Armed Forces. When one of these sol-diers is spotted by the hierarchy, he or she is considered as having a medical problem and therefore is referred to a medical doctor. The physician is the only authority to determine if the person concerned is fit or unfit for military service.

In the case of an active duty member, . . . if the physician does not find him or her unfit for military service, the commander will advise him/her to resign but cannot force him to leave the service.

Royal Danish Embassy   14 Aug 1990

In short we do not have special problems with homosexuals serv-ing in the Danish Armed Forces, and we do not have a stated written policy in this area.

We do not ask the military personnel about their sexual habits, and we do not expel them from service or diminish their career chances, if they tell us about their homosexuality.

Finally, . . . we do not have special organizations with respect to homosexuals serving in the Danish Armed Forces.

Embassy of Switzerland   25 September 1990

If the reputation of the army or the conduct of service suffer, especially if the homosexuals are not able to control themselves or are
conspicuous during their service through their behavior or the formation of cliques: *unfit for service.*

Embassy of Sweden   August 14, 1990

[T]here exist no regulations in the military with respect to homosexual men and women. . . . As we have no regulations, we take no
action. The individuals have their right to do what he or she wants to
do in their free time.

Royal Netherlands Embassy   October 3, 1990

Military Personnel policy does not discriminate on the basis of
sexual orientation.
Homosexual orientation gives no grounds to be found unfit for
service in the Netherlands armed forces.

Embassy of Belgium   October 5, 1990

The Belgian Penal Code does not object to homosexuality as
such. . . .
Homosexuality is not a reason for exclusion from the armed forces
in the Belgian conscript system. . . .

Embassy of Finland   August 22, 1990

[T]here are no special rules or regulations concerning homosexuals within the armed forces. . . .
In Finland, generally speaking, the homosexual acts are legal if the
individuals concerned are 18 years of age or older or 21 years or
older, if they are under the guardian of some person or organization.
This same law naturally applies to the armed forces.

Royal Norwegian Embassy   24 August 1990

There is no stated written policy concerning the acceptability of
gay men and lesbian women in the Norwegian Armed Forces, and
there has been no need for any. The practice is that every conscript

does military service as long as he or she does not have any psychical problems because of his or her inclination. Those who get problems consult the military doctor and are normally found unfit for service due to psychical health. . . .

In the Norwegian Penal Code there are two paragraphs dealing with the question:

Para 135A

Anyone who in written or oral form are threatening, scorning, prosecuting or despiting a gay or lesbian person will be punished with fines or with prison for up to two years.

Para 349A

Any individual who in its occupational activity are denying a person goods and services, because of this person's sexual preferences, on the same conditions as for other individuals, will be punished with fines or with prison for up to 6 months.

Regarding the Norwegian Armed Forces, as stated above, there are no particular regulations dealing with this question.

The Armed Forces simply comply with "the law of the land."

Department of Justice

MEMORANDUM IN RESPONSE

Reply Memorandum in Support of Defendants' Motion for Judgment on the Pleadings or, in the Alternative, for Summary Judgment and in Opposition to Plaintiff's Cross-motion for Summary Judgment

Preliminary Statement

IN THIS CASE, plaintiff challenges on equal protection grounds the administrative rules that required his separation from the United States Naval Academy following his admission of homosexuality. Relying on the extensive case law on point, defendants have shown that the aforementioned rules do not run afoul of the equal protection component of the Fifth Amendment. In his recent memorandum, plaintiff has sought to refute defendants' showing. As is demonstrated below, his attempt to do so is unpersuasive.

As a secondary matter, plaintiff argues that his separation from the Naval Academy was improper because, during his tenure at the Academy, ten midshipmen were permitted to graduate even though they, like he, were noncommissionable. In making this argument, plaintiff camouflages the fact that all of the midshipmen to whom he refers suffered from disabling medical conditions, and that none was a homosexual. As a result, his argument is without merit, and the case should be dismissed.

The Regulatory Scheme

A. *The Department of Defense (DOD) Directives.* The separation from the armed services of homosexual personnel is governed by two DOD directives, No. 1332.14 (Jan. 28, 1982) (enlisted personnel) and No. 1332.30 (Feb. 12, 1986) (commissioned officers). With certain exceptions, these directives provide that an individual shall be separated from the military if he or she is found to have "stated that he or she is a homosexual," or if he or she is found to have "engaged in, attempted to engage in, or solicited another to engage in a homosexual act or acts." The directives define a homosexual as "a person, regardless of sex, who engages in, desires to engage in, or intends to engage in homosexual acts."

The rationale for the above directives is as follows:

> Homosexuality is incompatible with military service. The presence in the military environment of persons who engage in homosexual conduct or who, by their statements, demonstrate a propensity to engage in homosexual conduct, seriously impairs the accomplishment of the military mission. The presence of such members adversely affects the ability of the Military Services to maintain discipline, good order, and morale; to foster mutual trust and confidence among servicemembers, to ensure the integrity of the system of rank and command; to facilitate assignment and worldwide deployment of servicemembers who frequently live and work under close conditions affording minimal privacy; to recruit and retain members of the Military Services; to maintain the public acceptability of military service; and to prevent breaches of security.

B. *The Naval Academy Rules.* The rules of the Naval Academy contain a list of "examples of problems which severely limit a midshipman's aptitude and potential for commissioned service" and which are "sufficient in and of themselves to warrant separation from the Naval Academy." Among other things, the aforementioned list provides that a midshipman shall be separated from the Academy for "engaging in, attempting to engage in, or soliciting another to engage in a homosexual act or acts" or for making "statements that he or she is homosexual." With limited exceptions, the aforementioned list does not require the separation of midshipmen suffering from medical disabilities.

ARGUMENT

DEFENDANTS' MOTION FOR JUDGMENT ON
THE PLEADINGS OR, IN THE ALTERNATIVE,
SUMMARY JUDGMENT, SHOULD BE
GRANTED. PLAINTIFF'S CROSS-MOTION FOR
SUMMARY JUDGMENT SHOULD BE DENIED.

Plaintiff Has Not Shown That the Administrative Rules That Required His Separation from the Naval Academy Violated His Constitutional Right to Equal Protection.

The constitutional validity of the administrative rules that plaintiff challenges—the rules requiring the separation of homosexuals from the military—rests on a trio of principles. First, "the military has needs for discipline and good order justifying restrictions that go beyond the needs of civilian society." In addition, "[o]rderly government requires that the judiciary be as scrupulous not to interfere with legitimate Army matters as the Army must be scrupulous not to intervene in judicial matters." *Orloff* v. *Willoughby* (1953). As a result, "when evaluating whether military needs justify a particular restriction" on the constitutional rights of servicemembers, "courts must give great deference to the professional judgment of military authorities concerning the relative importance of a particular military interest." *Goldman* v. *Weinberger* (1986). This deference extends to administrative rules restricting the right of homosexuals to serve in the military.

Second, for purposes of the Constitution's equal protection guarantees, homosexuals have generally been treated neither as a "suspect" nor a "quasi-suspect class." Accordingly, restrictions on the right of homosexuals to serve in the military have been held to be valid for equal protection purposes provided that they were "rationally related to a permissible end."

Third, the rationale contained in DOD Directive 1332.14 for the military's policy on homosexuality provides a rational basis therefor.

As the court said in *Woodward* v. *United States* (1989):

> The Navy's challenged practice regarding homosexuals need only be rationally related to a permissible governmental end to pass constitutional muster. Although this issue was not specifically argued by Woodward, we assume it to be inherent in his claim to be a member of a suspect class entitled to heightened scrutiny.
> We are convinced that the Navy's policy on homosexuality is rationally related to a permissible end. As stated in *Dronenburg:*

> > The Navy's policy requiring discharge of those who engage in homosexual conduct serves legitimate state interests which include the maintenance of "discipline, good order and morale[,] . . . mutual trust and confidence among service members, . . . insur[ing] the integrity of the system of rank and command, . . . recruit[ing] and retain[ing] members of the naval service . . . and . . . prevent[ing] breaches of security." SEC/ NAV 1900.9D (Mar. 12, 1981). We believe that the policy requiring discharge for homosexual conduct is a rational means of achieving those legitimate interests. The unique needs of the military, "a specialized society separate from civilian society," *Parker* v. *Levy*, justify the Navy's determination that homosexual conduct impairs its capacity to carry out its mission.

In this case, plaintiff has sought to refute each of the principles identified above. As is demonstrated below, however, he is unable to do so.

Plaintiff Has Not Shown That the Deference Traditionally Afforded to the Judgment of the Military Should Be Withheld in This Case.

As a threshold matter, plaintiff argues that it is inappropriate for the Court to "defer to . . . expert military judgment in deciding this case." The core of plaintiff's argument is that deference to the military's judgment is inappropriate because this case involves an equal protection claim. However, plaintiff's argument is without merit.

In *Goldman* v. *Weinberger* (1986), the Supreme Court upheld against First Amendment challenge a policy of the military that prohibited the wearing of yarmulkes by military personnel. In doing so, the Court said:

> Our review of military regulations challenged on First Amendment grounds is far more deferential than constitutional review of similar laws or regulations designed for civilian society. The military need not encourage debate or tolerate protest to the extent that such tolerance is required of the civilian state by the First Amendment; to accomplish its mission the military must foster instinctive obedience, unity, commitment, and esprit de corps. The essence of military service "is the subordination of the desires and interests of the individual to the needs of the service." *Orloff* v. *Willoughby*.
>
> These aspects of military life do not, of course, render entirely nugatory in the military context the guarantees of the First Amendment. But "within the military community there is simply not the same [individual] autonomy as there is in the larger civilian community." *Parker* v. *Levy*. In the context of the present case, when evaluating whether military needs justify a particular restriction on religiously motivated conduct, courts must give great deference to the professional judgment of military authorities concerning the relative importance of a particular military interest. Not only are courts " 'ill-equipped to determine the impact upon discipline that any particular intrusion upon military authority might have,' " but the military authorities have been charged by the Executive and Legislative Branches with carrying out our Nation's military policy. "[J]udicial deference . . . is at its apogee when legislative action under the congressional authority to raise and support armies and make rules and regulations for their governance is challenged." *Rostker* v. *Goldberg*.

In this case, plaintiff argues that the standard of deference propounded in *Goldman* is inapposite because *Goldman* involved a challenge to military policy based on the First Amendment while this case involves a challenge to military policy based on the equal protection component of the Fifth Amendment. However, plaintiff does not explain why the right of a Jewish serviceman to wear a yarmulke should be treated as less fundamental, for purposes of constitutional adjudication, than that of a homosexual to serve in the military *vel non*. As a result, plaintiff does not explain why the judgment of the military should be given greater deference in First Amendment cases than it is in equal protection cases. Nor have the courts been able to discern any difference between the two types of cases. Indeed, in a series of cases, the standard of deference propounded in *Goldman* has been held to be as applicable to equal protection claims as it is to First Amendment claims. As a result, plaintiff's claim that the Court should not "defer to ... expert military judgment in deciding this case" should be rejected.

Plaintiff Has Not Shown That the Military's Policy on Homosexuality Should Be Subjected to a Heightened Standard of Scrutiny.

A second argument made by plaintiff is that the Court should not use the "rational basis test" to determine the validity of the military's policy on homosexuality. According to plaintiff, homosexuals constitute a "suspect or quasi-suspect class." As a result, plaintiff argues that the military's policy must withstand "strict scrutiny" in order to be upheld.

In making this argument, plaintiff ignores the extensive case law that goes against him. For purposes of equal protection analysis, homosexuals have repeatedly been held to constitute neither a "suspect" nor a "quasi-suspect" class. *High Tech Gays* v. *Defense Indus. Sec. Clearance Office* (1990); *Ben-Shalom* v. *Marsh* (1989); *Woodward* v. *United States* (1989); *Padula* v. *Webster* (1987); *Gay Inmates of Shelby County Jail* v. *Barksdale* (1987); *Rich* v. *Secretary of the Army* (1984); *Secora* v. *Fox* (1989); *Todd* v. *Navarro* (1988). As a result, the use of the "rational basis test" to determine the validity of the military's policy on homosexuality is completely appropriate.

Nor has plaintiff made a persuasive showing to the contrary. To demonstrate that homosexuals constitute a "suspect" or "quasi-suspect" class, plaintiff uses a five-pronged test that requires him to show, among other things, that homosexuality is an "immutable trait" and that homosexuals "lack the political power necessary to obtain redress through the political process." Although plaintiff has attempted to make these showings, his attempts to do so fail.

To begin with, plaintiff's claim with respect to the "immutability" of homosexuality is undercut by the rejection of the same claim in *Woodward* and in *High Tech Gays*. As the court said in *Woodward*:

Homosexuality, as a definitive trait, differs fundamentally from those defining any of the recognized suspect or quasi-suspect classes. Members of recognized suspect or quasi-suspect classes, *e.g.*, blacks or women, exhibit immutable characteristics, whereas homosexuality is primarily behavioral in nature. The conduct or behavior of a recognized suspect or quasi-suspect class has no relevance to the identification of those groups.

Furthermore, to demonstrate the purported "immutability" of homosexuality, plaintiff places extensive reliance on the declaration of Dr. Richard Green. However, Dr. Green acknowledges in his declaration that changes in sexual orientation have frequently occurred as a result of therapy. For example, Dr. Green discusses one study in which a "'shift from homosexuality to exclusive heterosexuality'" was reported for "'27 percent of the patients'" studied and treated. For such a shift to have occurred flies in the face of plaintiff's contention that homosexuality is an "immutable" characteristic.

Similarly unpersuasive is plaintiff's argument that homosexuals lack sufficient power to obtain redress of their grievances through the political process. Indeed, plaintiff's argument is undercut by recent events in this case. On June 13 and 21, 1991, defendants served plaintiff with two supplemental responses to Plaintiff's Second Document Request. In doing so, defendants gave notice of their decision to withhold a limited number of records pursuant to the attorney-client and deliberative-process privileges. On June 28, 1991, thirty-two members of Congress responded to the above decision by sending a letter—a letter bearing the signatures of all thirty-two senders—to the secretary of defense. There, the senders of the letter "specifically request[ed] copies of the eight documents itemized in DOD's Supplemental Responses in the Steffan case" and said: "To the extent reconsideration is underway, we applaud it."

The mere existence of the above letter—a letter demonstrating the ability of plaintiff and his counsel to mobilize thirty-two members of the House of Representatives on a week's notice—gives great force to something that the court said in *Ben-Shalom:*

> In these times, homosexuals are proving that they are not without growing political power. It cannot be said "they have no ability to attract the attention of the lawmakers." *Cleburne,* 473 U.S. at 445, 105 S. Ct. at 3257. A political approach is open to them to seek a congressional determination about the rejection of homosexuals by the Army.

In view of the foregoing, plaintiff's claim that homosexuals "lack the political power necessary to obtain redress through the political process"—and his further claim that the military's policy on homosexuality must meet a standard of scrutiny beyond the rational basis test—should be rejected.[1]

Plaintiff Has Not Shown That the Military's Policy on Homosexuality Fails to Meet the Rational Basis Test.

Plaintiff's third claim is that the military's policy on homosexuality among servicemembers lacks a rational basis. Accordingly, plaintiff argues that the policy cannot be upheld, regardless of the applicable test.

The main obstacle to plaintiff's argument is the long series of judicial decisions—*Ben-Shalom, Woodward, Dronenburg, Rich,* and *Steffan II*—in which the military's policy has been held to have a rational basis. Although plaintiff has made a strenuous series of efforts to respond to these cases, once again he is unable to do so.

Plaintiff's claim that the military's policy on homosexuality cannot be found to have a rational basis because of the recent opinion of the Ninth Circuit in *Pruitt* v. *Cheney* is meritless. In *Pruitt,* the Ninth Circuit held that the military's policy on homosexuality could not be held to meet the rational basis test until the military had "establish[ed] on the record that its policy had a rational basis." In reaching this conclusion, the Ninth Circuit distinguished some, but not all, of the cases in which the military's policy had been held to have a rational basis. According to the Ninth Circuit, the aforementioned cases were distinguishable because they involved homosexual conduct rather than homosexual status, or failed to give appropriate consideration to whether the military's policy on homosexuality was based on private prejudices.

One case that *Pruitt* did *not* attempt to distinguish is *Ben-Shalom.* This failure is of crucial importance, because *Ben-Shalom* addressed both of the issues that *Pruitt* considered essential. First, *Ben-Shalom* held that the military's policy on homosexuality could be applied with equal force to cases involving admissions of homosexuality and cases involving actual homosexual conduct. As *Ben-Shalom* states:

> It is true that actual lesbian conduct has not been admitted by plaintiff on any particular occasion, and the Army has offered no evidence of any such

conduct. Judge Gordon found no reason to believe that the lesbian admission meant that plaintiff was likely to commit homosexual acts. We see it differently. Plaintiff's lesbian acknowledgment, if not an admission of its practice, at least can rationally and reasonably be viewed as reliable evidence of a desire and propensity to engage in homosexual conduct. Such an assumption cannot be said to be without individual exceptions, but it is compelling evidence that plaintiff has in the past and is likely to again engage in such conduct. To this extent, therefore, the regulation does not classify plaintiff based merely upon her status as a lesbian, but upon reasonable inferences about her probable conduct in the past and in the future. *The Army need not shut its eyes to the practical realities of this situation, nor be compelled to engage in the sleuthing of soldiers' personal relationships for evidence of homosexual conduct in order to enforce its bans on homosexual acts, a ban not challenged here. Plaintiff does not deny that she has engaged or will engage in homosexual conduct. Plaintiff has admitted that she has a homosexual desire, but not necessarily that she intends to commit homosexual acts. The Army need not fine tune a regulation to fit a particular lesbian's subjective thoughts and propensities.* [Emphasis added.]

Second, the court in *Ben-Shalom* held that impermissible private prejudices did not underlie the military's policy on homosexuality. Referring to the concurring opinion of Judge Norris in *Watkins* v. *United States Army*, the court said:

Judge Norris further rejected the Army's asserted justifications because he explained that they illegitimately cater to private biases. *Watkins.* We *respectfully disagree, as we believe that this particular classification is supported by military considerations and should be left to the Army. We do not believe that the concerns set forth in the military policy and regulation can so easily be dismissed as mere prejudice, though individual prejudice no doubt exists in the military and elsewhere. The new regulation, we find, clearly promotes a legitimate government interest sufficient to survive rational basis scrutiny.* We agree with Judge Hall, who wrote in dissent in *Watkins,* that "[t]here is no doubt that the majority's intrusion into military affairs, unjustified by important federal interests, will have a disruptive effect upon military discipline." *Watkins.* We need not pursue all the equal protection avenues thoroughly explored by Judge Norris in his concurrence as we find them unpersuasive in the military context. On this controversial subject unanimity is not to be expected as respectable arguments may be made on both sides of the issue.

Homosexuals have suffered a history of discrimination and still do, though possibly now to less degree. We do not see, however, that the new regulation embodies a gross unfairness in the military context so inconsistent with equal protection as to be termed "invidious." In these times, homosexuals are proving that they are not without growing political power. It cannot be said "they have no ability to attract the attention of the lawmakers." *Cleburne.* A political approach is open to them to seek a congressional determination about the rejection of homosexuals by the Army. We are, however, unwilling to substitute a mere judge-made rule for the Army's regulation or to act in an executive or legislative fashion. [Emphasis added.]

Because *Ben-Shalom* addressed the two aspects of the military's policy on homosexuality that *Pruitt* found troubling—and because *Pruitt* makes no effort to distinguish *Ben-Shalom*—the persuasiveness of *Pruitt* is seriously undermined. As a result, the Court should decline to follow *Pruitt* and should hold, on the basis of *Ben-Shalom, Woodward, Dronenburg, Rich,* and *Steffan II,* that the military's policy on homosexuality has a rational basis. The claims of plaintiff to the contrary should therefore be rejected.[2]

Defendants Did Not Act Improperly by Permitting Ten Midshipmen with Disabling Medical Conditions to Graduate from the Naval Academy.

During plaintiff's tenure at the Naval Academy, ten midshipmen who had entered their fourth year of instruction were permitted to graduate from the Academy, even though they suffered from disabling medical conditions that rendered them noncommissionable. In this case, plaintiff argues that the Academy lacked a rational basis for permitting the aforementioned midshipmen to graduate but requiring plaintiff to be separated from the Academy. Accordingly, plaintiff argues that the Academy violated the equal protection component of the Fifth Amendment and similarly violated 5 U.S.C. § 706(2)(A) by failing to treat plaintiff like the aforementioned midshipmen.

Plaintiff's argument founders on the fact that homosexual midshipmen are different from midshipmen who suffer from medical conditions that render them noncommissionable. The separation of homosexuals from the armed services has been held to bear a rational relationship to the advancement of "legitimate state interests which include the maintenance of 'discipline, good order and morale[,] ... mutual trust and confidence among service members, ... insur[ing] the integrity of the system of rank and command, ... recruit[ing] and retain[ing] members of the naval service ... and ... prevent[ing) breaches of security.' " Such interests are not advanced by the separation of personnel who suffer from disabling medical conditions like ulcerative colitis, diabetes, back, shoulder and eye problems, and somnambulism. Accordingly, an administrative rule like COMDTMIDNINST 1610.6F, § 2.15.3—the rule that required the separation of plaintiff from the Naval Academy for lack of "aptitude and potential for commissioned service" but did not require the separation of the midshipmen with the disabling medical conditions— is not irrational. The claim of plaintiff to the contrary should be rejected.[3]

Conclusion

For the foregoing reasons, defendants' motion for judgment on the pleadings or, in the alternative, summary judgment should be granted. Plaintiff's cross-motion for summary judgment should be denied.

Reply Memorandum in Support of Plaintiff's Cross-motion for Summary Judgment

THIS REPLY memorandum is respectfully submitted on behalf of plaintiff in support of his cross-motion for summary judgment.

Preliminary Statement

Defendants' response to plaintiff's cross-motion for summary judgment is more notable for what it omits than for what it includes. Nowhere is there any response to plaintiff's statement of undisputed facts. Nowhere is there any attempt to distinguish *Pruitt v. Cheney*, the one-month-old precedent that holds that the precise equal protection claim raised here cannot be disposed of on a motion to dismiss as defendants urge. Nowhere is there any explanation as to why it is that discrimination on the basis of sexual orientation is necessary to preserve good order, discipline, and morale or to prevent security breaches. And nowhere is there any explanation as to why Steffan had to be railroaded out of the United States Naval Academy in one week when the Navy has a "goal" of processing discharges for homosexuality in 120 days.

All of these omissions are of a piece. Defendants simply cannot respond to plaintiff's showing on these matters because if they did, they would have to admit that Steffan's discharge was deemed to be "necessary" because his mere presence could upset those whose prejudice can find no legal or moral basis. And on that basis, under *Palmore* v. *Sidoti*, defendants concede that they must lose.

As in their opening memorandum, rather than address the record in this case, defendants do little more than retype long portions of *Ben-Shalom* v. *Marsh* and pretend that a number of other cases that uphold military regulations discriminating on the basis of homosexual conduct control a challenge to discrimination solely on the basis of status. The D.C. Circuit itself, however, in *Doe* v. *Casey*, has rejected defendants' contention that status and conduct can be equated. And the D.C. Circuit *in this case* has also already held that *Ben-Shalom* is distinguishable on its facts.

Defendants' opposition to plaintiff's motion for summary judgment should thus be seen for what it is—a superficial attempt to avoid addressing the "difficult issue" that is raised squarely in this case. Defendants pretend that there is no evidentiary record because to do otherwise would require them to concede that plaintiff's proofs cannot be refuted. Defendants do not attempt to explain why it is that the very same words used to justify the military's discrimination against blacks are used to justify the discrimination challenged here because the only explanation available is that the long-abandoned policy discriminating against blacks and the frequently overlooked policy discriminating against gays both rest on prejudice. And defendants do not attempt to explain why Steffan could not be permitted to finish the remaining six weeks of his academic career when the Navy itself, as a matter of policy and practice, takes several months to discharge officers on the basis of homosexuality, because no explanation is available.

The simplistic and superficial course that defendants urge on this Court, however, is one that cannot and should not be followed. By reversing this court's prior decision dismissing this case, by distinguishing *Ben-Shalom* in a footnote after defendants had argued that it was both controlling and dispositive, and by holding that the question of "whether an agency of the federal government can discriminate against individuals merely because of sexual *orientation*" (emphasis in original) is undecided in this circuit, the court of appeals has made it clear that a searching inquiry is required to decide the "difficult issue" raised by this case. As shown in plaintiff's opening memorandum and below, that searching inquiry can lead to only one conclusion: that plaintiff's motion should be granted in all respects.

Argument

Point 1. Defendants' Attempt to Avoid* Pruitt *and Their Argument That* Ben-Shalom *Is Controlling Cannot Be Accepted.

Defendants concede, as they must, that if this court were to follow *Pruitt* v. *Cheney,* their motion to dismiss would have to be denied. *See also Dubbs* v. *CIA* (equal protection challenge to CIA ban on employment of homosexuals cannot be decided on motion to dismiss; CIA must demonstrate a rational relationship between policy and the ends it is designed to serve). Faced with *Pruitt,* defendants can only argue that *Pruitt* is not persuasive and that it should not be followed. Their contention should be rejected.

Two principles stand at *Pruitt's* core. The first is that once a plaintiff has made a showing of discrimination, it is incumbent upon the government "to establish *on the record* that its policy had a rational basis," something that defendants studiously refuse to do. In reaching this conclusion, the Ninth Circuit relied squarely on the Supreme Court's decision in *City of Cleburne* v. *Cleburne Living Center, Inc. Cleburne* was decided in the district court only after the defendants in that case were put to their proof in a bench trial.

In deciding *Cleburne,* the Supreme Court repeatedly focused on the record developed in the district court and emphasized that the defendants had failed to show on that record that there was any rational and legitimate basis for their regulations. *Cleburne,* moreover, did not depend on the existence of a "suspect" or even "semisuspect" class. The majority declined to extend such status to the mentally retarded, and held that a "rational basis" level of scrutiny required a showing on the record that the means were rationally related to a legitimate governmental objective.

Not surprisingly, the law of this circuit is fully consistent with *Cleburne* and *Pruitt.* The court of appeals has already held in *Doe* v. *Casey* that it is incumbent upon the defendants in an action challenging regulations discriminating on the basis of sexual orientation to demonstrate that such discrimination is necessary or advisable.

The second principle that lies at *Pruitt's* core is the proposition that it is impermissible for governmental discrimination against any group to be justified on the basis of private prejudice. Defendants themselves concede, as they must, that the applicable Supreme Court precedents support this aspect of *Pruitt.* Defendants claim, however, that *Pruitt* is defective because it fails to recognize that *Ben-Shalom* v. *Marsh* holds that the military regulations at issue here are not designed to cater to private prejudice.

The defect, however, is in the reasoning of *Ben-Shalom*, not *Pruitt.* For while *Ben-Shalom* does take issue with Judge Norris's conclusion in *Watkins* that "the Army's asserted justifications ... illegitimately cater to private biases," there is no explanation in *Ben-Shalom* as to *why* that court apparently believed that good order, morale, and discipline *are* somehow served by discriminating on the basis of sexual orientation. To be sure, good order, morale, and discipline are all laudable objectives for a military regulation. But the mere fact that a legitimate governmental objective is *asserted* to be involved does not excuse the defendants from *showing* that there is a rational relationship between the asserted objective and the means chosen to advance that objective. Nor is it permissible for defendants to attempt to "solve" problems—whether perceived or real—resulting from private biases by kowtowing to the naked prejudice that is at the root of the problem and denying members of a disfavored minority group "'rights created or protected by the Federal Constitution.'"

Because the City of Cleburne failed to provide any rational justification for its requirement that mentally retarded persons obtain a permit to build a group home, the Supreme Court concluded that singling out the mentally retarded rested on "irrational prejudice." A similar lack of justification was the basis for the Ninth Circuit's conclusion in *Pruitt. Pruitt* correctly followed the reasoning in *Cleburne. Ben-Shalom* did not. The absence of any justification in the record in this case warrants the same conclusion reached in *Cleburne* and *Pruitt*—the removal of Steffan from the service was based on "irrational prejudice."

Point 2. DOD Directives 1332.14 and 1332.30 and Their Progeny Should Be Declared Unconstitutional.

Plaintiff's opening memorandum demonstrated that the military regulations at issue in this case must be judged under the heightened scrutiny required when a suspect or quasi-suspect classification is involved. Plaintiff also demonstrated that whatever level of scrutiny is applied, defendants' regulations must fail because they are designed to cater to private prejudice and that no special deference is due to the military "judgments" in issue here. Nothing in defendants' opposition provides any cogent arguments to the contrary.

A. Defendants' Regulations Should Be Subjected to a Heightened Level of Scrutiny.

Defendants concede, as they must, that the Supreme Court has considered five factors in determining whether a suspect or quasi-suspect class is involved. Instead, they contend that "extensive case law" holds that homosexuals—when defined by status—do not constitute a suspect or quasi-suspect class. Virtually all of the cases that defendants cite, however, address conduct, *not* status. As the D.C. Circuit recognized in *Doe* v. *Casey*, defendants are simply wrong in asserting that cases involving a class defined by conduct control the question of whether a classification defined by homosexual orientation is suspect or quasi-suspect.

1. Sexual Orientation Is an "Immutable Characteristic."

Defendants also have failed to succeed in their attempt to refute some of plaintiff's proofs as to two of the five factors governing whether a particular group is a suspect or quasi-suspect class.[1] Purporting to rely on Dr. Green's declaration, defendants claim that homosexual status is not an "immutable characteristic." Yet Dr. Green himself explains in his reply declaration that defendants' reliance is wholly misplaced.

Of course, as Dr. Green concludes in his initial declaration, even if one were to accept "that one can with great effort graft apparently heterosexual behavior over an earlier homosexual orientation" with the use of electrical shock aversion "therapy," it does not "mean that sexual orientation is mutable." To the contrary, a review of the studies that defendants purport to rely upon shows that "'treatments may reduce or eliminate homosexual behavior and awareness of homosexual feelings without altering the sexual orientation.'" Moreover, men can be transformed into women through sex change operations and vice versa, skin pigmentation can be altered with drugs and bleaching creams by blacks who wish to "pass" as white, aliens can become citizens, and illegitimate children can be adopted. Yet no one can question that sex, race, alien status, and illegitimacy are "immutable characteristics" for purposes of constitutional analysis. What homosexual orientation has in common with all of these other characteristics is that it is not consciously chosen but rather is a basic part of an individual's being that is established prior to birth.

2. *Gays Are Relatively Politically Powerless and Are Underrepresented in the Political Process.*

Similarly ludicrous is defendants' attempt to claim that gays are not relatively politically powerless because thirty-two Congressmen—decidedly less than a majority of the House—wrote a single letter addressing the issue of gays in the military, because one of only two openly gay members of Congress asked Secretary of Defense Cheney a question on the issue at a hearing on an unrelated matter, and because those two openly gay Congressmen wrote a series of letters to a number of foreign embassies.

The point of *Frontiero* v. *Richardson* is not that a particular group may fall into a suspect or quasi-suspect class if it has *no* access at all to political redress but, rather, that such a group may be so classified if it has relatively little access to political channels. So, for example, in *Cleburne*, the Supreme Court considered the fact that the Congress had adopted three separate statutes addressing the "difficulties" of the retarded and that this fact "belies" the claim that there is "a continuing antipathy or prejudice and a corresponding need for more intrusive oversight by the judiciary."

The same cannot be said here. To the contrary, *no* federal legislation addresses discrimination against gays. And as Professor Sherrill discusses in his declaration, it is precisely because gays are the subject of widespread opprobrium and violence in our society that none is likely to be forthcoming.

B. DEFENDANTS' REGULATIONS CANNOT WITHSTAND ANY LEVEL OF SCRUTINY.

As shown in plaintiff's opening memorandum, whatever level of scrutiny is applied, it is plain that defendants' discrimination on the basis of sexual orientation must be held unconstitutional. Defendants have utterly failed to refute plaintiff's showing on this score. Overlooking *Pruitt*, defendants again cite to what they claim is a "long series of judicial decisions" consisting of *Ben-Shalom, Woodward, Dronenburg*, and *Rich*, which uphold the "rational basis" for their regulations. And again, all of the cases that defendants cite involve conduct, not status.

Their miscitation of authorities aside, the most glaring deficiency in defendants' argument comes when they blithely assert that "impermissible private prejudices [do] not underlie the military's policy on homosexuality." For nowhere in defendants' opposition is there any explanation—by affidavit or otherwise—as to what *does* "underlie" the military's ban. The reason for this omission is obvious and is provided by the documents that defendants sought to conceal in discovery: the exclusion of gays is deemed to be necessary because "the vast majority of Americans in general and servicemembers in particular strongly disapprove of homosexuals."[2]

There is no mystery here. At the September 14, 1989, hearing concerning, inter alia, plaintiff's desire to depose a representative of the Navy, the underlying rationale for the military's policy was obvious to the Court:

> MR. WOLINSKY: Your Honor, the policy of the Navy is that—one of the policies of the Navy is that the regulation is required to preserve the morale—the good morale and order of the service and if I ask a witness at a deposition why is the regulation necessary to preserve the good order and morale of the service—
>
> THE COURT: It ought to be obvious to you why they need such a regulation.
>
> MR. WOLINSKY: He's going to say that the reason is because other servicemen will be uncomfortable or unhappy serving with a gay service member.
>
> THE COURT: And that will be true.

However "true" the underlying rationale may be, defendants concede that their regulation must fail if nothing more than the private prejudice that was obvious to this court underlies its rationale. Yet when challenged to provide a rationale other than private prejudice, defendants conspicuously fail to do so. Thus, quite apart from the fact that the asserted justifications for the regulations are erroneous, the court should hold those regulations unconstitutional because they further goals that our Constitution does not permit the government to dignify.

C. THERE IS NO BASIS FOR THIS COURT TO DEFER TO MILITARY JUDGMENTS DESIGNED TO CATER TO PRIVATE PREJUDICES.

Plaintiff demonstrated in his opening memorandum that no special deference is due to military judgments as a general matter in the context of equal protection and more specifically in the context of this case. This showing stands unrefuted.

Thus, as an initial matter, defendants cite no Supreme Court authority that holds that the deference that the Court has shown to military judgments in the First Amendment context has been extended to the context of equal protection. No such case exists. To the contrary, in *Rostker* v. *Goldberg*—a case that defendants cite extensively in their memorandum—the Supreme Court noted that "a different equal protection test" does *not* apply simply because a case arises in "the military context."

Faced with this Supreme Court authority, defendants can only argue that plaintiff has not presented any reason why there is a difference between the First Amendment context and equal protection. The difference is obvious. As the Supreme Court recognizes in the First Amendment context, there is an inherent tension between free speech—and the debate and protest that is attendant to free speech—and the discipline and obedience deemed to be necessary for an effective military organization. There is no such inherent tension in the equal protection context. This difference is critical: while the military can exclude Jews who violate military regulations by wearing yarmulkes or refusing to work on the Sabbath, it cannot exclude Jews because they have a "propensity" to wear yarmulkes or a "desire" to observe Jewish holidays.

More important for purposes presented here, defendants have *conceded* that whatever deference may be due to so-called judgments by the military as a general matter, no deference is due to military judgments that rely on nothing more than "impermissible private prejudices" and archaic stereotypes. It is precisely this type of naked prejudice that underlies the regulations at issue here.

Point 3. Defendants' Refusal to Permit Steffan to Graduate Was Unlawful.

Defendants have admitted that they have a policy of permitting senior midshipmen who are deemed to be uncommissionable to graduate from the Academy. They also tacitly concede that Steffan could never have been processed for discharge within one week if he were a regular officer. Despite these concessions, defendants continue to claim—without providing any evidentiary showing—that it was rational to conclude that it was necessary to "railroad" Steffan out of the Academy because it would advance the same laundry list of platitudes that the military used to justify its discrimination against blacks. Defendants' argument should be rejected for three reasons.

First, as shown in plaintiff's opening memorandum and above, defendants' discrimination on the basis of sexual orientation as a general matter cannot withstand constitutional scrutiny. The policy rests on archaic and overbroad stereotypes and unlawfully caters to bigotry.

Second, defendants are simply wrong when they claim that all of the other uncommissionable midshipmen suffered from physical ailments. One of the midshipmen was discharged for somnambulism, a condition that is characterized as a "personality disorder" under the Diagnostic and Statistical Manual of Mental Disorders, the manual that the Academy relies on in classifying psychological conditions. Thus, under Academy regulations, the somnambulist midshipman was subject to involuntary discharge under the same regulations that required Steffan's discharge. And like the regulations concerning homosexuality, the regulations requiring the discharge of servicemembers suffering from personality disorders is deemed to be necessary to "sustain the traditional concepts of honorable military service and of special trust and confidence."

Third, defendants not only treated Steffan differently from other midshipmen who are deemed to be uncommissionable, they also treated him differently from other servicemembers who are to be discharged for homosexuality. Homosexual servicemembers generally are given thirty days' notice of the initial hearing on their discharge. Steffan was given twenty-four hours' notice. Homosexual servicemembers generally are afforded a military attorney to defend them at any hearing. Steffan had no such right. And homosexual servicemembers generally are discharged under a policy that states that it is a "goal" for the proceedings to be concluded within four months. Steffan was processed for discharge in one week.

Thus, while defendants do offer a "rationale"—albeit an illegitimate one—for their ban on gays generally, they offer no "rationale" for the exceedingly harsh treatment that Steffan was subjected to, treatment that was decidedly more harsh than that afforded other homosexual servicemembers. If the same timetable established as a general matter had been followed in Steffan's case, he would have received his degree. On this ground alone, Steffan should be awarded a diploma.

Conclusion

For the reasons set forth herein, plaintiff's cross-motion for summary judgment should be granted in all respects.

Richard Green

AFFIDAVIT II

On Recent Developments in the Field of Brain Research

1. On August 29, 1991, I submitted a declaration in this action that explained the basis for my opinion that homosexual orientation is an "immutable characteristic" that is largely determined by genetic, neurological, hormonal, and environmental factors prior to birth. On the basis of my declaration, defendants argue that homosexual orientation is not an immutable characteristic, claiming that I acknowledge in my declaration that "changes in sexual orientation have frequently occurred as a result of therapy." In fact, my declaration does nothing of the sort and cannot provide any comfort to defendants.

2. My declaration does discuss a number of studies that purport to present instances in which a small number of highly motivated "homosexuals" were "converted" into "heterosexuals." It goes on, however, to review these studies critically and point out that there are substantial defects in their methodology and that the follow-up data tend to show that these "conversions" either did not actually take place or were temporary. Because of these defects and on the basis of these follow-up studies, experts in the field have generally concluded that the reports of "conversion" are not reliable. Consider for example, the Bieber study discussed by defendants.[1]

Psychoanalytic treatment of homosexuality is exemplified by the work of Bieber et al. (1962), who advocate intensive long-term therapy aimed at resolving the unconscious childhood conflicts responsible for homosexuality. Bieber's methodology has been widely criticized on numerous grounds. First, his sample is entirely a clinical one. Second, all outcomes are based upon subjective therapist impression, not externally validated data or even self-report. Last, follow-up data have been poorly presented and not at all empirical in nature. Nevertheless, Bieber et al. (1962) report a meager 27% success rate in heterosexual shift after long-term therapy. Of these, however, only 18% were exclusively homosexual in the first place; 50% were bisexual. This blending of "apples and oranges" is quite common in conversion studies, and renders misleading these claims of success, which are, in this study, not impressive in the first place.

3. Similarly unavailing is defendants' attempt to rely on my own work for the proposition that changes in homosexual orientation "have frequently occurred as a result of therapy." As I discuss in my declaration, part of my research has focused on a group of sixty-six boys between ages four through twelve who displayed extensive cross-gender behaviors. As defendants note, three-quarters of this group manifested a homosexual or bisexual orientation in adulthood. That does not mean, however, that the remaining 25 percent were "converted" from a homosexual to a heterosexual orientation as defendants claim. The fallacy in defendants' contention is that all sixty-six of the boys who displayed cross-gender behaviors were in fact homosexual. There is no basis for this assumption. Indeed, what is particularly remarkable about defendants' attempt to rely on my work to support their position is that they ignore the fact (discussed in my declaration) that one-third of the cross-gender boys that I studied were involved in psychotherapy directed at changing sexual identity. Strikingly, the rate of homosexual or bisexual orientation in the "treated" group was the same as that of the "untreated" group.

4. The study that perhaps is most damaging to defendants' position appeared shortly after I submitted my declaration in this action. Specifically, in the August 31, 1991, issue of the prestigious journal *Science*, Dr. Simon LeVay of the Salk Institute for Biological Studies reported differences between male heterosexuals versus male homosexuals and women in a region of the brain associated with male sexual behavior in nonhumans. In his study, Dr. LeVay obtained brain tissue at autopsy from forty-one subjects. Nineteen were homosexual men who died of AIDS (one was bisexual). Sixteen were presumably heterosexual men, six of whom died of AIDS. Six were presumably heterosexual women, one of whom died of AIDS. The subjects were close in age at the time of death. The volume of the nuclei of cells in a region of the anterior hypothalamic portion of the brain (INAH 3) was more than twice as large in the group of presumably heterosexual men compared to the groups of homosexual men and presumably heterosexual women. The difference remained

statistically significant when comparing only the males who died of AIDS. Furthermore, the bisexual male's nucleus was in the heterosexual male range.

5. While further research is suggested by Dr. LeVay's findings, the study provides significant additional scientific support for my opinion that homosexual orientation is an "immutable characteristic" that is not consciously chosen.

Judge Oliver Gasch

OPINION

United States District Court for the District of Columbia

Memorandum

THIS MATTER is before the Court on defendants' Motion for judgment on the pleadings, or in the alternative, for summary judgment. The plaintiff has filed a cross-motion for summary judgment. The case has been fully briefed and argued in open court.

This suit is about the constitutionality of classifications by the military on the basis of sexual orientation. The plaintiff is suing for his diploma from the Naval Academy, his commission as an Ensign in the United States Navy, a declaration that his resignation was null and void, and for a declaration that the Department of Defense Directives 1332.14 and 1332.30, and all other regulations applied to the plaintiff prohibiting those with a homosexual orientation[1] from serving in the Navy or attending the Naval Academy, are violations of the equal protection component of the fifth amendment to the Constitution.[2]

On the merits, the Court has concluded for the reasons stated below that defendants are entitled to judgment as a matter of law. The Court will therefore grant defendants' Motion for summary judgment.

Background

The plaintiff was a midshipman in good standing at the United States Naval Academy in Annapolis, Maryland, when in March 1987, a few months before his expected graduation, he learned that he was under investigation by the Naval Investigative

Service ("NIS") for his alleged homosexuality. The NIS had received a report from the Academy that plaintiff had admitted his homosexuality to another midshipman. Upon learning of the NIS investigation, the plaintiff sought advice from a friend, a Chaplain at the Academy. After plaintiff admitted his homosexuality to the Chaplain, the Chaplain offered to help plead his case for a timely graduation with the Commandant of Midshipmen. This was accomplished, but on March 23, 1987, plaintiff was told by the commandant that graduation was not going to be possible because of the servicewide regulations promulgated in 1981 under Department of Defense ("DOD") Directive 1332.14, pt.1, § H, ¶ 1(a), which prohibit homosexuals from serving in the Armed Forces.

After hearing from the Commandant himself that graduation was impossible, plaintiff indicated that he would want to leave the Academy "as soon as possible." As a courtesy to an accomplished young man, the Commandant arranged for an expedited review process for plaintiff in order to accommodate his wishes. The Brigade Military Board met the following day, March 24, 1987, to review the Steffan case. At that hearing plaintiff admitted his homosexuality on the record and stated that he did not "desire to be commissioned as an officer of the Naval service by continuing as a midshipman of the Naval Academy." When asked by Captain Habermeyer on March 23, 1987, "Are you willing to state at this time that you are a homosexual?", plaintiff responded, "Yes, sir." At the Brigade Military Performance Board on March 24, 1987, Deputy Commandant, Captain Konetzni asked plaintiff: "I'd like your word, are you a homosexual?" Again plaintiff responded: "Yes, sir."

On April 1, 1987, the Naval Academy Academic Board convened to consider the plaintiff's case. By unanimous vote the Academic Board determined that the plaintiff had "insufficient aptitude to become a commissioned officer in the naval service." The Superintendent of the Academy wrote the plaintiff a memorandum that same day and advised the plaintiff of his intention to recommend a discharge to the Secretary of the Navy. The Superintendent, however, gave the plaintiff the option of submitting a qualified resignation to the Secretary, in which case the Superintendent would forego submitting his recommendation of discharge. The benefits of resignation were discussed with plaintiff. If he resigned, he would be honorably discharged; if not, his would be an involuntary discharge. It was made clear to plaintiff that an involuntary discharge would have a notation on his record that would indicate the plaintiff was a homosexual, whereas, if he resigned, no such notation would appear.

On April 1, 1987, the plaintiff submitted his qualified resignation. On May 6, 1987, it was accepted by an Assistant Secretary of the Navy. More than eighteen months later, on December 9, 1988, the plaintiff wrote the Secretary of the Navy requesting that his resignation be withdrawn. The present action was filed December 28, 1988. The Secretary denied the request to withdraw the resignation in February of 1989.

Discussion

I. Equal Protection

This is not a case of first impression. This may be the first time that a student at one of the service academies of the United States Armed Forces was not permitted to graduate because of his admitted status as a homosexual, but it is certainly not the first time that the regulations in question have been reviewed for their lawfulness on an equal protection challenge under the fifth amendment. *Ben-Shalom* v. *Marsh* (7th Cir. 1989) (lesbian denied re-enlistment in Army); *Dronenburg* v. *Zech* (D.C. Cir. 1984) (Naval petty officer discharged for admitted homosexual conduct with recruit on Navy property); *High Tech Gays* v. *Defense Indus. Sec. Clearance Office* (9th Cir. 1990) (class of homosexuals working in defense industries subject to expanded investigations for security clearances); *Woodward* v. *United States* (Fed. Cir. 1989) (Navy reserve released from active duty after being seen associating with an enlisted man awaiting discharge for homosexuality); *Rich* v. *Secretary of Army* (10th Cir. 1984) (serviceman honorably discharged for fraudulent enlistment when Army later learned he was homosexual despite earlier denial upon enlistment).

The plaintiff maintains that homosexuals, gay men and lesbians if you will, are a "suspect" or "quasi-suspect" class of persons who as a result of such classification are entitled to have the government action complained of, or regulation as applied as in this case, subject to a form of heightened scrutiny on an equal protection challenge. Plaintiff seeks to distinguish all of the cases cited above, as well as others, on the grounds that each involved some kind of homosexual

conduct, while in this case it is the plaintiff's *status* as a homosexual
that is at issue.

From the landmark classification case of *Cleburne* v. *Cleburne Living Center, Inc.*, there are three recognized levels of review that are used in equal protection cases: "strict scrutiny," "heightened review" (also called "intermediate scrutiny") and rational basis review. As stated in *Ben-Shalom* v. *Marsh*, "[i]n general, a government regulation will be presumed to be valid under equal protection analysis as long as the classification drawn by the regulation 'rationally furthers some legitimate, articulated state purpose.'"

Rational basis review is a deferential standard of scrutiny that is "grounded in a constitutional presumption that 'improvident [classifications] will eventually be rectified by the democratic processes.'" The warning in *Cleburne* is clear, however. When government conduct or a regulation makes classifications that are based on "factors which are so seldom relevant to the achievement of any legitimate state interest that laws grounded in such considerations are deemed to reflect prejudice and antipathy," then a form of heightened scrutiny is used in lieu of rational basis review.

In the case at bar, as in *Ben-Shalom*, the issue has been a bit clouded by a debate and discovery over whether the defendants' classification of the plaintiff went to his *conduct* as a homosexual or his *status* as a homosexual. The ongoing NIS investigation of plaintiff's homosexual conduct was discontinued upon the acceptance of his resignation from the Navy. Plaintiff declined to answer questions at deposition about whether he had engaged in homosexual conduct at the Academy. As a result, this is primarily a case about the plaintiff's status as a homosexual.

A. HOMOSEXUALS NOT A "SUSPECT" OR "QUASI-SUSPECT" CLASS

The district court in *Ben-Shalom* held that homosexuals were a suspect class, a holding which was subsequently reversed by the Seventh Circuit. There is ample authority to support the defendants' position in this case that those with a homosexual orientation are not a suspect class. The best way, however, to determine if the plaintiff is a member of a suspect class is to review the analysis used in *Bowen* v. *Gilliard*.

Under *Bowen* the plaintiff must: 1) have suffered a history of discrimination; 2) exhibit obvious, immutable, or distinguishing characteristics that define him as a member of a discrete group; and 3) show that the group is a minority or politically powerless, or alternatively show that the statutory classification at issue burdens a fundamental right.

1. History of Discrimination

Using the *Bowen* test, then, plaintiff alleges that those with a homosexual orientation have, in fact, suffered a history of discrimination.

The court in *Ben-Shalom* however, held that discrimination was *not* responsible for the military's policy of excluding homosexuals. With reference to the concurring opinion of Norris, J., in *Watkins* v. *United States Army*, (9th Cir. 1989) (en banc), the Seventh Circuit said: "Homosexuals have suffered a history of discrimination and still do, though possibly now to a less degree. We do not see, however, that the new regulation embodies a gross unfairness in the military context so inconsistent with equal protection as to be termed 'invidious.'"

2. Distinguishing Characteristics

The next question concerns obvious, immutable or distinguishing characteristics that define those with a homosexual orientation as a discrete or separate group. Plaintiff argues eloquently that there is no way to distinguish those persons with a homosexual orientation by way of performance of their duties. The plaintiff himself is an example of this point; academically he was in the top ten percent of his class at the Academy, and he was slated for one of the most prestigious assignments after graduation, duty on a nuclear submarine. Beyond all that, he is a talented young performer and singer who made the Academy and our country proud on several occasions. It can fairly be said that there is nothing obvious or distinguishing about plaintiff's homosexual orientation which sets him apart.

Even if it were maintained that his sexual preference for men was a distinguishing characteristic, nothing in the record indicates that the plaintiff overtly "exhibited" such a characteristic. In fact, he kept his sexual preference secret between the time he determined his preference in his third class (second or sophomore) year, and February or March of 1987 when he told a fellow midshipman, despite knowing all the while that the DOD and the Academy had regulations prohibiting homosexual orientation or conduct.[3]

3. *Immutability*

Whether homosexual orientation is an immutable characteristic is difficult to analyze. The Federal Circuit in *Woodward* found homosexuality to be "primarily behavioral in nature." In *High Tech Gays* the Ninth Circuit came to a similar conclusion. Each of those cases, however, dealt with fact situations where some homosexual conduct was part of the record. This case is different. The Court is, however, convinced that homosexual orientation is neither conclusively mutable nor immutable since the scientific community is still quite at sea on the causes of homosexuality, its permanence, its prevalence, and its definition.[4]

On the matter of suspect classifications, the Supreme Court seems to focus on the question of whether an individual *chooses* the characteristic that defines the class or not. One's race is determined genetically, and one's gender is—unless there is new evidence worthy of a Nobel prize—commonly believed to be a random event. One's national or ethnic origin and whether one was born out of wedlock are characteristics similarly not subject to choice by the person being so classified. In the *Plyler* case, the Supreme Court subjected a Texas statute denying public school education to children of illegal aliens to heightened scrutiny and found that Texas had denied the children their right to equal protection of the laws. The Court noted that illegal aliens who are adults are not a suspect class since the conduct that defines the class is unlawful, and their status as illegal and as aliens is not immutable. Minor children of illegal aliens, on the other hand, do not consciously choose their status, nor can they very well alter it by leaving the country on their own accord.

Seeing how the choice of the characteristic influences the decision on whether or not the class that bears the characteristic is "suspect" or "quasi-suspect," the court turns to the case at bar. Homosexual orientation, plaintiff asserts, is not a matter of choice. Defendants, on the other hand, agree with the Federal Circuit in *Woodward* that the characteristic is primarily behavioral in nature, and that if man is a mammal in control of his own behavior, he therefore chooses his sexual orientation. As aforementioned, the scientific community is unclear and unsure about many of the causes and attributes of sexual orientation. It is not for this Court to say definitively whether sexual orientation is *always* chosen by the individual, but it is apparent that *sometimes* it is chosen. This realization puts sexual orientation closer to the category of alien adults who are not a suspect class under *Plyler*, than to their children who did not choose their status.

4. Fundamental Rights

On the question of a fundamental right, in *Bowers* v. *Hardwick* (1986), the Supreme Court upheld a Georgia criminal sodomy statute as applied to a consenting adult homosexual male found engaging in homosexual sodomy in his home. It was determined in *Bowers* that there was no fundamental right to engage in that kind of activity. Since plaintiff does not maintain that he has a fundamental right to have a homosexual orientation under the Constitution, we need not reach that issue.

5. Political Power

The last issue concerning a suspect class is political powerlessness. Even *if* it were proven that homosexual orientation was immutable, or indeed, not subject to individual choice, it is still very clear that homosexuals as a class enjoy a good deal of political power in our society, not only with respect to themselves, but also with respect to issues of the day that affect them.[5]

It is beyond doubt that the homosexual community has been able to reach out and gain the attention of politicians of all sorts.[6] One need only remember St. Patrick's Day 1991 in New York City to see Mayor David Dinkins marching in the traditionally Irish-Catholic parade with homosexual groups and activists who were important supporters during his tough mayoral campaign. There are many other important and high visibility issues which have brought the homosexual community into the political landscape in this country and in the states, not the least of which is the AIDS epidemic and the related issues of funding for research and drugs, school attendance for children who are HIV-positive, and insurance coverage for victims.

Assuming *arguendo* that there is continuing antipathy and prejudice exhibited towards the plaintiff's class, it cannot successfully be maintained that the political branches are not paying attention to homosexuals or those who advocate legislation favorable to them. Just because there are only a few members of Congress who are openly homosexual does not mean that homosexuals as a class are without influence. There are not many medical doctors in Congress either, and yet that profession is exceptionally well represented on

Capitol Hill. It is far more important to notice that references to sexual orientation, sexual preference and AIDS show up from time to time in the law of the various states, localities, and in the federal law. In *Ben-Shalom*, the court was succinct:

> In these times, homosexuals are proving that they are not without growing political power. It cannot be said "they have no ability to attract the attention of the lawmakers." *Cleburne*, 473 U.S. at 445. A political approach is open to them to seek a congressional determination about rejection of homosexuals by the Army. We are, however, unwilling to substitute a mere judge-made rule for the Army's regulation or to act in an executive or legislative fashion.

The example of political power exercised by the plaintiff that is most readily available is the discovery phase of this very case. Thirty-two Members of Congress personally signed a letter written by Congressman Studds urging the Secretary of Defense, a defendant in this case, to comply with certain discovery requests.[7] Given that plaintiff and the homosexual community have been able to move well and gain attention in political circles, under *Bowen* then, plaintiff has not been able to show that he is a member of a suspect class.

As a final note on this subject of whether plaintiff is a member of a suspect class, in *Cleburne* Justice White raised the question of whether there is a principled way to distinguish between the plaintiff's class and others, for example, the aging, the infirm, or the mentally ill. All these groups suffer from some form of discrimination, they all have immutable characteristics which set them apart from most other people, and they all have a diminished capacity to mandate legislative responses helpful to their class. The Supreme Court in *Cleburne* specifically declined the opportunity of walking down that difficult path with respect to the aging and other groups.

Putting aside the conclusions above for the sake of argument, even if plaintiff could satisfy the requirements for suspect classification under *Bowen*, nothing has been presented by him which suggests a difference relevant to an equal protection analysis between those with a homosexual orientation and the aging, for example. Both classes have suffered historical discrimination on a variety of levels in society and in many forms. Both characteristics which define the class are arguably immutable. And it is argued that both groups suffer from underrepresentation in Congress and general political powerlessness. Yet the Supreme Court specifically declined to extend the fifth amendment equal protection considerations to include groups like the aging and the mentally retarded. Classification principles established in *Cleburne* are equally applicable to non-practicing homosexuals.

Given the clear logic of this analysis and the weight of authority, no lower federal court could come to another conclusion, but that the plaintiff is not a member of a suspect class entitled to a higher level of judicial scrutiny. Rational basis review is the applicable standard of review for this case.

B. RATIONAL BASIS FOR THE REGULATIONS

The defendants in this case must show that there is a rational basis for the regulations which caused the plaintiff to be encouraged to resign from the Naval Academy and denied his commission in the Navy. In equal protection cases using rational basis review, the Supreme Court has held that the regulation must bear a rational relationship to a legitimate state end, and "statutory classifications will be set aside only if no grounds can be conceived to justify them." In addition, defendants must articulate the state purpose of the regulation.

Arguing that the DOD Directives at issue are not rational as a matter of law, plaintiff relies heavily on the recent Ninth Circuit decision in *Pruitt* v. *Cheney*, saying that "the Ninth Circuit squarely rejected the position that defendants advance here. *Pruitt*, like this case, presented an Equal Protection challenge to military regulations that require the discharge of servicemembers solely on the basis of homosexual orientation."

In *Pruitt* the district court granted the defendants' motion to dismiss for failure to state a claim under Rule 12(b)(6) of the Federal Rules of Civil Procedure. The Ninth Circuit agreed with the district court that the plaintiff had not stated a first amendment challenge, but disagreed with the district court and concluded that an equal protection claim had been stated. Contrary to the plaintiff's reading, *Pruitt* is not a case where the Ninth Circuit *held* anything other than that the plaintiff had stated an equal protection claim, and remanded the case to the district court for further proceedings.

Now that *Pruitt* is on remand, the defendants will have to articulate a rational basis for the regulations excluding Pruitt from reenlistment in the Army. In this case, the defendants have articulated a number of different bases for the regulations that affected plaintiff and his departure from the Naval Academy. The case at bar is procedurally a bit ahead of *Pruitt.* Plaintiff's reliance on it, as a result, is misplaced.

To survive rational basis review the government regulation need only "promote a legitimate government interest." The Army regulation at issue in *Ben-Shalom* was very close in wording to the DOD Directives 1332.14 and 1332.30 of which plaintiff complains. The Seventh Circuit found that the Army regulation "*clearly* promotes a legitimate government interest."

Surely the government has a legitimate interest in good order and morale, the system of rank and command, and discipline in the Military Services. Judging from Directive 1332.14, it is the determination of the Secretary of Defense and of the Congress of the United States which delegated such rule-making authority, that allowing admitted homosexuals to serve alongside heterosexual members and officers in the Armed Forces would jeopardize morale, discipline and the system of rank and command. Under the deferential standard of rational basis review, we cannot say that these are not in fact legitimate interests, or that the regulations in question do not promote them.

A controlling case in this Circuit is *Dronenburg v. Zech.* In his opinion for the court, Judge Robert Bork gave additional examples of what the military hoped to achieve with this regulation. He wrote:

> This very case illustrates dangers of the sort the Navy is entitled to consider: a 27-year-old petty officer had repeated sexual relations with a 19-year-old seaman recruit. The latter then chose to break off the relationship. Episodes of this sort are certain to be deleterious to morale and discipline, to call into question the evenhandedness of superiors' dealings with lower ranks, to make personal dealings uncomfortable where the relationship is sexually ambiguous, to generate dislike and disapproval among many who find homosexuality morally offensive, and, it must be said, given the powers of military superiors over their inferiors, to enhance the possibility of homosexual seduction.

In *Dronenburg* the same Navy regulations at issue in this case were considered rational when the issue was homosexual conduct. Of the reasons given by the Court of Appeals, quoted above, as to why the Navy's regulations were rational and the state purposes legitimate, all have equal application to this non-conduct case.

It is worth highlighting that if the Navy accepted those with a homosexual orientation, action plaintiff urges, it may still "generate dislike and disapproval among many who find homosexuality morally offensive." Recognizing that the *Dronenburg* court had homosexual conduct in mind rather than homosexual orientation when it spoke of "homosexuality," it has not been shown in this case that lifelong, or even career-long celibacy among those with a homosexual orientation is the rule rather than the exception. This is important because the regulation in question states that:

> The presence in the military environment of persons who engage in homosexual conduct or who, by their statements, *demonstrate a propensity to engage in homosexual conduct*, seriously impairs the accomplishment of the military mission.

The plaintiff has stated his sexual preference for people of the same gender as himself and has thereby demonstrated a propensity to engage in conduct which both parties agree is clearly regulable under *Dronenburg*. Unless it can be shown that the plaintiff has some commitment to celibate living, the presumption must be, and it is rational for the Navy to believe, that plaintiff could one day have acted on his preferences in violation of regulations prohibiting such conduct.

Plaintiff argues that defendants maintain the regulations in question out of impermissible prejudice towards plaintiff and those similarly situated. If, however, the Court of Appeals is correct in its conclusion that many would find the Navy's approval of a homosexual orientation among its fighting forces to be morally offensive, then it is not prejudice which is responsible for the regulations, but rather a standard of morality. And so, as Judge Bork so eloquently said in *Dronenburg*: "If the revolution in sexual mores that appellant proclaims is in fact ever to arrive, we think it must arrive through the moral choices of the people and their elected representatives, not through the ukase of this court." This cogent statement in *Dronenburg* has its constitutional underpinnings in Article I, section 8: "The Congress shall have power ... [t]o provide and maintain a Navy," and "[t]o make Rules for the Government and Regulation of the land and naval forces."

Finally, a word about the military interest in maintaining a semblance of privacy for its members despite each member's commitment to a career or period of service which affords minimal privacy. DOD Directive 1332.14 states in part, with reference to those who by their statements demonstrate a propensity to engage in homosexual conduct: "The presence of such members adversely affects the ability of the Military Services to . . . facilitate assignment and worldwide deployment of servicemembers who frequently must live and work under close conditions affording minimal privacy." In the Military Establishment and for those who attend the Naval Academy, the policy of separating men and women while sleeping, bathing and "using the bathroom" seeks to maintain the privacy of officers and the enlisted when in certain states of undress.[8] The embarrassment of being naked as between the sexes is prevalent because sometimes the other is considered to be a sexual object. The quite rational assumption in the Navy is that with no one present who has a homosexual orientation, men and women alike can undress, sleep, bathe, and use the bathroom without fear or embarrassment that they are being viewed as sexual objects.

II. Health and Welfare of the Military

There is another justification for the policy of excluding homosexuals from service in the United States Armed Forces, and more precisely, in the United States Navy. Though not mentioned in the papers of either party or indeed in the DOD Directive itself, there is a fact that can be judicially noticed: far and away the highest risk category for those who are HIV-positive, a population who will with a high degree of medical certainty one day contract AIDS, is homosexual men.[9]

The taking of judicial notice of facts which justify a certain classification is a time-honored practice under the seminal case *Pacific States Box & Basket Co.* v. *White.* Justice Brandeis for a unanimous Court said:

> When such legislative action "is called in question, if any state of facts reasonably can be conceived that would sustain it, there is a presumption of the existence of that state of facts, and one who assails the classification must carry the burden of showing by a resort to common knowledge or other matters which may be judicially noticed, or to other legitimate proof, that the action is arbitrary."

Of course the obvious objection is that the DOD Directive in this case was not a "legislative action." The Court in *Pacific States* continued:

> The question of law may always be raised whether the legislature had power to delegate the authority exercised. . . . But where the regulation is

within the scope of authority delegated, the presumption of the existence of facts justifying its specific exercise attaches alike to statutes, to municipal ordinances, and to orders of administrative bodies.

In the case at bar, the defendants have argued that military judgments which prohibit homosexuals from serving in the Armed Forces, are, like most military judgments, entitled to deference from the judicial branch. *Goldman* v. *Weinberger*. Though *Goldman* was a first amendment case concerning an Orthodox Jewish servicemember's right to wear a yarmulke indoors against regulations under the free exercise clause, defendants in this case quote the *Goldman* Court saying that "courts must give great deference to the professional judgment of military authorities concerning the relative importance of a particular military interest." In *Burns* v. *Wilson* (1953) (plurality opinion), Chief Justice Vinson wrote: "[T]he rights of men in the armed forces must perforce be conditioned to meet certain overriding demands of discipline and duty, and the civil courts are not the agencies which must determine the balance which must be struck in this adjustment. The Framers expressly entrusted that task to Congress."

Likewise, legislative determinations are entitled to great deference from the judiciary using the rational basis test. In *Vance* v. *Bradley* (1979), the Supreme Court held that Section 632 of the Foreign Service Act of 1946, a scheme which requires retirement at age 60 for members of the Foreign Service while no mandatory retirement age is established for Civil Service employees, was not a violation of the equal protection component of the Due Process Clause of the fifth amendment. On the issue of deference to the legislature, the Court said:

> The Constitution presumes that, absent some reason to infer antipathy, even improvident decisions will eventually be rectified by the democratic process and that judicial intervention is generally unwarranted no matter how unwisely we may think a political branch has acted. Thus, we will not overturn such a statute unless the varying treatment of different groups or persons is so unrelated to the achievement of *any combination of legitimate purposes* that we can only conclude that the legislature's actions were irrational.

There are no reasons to "infer antipathy" between Congress and those homosexuals who are not practicing or exhibiting their orientation through sexual conduct in the Armed Forces as such was the case with plaintiff. Congress is, and for most of this century has been, controlled by a majority party which has taken a great deal of pride in giving legislative aid to those groups in society who have been discriminated against, taken advantage of, or downtrodden. Furthermore, Congress and the various state legislatures around the nation have responded to the homosexual community on numerous occasions in the last decade with respect to the HIV epidemic.

And so it is with deference to the military and its professional judgment, with deference to the legislature, and under the teaching of *Pacific States* that the Court takes judicial notice of the widely praised and accepted final report of the Presidential Commission on the Human Immunodeficiency Virus Epidemic [hereinafter Presidential Report].

In that report it was stated that the HIV "epidemic has predominantly been confined to people participating in behaviors such as homosexual sex and intravenous drug abuse." The latest figures available from the Centers for Disease Control show that of the AIDS cases reported through August 1991, 59% of all adults and adolescents were exposed because they were men who had sex with other men. Among males, 65% of adults and adolescents were exposed to HIV and subsequently contracted AIDS because of sex with other males.[10]

Article I, Section 8, gives the Congress the power to "raise and support Armies" and "provide and maintain a Navy," and "[t]o make Rules for the Government and Regulation of the land and naval forces." Implicit in the power to support armies is the power to make rules concerning their health and welfare. Regulations designed to protect the health of the nation's Armed Forces are not new. During World War I, Congress authorized the Secretary of War to make regulations to suppress "houses of ill-fame" in the vicinity of military camps. In *McKinley* v. *United States* (1919), the plaintiffs in error were convicted of keeping such a house within five (5) miles of a camp, in violation of the regulations. Plainly, since Congress is empowered to raise and support armies, it may do whatever is necessary to protect the health and welfare of those armies, however much its legislation and regulations promulgated pursuant thereto might impinge on what would otherwise be the subject of police power reserved exclusively to the States. The Supreme Court in *McKinley* sustained the convictions.

The power to protect the Armed Forces from venereal disease is ample to sustain the power to protect them from what is now known to be a fatal and incurable virus, the HIV. Given that at least 59% of all those who have contracted HIV have done so due to homosexual or bisexual activity, surely it does not require extended discussion in the dialectic and sterile *cliches* of "how equal the Equal Protection Clause's protection must be" to show that the exclusion of homosexuals from the Armed Forces constitutes a reasonable step towards the protection of those forces' health.

To be sure, there is no evidence in this case about the plaintiff having had sex with anybody, male or female. But the defendants' policy of excluding homosexuals is rational in that it is directed, in part, at preventing those who are at the greatest risk of dying of AIDS from serving in the Navy and the other armed services.[11] This is understandable in light of the overall military mission of defending the Nation. The interest we as a Nation have in a healthy military cannot be underestimated or discounted.

Conclusion

The Department of Defense's regulations that prohibit homosexuals from serving in the Navy and the other armed services establish classifications that rationally further legitimate state purposes. Those purposes include the maintenance of discipline, morale, good order, a respected system of rank and command, a healthy military force, morality and respect for the privacy interests of both officers and the enlisted. Plaintiff is not a member of a suspect class entitled to heightened scrutiny. Under the deferential standard of rational basis review, coupled with judicial deference to the military and the legislature, the regulations in question are not violative of the equal protection component of the Due Process Clause of the fifth amendment. The Court reaches these conclusions without reference to the final report of the Presidential Commission on the HIV (Watkins Report), the Center for Disease Control statistics or the *Pacific States* precedent; however, it notes that these factors strengthen the conclusions heretofore reached.

December 9, 1991   Judge Oliver Gasch

TABLE OF CASES

Introduction

1. Richard Posner, *Sex and Reason* (Harvard University Press, 1992).

Brief for Joseph Steffan

1. The difference between status and conduct is one recognized by science as well as law. As Green explains in his affidavit, "homosexual orientation is separate and distinct from homosexual conduct" and "a person's sexual behavior does not necessarily define his or her orientation." Green states that "heterosexual conduct is common among individuals who identify themselves as lesbian or gay" and vice versa. He also explains that "[w]hile sexual activity among heterosexuals and homosexuals is common and diverse, significant portions of both populations engage in little or no interactive sexual conduct, both temporarily and for long periods of time for various reasons." Affidavit of Green, par. 4–7. Thus, as a matter of fact, it cannot be presumed that a servicemember who identifies him or herself as a "homosexual" is regularly (or even irregularly) engaging in homosexual conduct.

2. A 1988 study commissioned by the military similarly concluded that the fact that the worldwide prevalence of homosexuality is constant in the male population regardless of varying cultural attitudes "suggests that biological factors may be the fundamental source of homosexual orientation."

3. In contrast, homosexual orientation *was* criminalized in Nazi Germany and provided the justification for the genocide of gays along with Jews, Gypsies, Jehovah's Witnesses, and the mentally retarded. See F. Rector, *The Nazi Extermination of Homosexuals* (Stein & Day, 1981), p. 119 (paragraph 175A of the German Penal Law defines homosexual acts to include homosexual fantasies). See also H. Heger, *The Men with the Pink Triangle* (Alyson, 1980).

4. See also *Korematsu v. United States* (1944)(Murphy, J., dissenting)("an accumulation" of "misinformation, half-truths and insinuations" provided the basis for the "military judgment" that Japanese-Americans be interned; "[a] military judgment based upon such racial and sociological considerations is not entitled to the great weight ordinarily given the judgments based upon strictly military considerations").

Affidavit I of John Boswell

1. 12 U.S.C. § 925.
2. See, e.g., St. Thomas Aquinas, *Summa theologica*, 1a2ae.31.7, and my discussion in John Boswell, *Christianity, Social Tolerance and Homosexuality* (University of Chicago Press, 1980), 324–30.

Affidavit II of John Boswell

1. Herzer, "Kertbeny and the Nameless Love," *Journal of Homosexuality* 12 (1985): 1–26; H. Kennedy, *Ulrichs: The Life and Works of Karl Henry Ulrichs, Pioneer of the Modern Gay Movement* (Alyson, 1988), 149–56; Feray, "Une Histoire Critique du Mot Homosexualite," *Arcadie* 28 (1981): 325.
2. See, e.g., E. M. Forster, *Maurice*, chap. 7.
3. See, e.g., art. 125, UCMJ, 10 U.S.C. § 925 (defining "sodomy" as "unnatural carnal copulation with another person of the same or opposite sex or with an animal"); *Black's Law Dictionary* (1979).
4. *Letters of C. S. Lewis* ed. W. H. Lewis (Harcourt Brace Jovanovich, 1966), 292.
5. Defendants' memorandum, 9, n.2.

Affidavit I of Richard Green

1. M. Weinberg and C. Williams, *Male Homosexuals: Their Problems and Adaptations* (Oxford University Press, 1974).
2. A. Bell and M. Weinberg, *Homosexualities: A Study of Diversity Among Men and Women* (Simon and Schuster, 1978); J. Reinisch, J. Sanders, and M. Ziemba-Davis, "Sex Research Around the AIDS Crisis," in B. Voller, J. Reinisch, and M. Gottlieb, *AIDS and Sex: An Integrated Biomedical Approach* (Oxford University Press, 1989).
3. J. Gonsiorek and J. Weinrich, "The Definition and Scope of Sexual Orientation," in J. Gonsiorek and J. Weinrich, *Homosexuality: Research Implications for Public Policy* (Sage, 1991), 3–5.
4. A. Kinsey, W. Pomeroy, and C. Martin, *Sexual Behavior in the Human Male* (W. B. Saunders, 1949), 623–30. Kinsey also found that 28 percent of the female population had homosexual responses and contacts. A. Kinsey, W. Pomeroy, C. Martin, and P. Gebhard, *Sexual Behavior in the Human Female* (W. B. Saunders, 1953), 474–75.
5. See A. Berube, *Coming Out under Fire: The History of Gay Men and Women in World War II* (Free Press, 1990).

6. R. Fieve, D. Rosenthal, and H. Brill, *Genetic Research in Psychiatry* (1975).

7. Sanders, "Homosexueele Tweellingen," *Nederl. Tijdschr. Geneesk* 78 (1934): 3346.

8. Kallman, *Comparative Twin Study on Genetic Aspects of Male Homosexuality, J. Nerv. Ment. Dis.* 115 (1952): 283.

9. Ibid., 290.

10. A. Kinsey, W. Pomeroy, and C. Martin, *Sexual Behavior in the Human Male.*

11. Kallman, *Heredity in Health and Mental Disorder* (1953).

12. Ibid., 154.

13. Heston and Shields, "Homosexuality in Twins," *Arch. Gen. Psychiatry* 18 (1968): 149.

14. See, McConaghy, "A Pair of Monozygotic Twins Discordant for Homosexuality: Sex-Dimorphic Behavior and Penile Volume Responses," *Arch. Sex. Behav.* 9 (1980): 123; Zuger, "Monozygotic Twins Discordant for Homosexuality—Report of a Pair and Significance of Phenomenon," *Comp. Psychiatry* 17 (1976): 661; Rainer, "Homosexuality and Heterosexuality in Identical Twins," *Psychosom. Med.* 22 (1960): 251; Friedman, "Psychological Development and Blood Levels of Sex Steroids in Male Identical Twins of Divergent Sexual Orientation," *J. Nerv. Ment. Dis.* 163 (1976): 282; Parker, "Homosexuality in Twins: A Report on Three Discordant Pairs," *Brit. J. Psychiatry* 110 (1964): 489.

15. See also Meyers, "Homosexuality, Sexual Dysfunction, and Incest in Male Identical Twins," *Can. J. Psychiatry* 27 (1982): 144; Holden, "Psychotherapy of a Shared Syndrome in Identical Twins," *Brit. J. Psychiatry* 111 (1965): 859.

16. Eckert, "Monozygotic Twins Reared Apart: Preliminary Findings of Psychiatric Disturbances and Traits," *Prog. Clin. Biol. Research* 69 (1981): 179.

17. Pillard and Weinrich, "Evidence of Familial Nature of Homosexuality," *Arch. Gen. Psychiatry* 43 (1986): 808.

18. G. W. Henry, *Sex Variants: A Study of Homosexual Patterns* (1941; repr., AMS Press).

19. Pillard, Poumadere, and Carretta, "A Family Study of Sexual Orientation," *Arch. Sex. Behav.* 11 (1982): 511.

20. R. Krafft-Ebing, *Psychopathia Sexualis* (1898).

21. See, Kolodny, "Plasma Testosterone and Semen Analysis in Male Homosexuals," *New Eng. J. Med.* 285 (1971): 1170; Pillard, "Plasma Testosterone Levels in Homosexual Men," *Arch. Sex. Behav.* 3 (1974): 453; and Starka, "Plasma Testosterone in Male Transsexuals and Homosexuals," *J. Sex. Res.* 11 (1975): 134.

22. Meyer-Bahlberg, "Psychoendocrine Research on Sexual Orientation: Current Status and Future Options," *Prog. Brain Res.* 61 (1984): 375.

23. See Rohde, "Plasma Basal Levels of FSH, LH and Testosterone in Homosexual Men," *Endokrinol.* 70 (1977): 241; Stahl, "Significantly Decreased Apparently Free Testosterone Levels in Plasma of Male Homosexuals," *Endokrinol,* 68 (1976): 115. One found an elevated level in homosexuals. Doerr, "Further Studies on Sex Hormones in Male Homosexuals," *Arch. Gen. Psychiatry* 33 (1976): 611.

24. Doerr, "Plasma Testosterone, Estradiol, and Semen Analysis in Male Homosexuals," *Arch. Gen. Psychiatry* 29 (1973): 829.

25. Newmark, "Gonadotropin, Estradiol, and Testosterone Profiles in Homosexual Men," *Amer. J. Psychiatry* 136 (1979): 767.

26. See generally Meyer-Bahlberg, "Psychoendocrine Research on Sexual Orientation: Current Status and Future Options," *Prog. Brain Res.* 61 (1984): 375.

27. Lorraine, "Patterns of Hormone Excretion in Male and Female Homosexuals," *Nature* 224 (1971): 552; Gartrell, "Plasma Testosterone in Homosexual and Heterosexual Women," *Amer. J. Psychiatry* 134 (1977): 1117; Sipova and Starka, "Plasma Testosterone Values in Transsexual Women," *Arch. Sex. Behav.* 6 (1977): 477.

28. Jost, "Recherches sur la Differenciation Sexuelle de l'Embryon de Lapin," *Arch. Anat. Microscop. Morphol. Exper.* 36 (1947): 151, 242.

29. Young, "Hormones and Sexual Behavior," *Science* 143 (1964): 212.

30. Phoenix, "Female Sexual Behavior Displayed by Androgenized Female Rhesus Macaques," *Horm. Behav.* 17 (1983): 146.

31. Ehrhardt and Baker, "Fetal Androgens, Human Central Nervous System Differentiation, and Behavior Sex Differences," in *Sex Differences in Behavior,* ed. R. Friedman, R. Richart, and R. Van de Wiele (1974).

32. Ehrhardt, "Influence of Androgen on Some Aspects of Sexually Dimorphic Behavior in Women with Late-Treated Adrenogenital Syndrome," *Johns Hop. Med. J.* 123 (1968): 115.

33. Money, Schwartz, and Lewis, "Adult Erotosexual Status and Fetal Hormonal Masculinization and Demasculinization: 46 XX Congenital Virilizing Adrenal Hyperplasia and 46 XY Androgen Insensitivity Syndrome Compared," *Psychoneuroend.* 9 (1984): 405.

34. Money, "Psychosexual Development and Absence of Homosexuality in Males with Precocious Puberty: Review of 18 Cases," *J. Nerv. Ment. Dis.* 148 (1969): 111; Money, "Homosexual/Heterosexual Status in Boys at Puberty: Idiopathic Adolescent Gynecomastia and Congenital Virilizing Adrenocorticism Compared," *Psychoneuroend.* 7 (1982): 339.

35. J. Money and A. Ehrhardt, *Man and Woman, Boy and Girl* (1972).

36. Imperato-McGinley, "Androgens and the Evolution of Male Gender Identity among Male Pseudohermaphrodites with 5a Reductase Deficiency," *New Eng. J. Med.* 300 (1979): 1233.

37. See generally B. McEwen, in R. Greep, "Reproductive Physiology IV," *Internat. Rev. Physiol.* 27 (1983).

38. Ehrhardt, "Sexual Orientation after Prenatal Exposure to Exogenous Estrogen," *Arch. Sex. Behav.* 14 (1985): 57.

39. Dorner, "A Neuroendocrine Predisposition for Homosexuality in Men," *Arch. Sex. Behav.* 4 (1975): 1.

40. Gladue, Green, and Hellman, "Neuroendocrine Response to Estrogen and Sexual Orientation," *Science* 225 (1984): 1496.

41. Gooren, "The Neuroendocrine Response of Luteinizing Hormone to Estrogen Administration in Heterosexual, Homosexual and Transsexual Subjects," *J. Clin. End. Metab.* 63 (1986): 583.

42. Ward, "The Prenatal Stress Syndrome: Current Status," *Psychoneuroend.* 9 (1984): 3.

43. Dorner, "Stressful Events in Prenatal Life of Bi- and Homosexual Men," *Exper. Clin. Endocrin.* 81 (1983): 83.

44. Swaab and Fliers, "A Sexually Dimorphic Nucleus in the Human Brain," *Science* 228 (1985): 1112.

45. McGlone, "Sex Differences in Human Brain Asymmetry: A Critical Survey," *Behav. Brain Sci.* 3 (1980): 215.

46. Entus, "Hemispheric Asymmetry in Processing of Dichotically Presented Speech," in *Language Development and Neurological Theory*, ed. S. Segalowitz and F. Gruber (1977).

47. Sanders and Ross-Field, "Sexual Orientation and Visuo-Spatial Ability," *Brain and Cognition* 5 (1986): 280.

48. Sanders and Ross-Field, "Sexual Orientation, Cognitive Abilities and Cerebral Asymmetry: A Review and 7 Hypotheses Tested," *Intl. J. Zool.* 20 (1986): 459.

49. *Brain and Cognition* 5: 288–89.

50. Breuer and Neischlag, "Antibodies to Hormones in Endocrinology," in *Immunization with Hormones in Reproduction Research*, ed. E. Neischlag (1975).

51. Fainstat and Bhat, "Recurrent Abortion and Progesterone Therapy," in *Progesterone and Progestins*, ed. C. Bardin, E. Milgrom, and P. Mauvais-Jarvis (Raven Press, 1983).

52. M. Wintrobe, *Clinical Hematology* (1956).

53. Slater, "Birth Order and Maternal Age of Homosexuals," *Lancet* 1 (1962): 69; Hare and Moran, "Parental Age and Birth Order in Homosexual Patients: A Replication of Slater's Study," *Brit. J. Psychiatry* 134 (1979): 178.

54. S. Freud, *The Psychogenesis of a Case of Homosexuality in a Woman* (1920; repr., 1957).

55. I. Bieber, *Homosexuality* (1962).

56. Ibid., 276.

57. Mayerson and Lief, "Psychotherapy of Homosexuals," in J. Marmor, *Sexual Inversion* (1965).

58. Coleman, "Toward a New Model of Treatment of Homosexuality," *J. Homosexuality* 3 (1978): 345.

59. Woodward, "The Diagnosis and Treatment of Homosexual Offenders," *Brit. J. Delinq.* 9 (1956): 44.

60. Curran and Parr, "Homosexuality: An Analysis of 100 Male Cases Seen in Private Practice," *Brit. Med. J.* 1 (1957): 797.

61. Fookes, "Some Experiences in the Use of Aversion Therapy in Male Homosexuality, Exhibitionism, and Fetishism-Transvestism," *Brit. J. Psychiatry* 115 (1969): 339.

62. MacCullough and Feldman, "Aversion Therapy in Management of 43 Homosexuals," *Brit. Med. J.* 2 (1967): 594.

63. Bancroft, "Aversion Therapy of Homosexuality," *Brit. J. Psychiatry* 115 (1969): 1417.

64. McConaghy and Barr, "Classical, Avoidance and Backward Conditioning Treatments of Homosexuality," *Brit. J. Psychiatry* 122 (1973): 151.

65. McConaghy, "Aversive and Positive Conditioning Treatments of Homosexuality," *Behav. Research Ther.* 13 (1975): 309.

66. Freeman and Meyer, "A Behavioral Alteration of Sexual Preferences in the Human Male," *Behav. Ther.* 6 (1975): 206.

67. Birk, "Avoidance Conditioning for Homosexuality," *Arch. Gen. Psych.* 25 (1971): 314.

68. Thorpe, "A Comparison of Positive and Negative (Aversive) Conditioning in the Treatment of Homosexuality," *Behav. Research Ther.* 1 (1963): 357.

69. Levin, "Treatment of Homosexuality and Heterosexual Anxiety with Avoidance Conditioning and Systematic Desensitization: Data and Case Report," *Psychotherapy: Theory, Research, Pract.* 5 (1968): 160.

70. Marquis, "Orgasmic Reconditioning: Changing Sexual Object Choice Through Controlling Masturbation Fantasies," *J. Beh. Ther. Exper. Psychiatry* 1 (1970): 263.

71. Barlow, "Biofeedback and Reinforcement to Increase Heterosexual Arousal in Homosexuals," *Behav. Research Ther.* 13 (1975): 45.

72. Conrad and Wincze, "Orgasmic Reconditioning: A Controlled Study of Its Effects upon the Sexual Arousal and Behavior of Adult Male Homosexuals," *Beh. Ther.* 7 (1976): 155.

73. Adams and Sturgis, "Status of Behavioral Reorientation Techniques in the Modification of Homosexuality: A Review," *Psychological Bull.* 84 (1977): 171.

74. K. Freund, "Some Problems in the Treatment of Homosexuality," in *Behaviour Therapy and the Neuroses,* ed. H. Eysenck (Pergamon repr., 1960).

75. McConaghy, "Is a Homosexual Orientation Irreversible?" *Brit. J. Psychiatry* 129 (1976): 556.

76. Ibid., 561.

77. Ibid.

78. Ibid.

79. Pattison and Pattison, "'Ex-Gays': Religiously Mediated Change in Homosexuals," *Amer. J. Psychiatry* 137 (1980): 1553.

80. Ibid., 1560.

81. Ibid.

82. Ibid.

83. Haldeman, "Sexual Orientation Conversion Therapy for Gay Men and Lesbians: A Scientific Examination," in J. Gonsiorek and J. Weinrich, *Homosexuality: Research Implications for Public Policy* (Sage, 1991), 149, 159.

84. R. Green, *The "Sissy Boy Syndrome" and the Development of Homosexuality* (1987).

85. E.g., A. Bell, M. Weinberg, and S. Hammersmith, *Sexual Preference: Its Development in Men and Women* (Indiana University Press, 1981); J. Money, *Gay, Straight and In-Between: The Sexology of Erotic Orientation* (Oxford University Press, 1988).

86. Harry, "Homosexual Men and Women Who Served Their Country," *Journal of Homosexuality* 10 (1984): 117, 121.

Affidavit of Kenneth Sherrill

1. Charles Beard *An Economic Interpretation of the Constitution of the United States* (Macmillan, 1913).

2. See Robert A. Dahl, *Who Governs?* (Yale University Press, 1961), *A Preface to Democratic Theory* (University of Chicago Press, 1956), and *Pluralist Democracy in the United States* (Rand McNally, 1967).

3. See Dahl, "The Concept of Power," *Behavioral Science* 2, no. 3 (July 1957): 201–15.

4. Harold D. Lasswell, *Politics: Who Gets What, When, How?* (1936), *Power and Personality* (1948), and *Democratic Character* (1951), all in *The Political Writings of Harold D. Lasswell* (Free Press, 1951).

5. V. O. Key, Jr., *Politics, Parties and Pressure Groups* (Crowell, 1964), 2.

6. Ibid., 3.

7. See David Truman, *The Governmental Process* (Knopf, 1963); and Bernard Berelson, Paul Lazarsfeld, and William McPhee, *Voting* (University of Chicago Press, 1954).

8. See Arthur Bentley, *The Process of Government* (1908); Dahl, *Who Governs?*; Michael Lipsky, "Protest as a Political Resource," *American Political Science Review* 62 (1968): 1144f.; Kenneth S. Sherrill and David J. Vogler, *Power, Policy, and Participation* (Harper and Row, 1977); Truman, *The Governmental Process*.

9. Alfred C. Kinsey, Wardell B. Pomeroy, and Clyde E. Martin, *Sexual Behavior in the Human Male* (W. B. Saunders, 1948), 357–61, 610–66.

10. Ibid., 65.

11. Ibid., 621.

12. Ibid., 621–22.

13. See Kenneth S. Sherrill, "Homosexuality and Civil Liberty," paper delivered at the Annual Meeting of the American Political Science Association in Atlanta, Georgia, 1989.

14. Kinsey, Pomeroy, and Martin, *Sexual Behavior*, 53.

15. Elisabeth Noelle-Neumann, *The Spiral of Silence* (University of Chicago Press, 1984), 6–7.

16. Ibid., 3.

17. Lasswell, *Democratic Character*, 477.

18. Ibid.

19. Ibid., 478.

20. Ibid.   .

21. Bureau of Justice Statistics, *Teenage Victims*, cited in *American Enterprise* 82 (July–August 1991).

22. D. Matthews and J. Prothro, *Negroes and the New Southern Politics* (Harcourt, Brace and World, 1966).

23. Ibid., 50.

24. Ibid., 49.

25. Harold W. Stanley and Richard G. Niemi, *Vital Statistics in American Politics* (CQ Press, 1988), 146.

26. Linda Garnets and Douglas Kimmel, "Lesbian and Gay Male Dimensions in the Psychological Study of Human Diversity," in *Psychological Perspectives on Diversity in America*, ed. D. Jacqueline Goodchilds, (American Psychological Association, 1991).

27. *1987 Congressional Quarterly Almanac*, 112-H.

28. See Michael Barone and Grant Ujifusa, *The Almanac of American Politics, 1990* (National Journal, Inc., 1989).

Affidavit of Gregory Herek

1. See D. W. Cory, *The Homosexual in America* (Greenberg, 1951).

2. See, e.g., M. Seeman, "Intergroup Relations," in M. Rosenberg and R. H. Turner, *Social Psychology: Sociological Perspectives* (Basic Books, 1981), 378–410; H. Tajfel, *Human Groups and Social Categories: Studies in Social Psychology* (Cambridge University Press, 1981).

3. See W. Paul, "Minority Status for Gay People: Majority Reactions and Social Context," in W. Paul, J. D. Weinrich, J. C. Gonsiorek, and M. E. Hotvedt, *Homosexuality: Social, Psychological, and Biological Issues* (Sage, 1982); 351–369.

4. See, e.g., D. Altman, *The Homosexualization of America, the Americanization of the Homosexual* (St. Martin's Press, 1982); J. D'Emilio, *Sexual Politics, Sexual Communities: The Making of a Homosexual Minority in the*

United States, 1940–1970 (University of Chicago Press, 1983); M. P. Levine, "Gay Ghetto," in M. P. Levine, *Gay Men: The Sociology of Male Homosexuality* (Harper and Row, 1979), 182–204.

5. L. Gross, S. K. Aurand, and R. Addessa, *Violence and Discrimination against Lesbian and Gay People in Philadelphia and the Commonwealth of Pennsylvania* (Philadelphia Lesbian and Gay Task Force, 1988); M. P. Levine, "Employment Discrimination against Gay Men," *International Review of Modern Sociology* 9 (1979): 5, 151–63; M. P. Levine and R. Leonard, "Discrimination against Lesbians in the Work Force," *Signs* 9 (1984): 700; "Results of Poll," *San Francisco Examiner*, June 6, 1989, A19.

6. G. M. Herek, "Hate Crimes against Lesbians and Gay Men: Issues for Research and Policy," *American Psychologist* 44 (1989): 948–55; G. M. Herek and K. T. Berrill, "Violence against Lesbians and Gay Men: Issues for Research, Practice, and Policy," *Journal of Interpersonal Violence* 5 (1990); Paul, "Minority Status for Gay People," 351–69.

7. H. M. Hacker, "Homosexuals: Deviant or Minority Group?" in E. Sagarin, *The Other Minorities* (Ginn and Co., 1971), 65–92.

8. G. M. Herek, "The Context of Anti-Gay Violence: Notes on Cultural and Psychological Heterosexism," *Journal of Interpersonal Violence* 5 (1990): 316; Paul, "Minority Status for Gay People," 351.

9. See M. M. Bierly, "Prejudice toward Contemporary Outgroups as a Generalized Attitude," *Journal of Applied Social Psychology* 15 (1985): 189; C. S. Gentry, "Social Distance Regarding Male and Female Homosexuals," *Journal of Social Psychology* 127 (1987): 199; G. M. Herek, "Beyond 'Homophobia': A Social Psychological Perspective on Attitudes toward Lesbians and Gay Men," *Journal of Homosexuality* 10 (1984): 1; G. M. Herek, "Religion and Prejudice: A Comparison of Racial and Sexual Attitudes," *Personality and Social Psychology Bulletin* 13 (1987): 56; A. D. Klassen, C. J. Williams, and E. E. Levitt, *Sex and Morality in the U.S.* (Wesleyan University Press, 1989); S. M. Maret, "Attitudes of Fundamentalists toward Homosexuality," *Psychological Reports* 55 (1984): 205; W. Schneider and I. A. Lewis, "The Straight Story on Homosexuality and Gay Rights," *Public Opinion* 7 (February/March 1984): 16.

10. For statements of the argument, see A. Bryant, *The Anita Bryant Story: The Survival of Our Nation's Families and the Threat of Militant Homosexuality* (Fleming H. Revell, 1977); Congregation for the Doctrine of the Faith, *Letter to the Bishops of the Catholic Church on the Pastoral Care of Homosexual Persons* (Congregation for the Doctrine of the Faith, 1986). For descriptions of anti-gay activism by church officials, see E. T. Rueda, *The Homosexual Network: Private Lives and Public Policy* (Devin, Adair, 1982), chap. 7.

11. See, e.g., Bierly, "Prejudice toward Contemporary Outgroups as a Generalized Attitude," 189; K. J. Gergen and M. M. Gergen, *Social Psychology* (Harcourt Brace Jovanovich, 1981).

12. M. E. Kite, "Sex Differences in Attitudes toward Homosexuals: A Meta-

analytic Review," *Journal of Homosexuality* 10 (1984): 69; Herek, "Beyond 'Homophobia,'" 1; Herek, "Heterosexuals' Attitudes toward Lesbians and Gay Men: Correlates and Gender Differences," *Journal of Sex Research* 25 (1988): 451.

13. B. Altemeyer, *Enemies of Freedom: Understanding Right-Wing Authoritarianism* (Jossey-Bass, 1988); Herek, "Heterosexuals' Attitudes toward Lesbians and Gay Men," 451; R. W. Hood, Jr., "Dogmatism and Opinions about Mental Illness," *Psychological Reports* 32 (1973): 1283; R. Karr, "Homosexual Labeling and the Male Role," *Journal of Social Issues* 34 (1978): 74; K. S. Larsen, M. Reed, and S. Hoffman, "Attitudes of Heterosexuals toward Homosexuality: A Likert-type Scale and Construct Validity," *Journal of Sex Research* 16 (1980): 245; A. P. MacDonald, Jr. and R. G. Games, "Some Characteristics of Those Who Hold Positive and Negative Attitudes toward Homosexuals," *Journal of Homosexuality* 1 (1974): 9; K. T. Smith, "Homophobia: A Tentative Personality Profile," *Psychological Reports* 29 (1971): 1091; H. Sobel, "Adolescent Attitudes toward Homosexuality in Relation to Self Concept and Body Satisfaction," *Adolescence* 11 (1976): 443.

14. Bierly, "Prejudice toward Contemporary Outgroups as a Generalized Attitude," 189; N. M. Henley and F. Pincus, "Interrelationships of Sexist, Racist, and Antihomosexual Attitudes," *Psychological Reports* 4 (1978): 83.

15. See, e.g., G. Allport, *The Nature of Prejudice* (Addison Wesley, 1954).

16. R. D. Ashmore and F. K. DelBoca, "Conceptual Approaches to Stereotypes and Stereotyping," in D. L. Hamilton, *Cognitive Processes in Stereotyping and Intergroup Behavior* (Lawrence Erlbaum, 1981), 1.

17. E.g., M. B. Brewer and R. M. Kramer, "The Psychology of Intergroup Attitudes and Behavior," *Annual Review of Psychology* 36 (1985): 219.

18. E.g., M. Snyder, "On the Self-perpetuating Nature of Social Stereotypes," in Hamilton, *Cognitive Processes*, 183.

19. E.g., Hamilton, *Cognitive Processes*.

20. E.g., Snyder, "On the Self-perpetuating Nature of Social Stereotypes."

21. See A. E. Gross, S. K. Green, J. T. Storck, and J. M. Vanyur, "Disclosure of Sexual Orientation and Impressions of Male and Female Homosexuals," *Personality and Social Psychology Bulletin* 6 (1980): 307.

22. See S. B. Gurwitz and M. Marcus, "Effects of Anticipated Interaction, Sex, and Homosexual Stereotypes on First Impressions," *Journal of Applied Social Psychology* 8 (1978): 47.

23. M. Snyder and S. W. Uranowitz, "Reconstructing the Past: Some Cognitive Consequences of Person Perception," *Journal of Personality and Social Psychology* 36 (1978): 941; *see also* Snyder, "On the Self-perpetuating Nature of Social Stereotypes."

24. L. J. Chapman and J. P. Chapman, "Illusory Correlation as an Obstacle to the Use of Valid Psychodiagnostic Signs," *Journal of Abnormal Psychology* 74 (1969): 271.

25. E.g., M. E. Kite and K. Deaux, "Attitudes toward Homosexuality: Assessment and Behavioral Consequences," *Basic and Applied Social Psychology* (1986): 137; M. E. Kite and K. Deaux, "Gender Belief Systems: Homosexuality and the Implicit Inversion Theory," *Psychology of Women Quarterly* 11 (1987): 83.

26. K. Deaux and L. L. Lewis, "Structure of Gender Stereotypes: Interrelationships among Components and Gender Label," *Journal of Personality and Social Psychology* 46 (1984): 991; M. D. Storms, M. L. Stivers, S. M. Lambers, and C. A. Hill, "Sexual Scripts for Women," *Sex Roles* 7 (1981): 699.

27. M. R. Laner and R. H. Laner, "Personal Style or Sexual Preference: Why Gay Men Are Disliked," *International Review of Modern Sociology* 9 (1979): 215; M. D. Storms, "Attitudes toward Homosexuality and Femininity in Men," *Journal of Homosexuality* 3 (1978): 257.

28. R. Karr, "Homosexual Labeling and the Male Role," *Journal of Social Issues* 34 (1978): 73.

29. B. D. Adam, *The Survival of Domination: Inferiorization and Everyday Life* (Elsevier, 1978).

30. H. A. Oberman, *The Roots of Anti-Semitism in the Age of Renaissance and Reformation*, trans. J. I. Porter (Fortress, 1984).

31. Adam, *The Survival of Domination.*

32. D. Newton, "Homosexual Behavior and Child Molestation: A Review of the Evidence," *Adolescence* 13 (1978): 29.

33. T. S. Szasz, *The Manufacture of Madness* (Harper and Row, 1970).

34. S. L. Gilman, *Difference and Pathology: Stereotypes of Sexuality, Race, and Madness* (Cornell University Press, 1985).

35. See ibid.

36. W. H. McNeill, *Plagues and Peoples* (Anchor, 1976).

37. See E. H. Erikson, *Childhood and Society* (Norton, 1963).

38. E.g., J. Boswell, *Christianity, Social Tolerance, and Homosexuality* (University of Chicago Press, 1980); J. J. McNeill, *The Church and the Homosexual* (Sheed Andrews and McMeel, 1976).

39. See, e.g., C. S. Gentry, "Social Distance regarding Male and Female Homosexuals," *Journal of Social Psychology* 127 (1987): 199; Herek, "Beyond 'Homophobia'"; Herek, "Heterosexuals' Attitudes toward Lesbians and Gay Men," 451; W. Schneider and I. A. Lewis, "The Straight Story on Homosexuality and Gay Rights," *Public Opinion* 7 (February–March 1984): 16.

40. B. Schneider, "Coming Out at Work: Bridging the Private/Public Gap," *Work and Occupations* 13 (1986): 463; T. S. Weinberg, *Gay Men, Gay Selves: The Social Construction of Homosexual Identities* (Irvington, 1983); J. W. Wells and W. B. Kline, "Self-disclosure of Homosexual Orientation," *Journal of Social Psychology* 127 (1987): 191.

41. See Schneider and Lewis, "The Straight Story on Homosexuality and Gay Rights," 16, 59–60.

42. M. R. Stevenson, "Promoting Tolerance for Homosexuality: An Evaluation of Intervention Strategies," *Journal of Sex Research* 25 (1988): 500.

43. J. A. Cerny and J. Polyson, "Changing Homonegative Attitudes," *Journal of Social and Clinical Psychology* 2 (1984): 366.

44. C. L. Anderson, "The Effect of a Workshop on Attitudes of Female Nursing Students toward Homosexuality," *Journal of Homosexuality* 7 (1981): 57; S. F. Morin, "Educational Programs as a Means of Changing Attitudes toward Gay People," *Homosexual Counseling Journal* 1 (1974): 160.

45. R. Goldberg, "Attitude Change among College Students toward Homosexuality," *Journal of American College Health* 30 (1982): 260.

46. L. M. Lance, "The Effects of Interaction with Gay Persons on Attitudes toward Homosexuality," *Human Relations* 40 (1987): 329; I. Pagtolun-An and J. M. Clair, "An Experimental Study of Attitudes toward Homosexuals," *Deviant Behavior* 7 (1986): 121.

47. Goldberg, "Attitude Change among College Students toward Homosexuality," 260.

48. Ibid.

49. W. J. Serdaheley and G. J. Ziemba, "Changing Homophobic Attitudes through College Sexuality Education," *Journal of Homosexuality* 10 (1984): 109.

50. P. A. Katz, ed., *Towards the Elimination of Racism* (Pergamon Press, 1976); W. G. Stephan, "Intergroup Relations," in *The Handbook of Social Psychology*, ed. G. Lindzey and E. Aronson (Random House, 1985).

51. E. Hooker, "The Adjustment of the Male Overt Homosexual," *Journal of Projective Techniques* 21 (1957): 17.

52. J. C. Gonsiorek, "Results of Psychological Testing on Homosexual Populations," *American Behavioral Scientist* 25 (1982): 385.

53. Ibid., 74. Similar conclusions were reached by M. Hart, H. Roback, B. Tittler, L. Weitz, B. Walston, and E. McKee, "Psychological Adjustment of Nonpatient Homosexuals: Critical Review of the Research Literature," *Journal of Clinical Psychiatry* 39 (1978): 604; and B. F. Reiss, "Psychological Tests in Homosexuality," in J. Marmor, *Homosexual Behavior: A Modern Reappraisal* (Basic Books, 1980), 296.

54. M. McDaniel, *Preservice Adjustment of Homosexual and Heterosexual Military Accessions: Implications for Security Clearance Suitability* (PERS-EREC, 1989).

55. Doc. no. 241, 81st Cong., 2d sess. (1950).

56. See J. Crocker and B. Major, "Social Stigma and Self-esteem: The Self-protective Properties of Stigma," *Psychological Review* 96 (1989): 608; E. Goffman, *Stigma: Notes on the Management of Spoiled Identity* (Prentice-Hall, 1963); E. E. Jones, A. Farina, A. H. Hastorf, H. Markus, D. T. Miller, and R. A. Scott, *Social Stigma: The Psychology of Marked Relationships* (W. H. Freeman, 1984).

57. Allan Bérubé, *Coming Out under Fire: The History of Gay Men and Women in World War II* (Free Press, 1990), 170–71.

58. See Goffman, *Stigma.*

59. *Federal Government Security Clearance Programs: Hearings before the Permanent Subcommittee on Investigations of the Committee on Governmental Affairs,* 99th Cong., 1st sess. (1985).

60. G. B. Melton, "Public Policy and Private Prejudice: Psychology and Law on Gay Rights," *American Psychologist* 44 (1989): 933.

61. M. Delaney and P. Goldblum, *Strategies for Survival: A Gay Men's Health Manual for the Age of AIDS* (St. Martin's Press, 1986); J. Preston and G. Swann, *Safe Sex* (New American Library, 1986); E. L. Sisley and B. Harris, *The Joy of Lesbian Sex* (Wallaby, 1977).

62. 10 U.S.C. § 925(a).

63. H. Hartshorne and M. May, *Studies in the Nature of Character,* 3 vols. (Macmillan, 1928–30).

64. See also R. V. Burton, "Honesty and Dishonesty," in T. Lickona, *Moral Development and Behavior: Theory, Research, and Social Issues* (Holt, Rinehart and Winston, 1976), 173.

65. M. Snyder and W. Ickes, "Personality and Social Behavior," in G. Lindzey and E. Aronson, *Handbook of Social Psychology* (Random House, 1985), 2: 883.

66. L. Kohlberg, "Moral Stages and Moralization: The Cognitive-Developmental Approach," in Lickona, *Moral Development and Behavior,* 31.

67. See, e.g., E. M. Brecher, *Love, Sex, and Aging* (Little, Brown, 1984); S. Hite, *The Hite Report: A Nationwide Study of Female Sexuality* (Knopf, 1976); S. Hite, *The Hite Report on Male Sexuality* (Knopf, 1981); A. C. Kinsey, W. B. Pomeroy, and C. E. Martin, *Sexual Behavior in the Human Male* (W. B. Saunders, 1948); A. C. Kinsey, W. B. Pomeroy, C. E. Martin, and P. H. Gebhard, *Sexual Behavior in the Human Female* (W. B. Saunders, 1953); L. Wolfe, *The Cosmo Report* (Arbor House, 1981).

68. A. P. Bell and M. S. Weinberg, *Homosexualities: A Study of Diversity among Men and Women* (Simon and Schuster, 1978); Levine, "Employment Discrimination against Gay Men," 151; Levine and Leonard, "Discrimination against Lesbians in the Work Force," 700; Schneider, "Coming Out at Work," 463; Wells and Kline, "Self-disclosure of Homosexual Orientation," 191.

Memorandum in Response of Department of Justice

1. In his recent memorandum, plaintiff attempts to draw extensive parallels between the current status of homosexuals in the military and the one-time status of blacks therein. Juridically speaking, however, the two groups are very different. As the Supreme Court has held, laws that classify on the

basis of race "are subjected to strict scrutiny and will be sustained only if they are suitably tailored to a compelling state interest." By contrast, the government need only establish a rational basis to justify classifications based on sexual orientation. As a result, rationales that may be insufficient to justify the differential treatment of racial minorities may be perfectly sufficient to justify the differential treatment of homosexuals.

2. In this case, plaintiff claims that defendants are engaging in nothing more than bigotry and prejudice when they claim that the exclusion of homosexuals from the military fosters "good order and morale," "mutual trust and confidence," the "integrity of the system of rank and command," the ability of the military to "recruit and retain members of the military service," and the "public acceptability of military service." For all of their lengthy declarations, however, plaintiff offers no evidence to show that the exclusion of homosexuals does not foster these things.

3. In this case, plaintiff makes much of the fact that he was separated from the Naval Academy six weeks prior to his scheduled graduation. However, plaintiff has admitted that he learned of his homosexuality "sometime during [his] sophomore year at Annapolis" and that he "generally knew before entering the Naval Academy that the Navy and military, in general, did not allow homosexuals to serve." In addition, plaintiff has admitted that, as a midshipman and a student leader, he knew and understood the rules of the Naval Academy prohibiting homosexual conduct, the seriousness of such conduct, and the policy of the military excluding homosexuals from service in the armed forces. Thus, plaintiff has admitted that he permitted himself to receive at least two years of higher education at the expense of the taxpayers, knowing that he had no right to receive it.

Reply Memorandum in Support of Joseph Steffan's Motion

1. Nowhere do defendants take issue with plaintiff's showing that (a) gays have suffered a history of purposeful discrimination; (b) homosexual orientation bears no relationship to an individual's ability to perform or contribute to society; and (c) gays have been saddled with unique disabilities because of prejudice and inaccurate or absurd stereotypes.

2. Defendants do not even attempt to defend the security rationale for the policy. This tactic is not surprising given Secretary Cheney's admission that the security rationale is "an old chestnut"; the security rationale can be traced to the post–World War II cold war hysteria; an assistant secretary of defense who is a close adviser to defendant Cheney is gay; the Department of Defense does not disqualify gays from holding security clearances; no homosexual in American history has ever betrayed his country under threat of

blackmail; and gays as a group are not unstable. Further evidence of the irrationality of the security rationale is provided by a memorandum dated January 9, 1991, which was prepared by the Department of Defense. Titled "Eligibility of Homosexuals for DOD Security Clearances," the memorandum concludes that there is no basis for denying a security clearance to an individual solely on the basis of his or her sexual orientation because of, among other things, "the general lack of enforcement" of sodomy laws to private consensual sodomy. It is also provided by a Defense Personnel Security Research and Education Center report, which concludes that "there is no basis for holding the belief that homosexuals as a group are less trustworthy or less patriotic than heterosexuals" and that "sexual orientation is unrelated to moral character."

Affidavit II of Richard Green

1. As discussed by Dr. Douglas Haldeman in his article, "Sexual Orientation Conversion Therapy for Gay Men and Lesbians: A Scientific Examination," in *Homosexuality: Research Implications for Public Policy*, ed. J. Gonsiorek and J. Weinrich (Sage, 1991).

Opinion of Judge Oliver Gasch

1. Plaintiff and counsel argue that there are definitional problems with the words "homosexual" and "homosexuality." Plaintiff urges use of the term "homosexual orientation" when talking about one's status as a homosexual, one's sexual preference, or one's desires for sexual gratification from those of the same gender. The terms "homosexual conduct" or "homosexual activity" are to be used to talk about sexual bodily contact between members of the same gender designed to elicit a sexual response or give sexual pleasure or gratification, and any other behavior that may induce or make welcome such contact.

2. The Equal Protection Clause of the fourteenth amendment is binding on the federal government, and the defendants in this case, by the fifth amendment's Due Process Clause. *Bolling* v. *Sharpe*. Equal protection claims under the fifth amendment are to be treated just as they are under the fourteenth amendment. *Weinberger* v. *Wiesenfeld*.

3. March of 1987 was during plaintiff's first class (senior) year. Plaintiff argues under Section 706(2)(A) of the Administrative Procedure Act ("APA") that he has not been treated fairly by the Naval Academy, and that the Navy has acted in an arbitrary and capricious manner since there were ten (10)

other midshipmen that year who were allowed to graduate, but who, because of various medical conditions discovered that year, were not commissioned in the Navy.

On the issue of immutability, discussed *infra*, plaintiff argues that homosexuality is not in fact a disease or illness of any kind. He says the scientific literature is clear on this point. If so, he is distinguishable under the Naval Academy Regulations which do not forbid graduation of midshipmen who have medical conditions which cause them not to be commissioned. Furthermore, plaintiff admits that he "discovered" his "condition" during his third class year which, if known to the Academy, under the Regulations would have caused a similarly situated midshipman with a medical condition to be discharged.

Plaintiff also argues that his resignation was obtained within the time period of one week while the Navy has as its goal the period of four months to process a discharge on the grounds of homosexuality. The speed of plaintiff's discharge proceedings and subsequent resignation, he argues, amounts to arbitrary and capricious action on the part of the Navy.

Because plaintiff had indicated that he did not desire to be commissioned in the Navy, that he was a homosexual, and that since graduation was impossible he would have to leave the Academy, it was neither arbitrary nor capricious for the Navy, as an accommodation to an accomplished young man, to save him the embarrassment and expense of duplicative, longer and more protracted discharge proceedings.

4. There is a continuum of sexuality recognized by the DOD and Navy regulations. For example, a midshipman who had only once engaged in some homosexual activity out of curiosity or due to intoxication, but who otherwise demonstrated indicia of heterosexual orientation, would normally be retained at the Academy.

The scientific literature on this subject suggests that there are those with a strict heterosexual orientation and whose lives and sexual experiences are strictly consistent with that orientation. On the other end of the spectrum, there are those who have a homosexual orientation and who have had nothing but homosexual sexual activity in their lives. A. Kinsey, W. Pomeroy, and C. Martin, *Sexual Behavior in the Human Male* (1948), 638–41. The great "in between" includes most lesbians and bisexual men, whether they have a homosexual or a heterosexual orientation. Note, "The Tradition of Prejudice versus the Principle of Equality: Homosexuals and Heightened Equal Protection Scrutiny after *Bowers v. Hardwick*," *Boston College Law Review* 31 (1990): 378, n.24, 379, n.25.

It is surely true that there are many stories behind why a particular individual has a homosexual orientation. It is not at all clear, as a scientific matter, whether one *chooses* one's sexual orientation or not. See Review, "Really, Dr. Kinsey?" *Lancet* 337 (1991): 547, citing Judith A. Reisman and Edward W.

Eichel, *Kinsey, Sex and Fraud: The Indoctrination of a People*, ed. John H. Court and J. Gordon Muir (1990) (Kinsey reports on male/female sexuality sharply criticized due to improper knowingly unethical use of unrepresentative populations); Review, "Kinsey's Sexreport: Dubious, Misleading, Fraud?" trans. Jurgen Benning, *German Medical Tribune*, July 19, 1991, 1, 6. No choice in the matter would argue for a conclusion of immutability, while some choice or a great deal of choice would tend to support a finding of mutability. Without a definitive answer at hand, yet confident that *some* people exercise *some* choice in their own sexual orientation, the Court does not regard homosexuality as being an immutable characteristic.

5. The latest statistics available, of which this Court takes judicial notice, show that 59% of adults and adolescents with the Human Immunodeficiency Virus ("HIV") contracted it through homosexual sodomy among males. The HIV is a virus which causes the Acquired Immune Deficiency Syndrome ("AIDS"). Homosexual activist groups have been highly involved in federal, state, and local efforts to deal with the epidemic. See, e.g., Jason DeParle, "Rude, Rash, Effective, Act-Up Shifts AIDS Policy," *New York Times*, Jan. 3, 1990, B1, col. 2, B4, col. 1 (AIDS coalition to unleash power—"ACT-UP"—well heeded by policymakers because of aggressive tactics); Bruce Lambert, "In Gay Parade, Pause to Recall AIDS Deaths," *New York Times*, July 1, 1991, B1, col. 5, B3, col. 1 (seventy thousand marchers and two hundred thousand onlookers for annual Gay and Lesbian Parade in New York City); Philip T. Hilts, "Landmark Accord Promises to Ease Immigration Curbs," *New York Times*, Oct. 26, 1990, A1, col. 4, A24, col. 1 (Lambda Legal Defense and Education Fund and Rep. Barney Frank helped get homosexuals and those with AIDS reduced restrictions on immigration); and Robert Pear, "Congress Authorizes $875 Million to Fight AIDS in Hard-Hit Areas," *New York Times*, Aug. 4, 1990, L1, col. 1 (despite no support from the President, authorization passed 95 to 4 in the Senate, and 408 to 14 in the House).

This is not to imply that only homosexuals will benefit from a solution to the HIV crisis, but simply to say that homosexual groups have been well publicized, heard and heeded by the political branches of our federal, state and local governments when it has come to dealing with the HIV epidemic and other related issues.

6. Atlanta, Boston, Chicago, Los Angeles, New York, Philadelphia, San Francisco, and Seattle are just some of the cities that have passed anti-discrimination regulations concerning homosexuals. California, Michigan, New York, and Wisconsin all have various statewide legislation or regulations which benefit homosexual groups. "Developments in the Law—Sexual Orientation and the Law," *Harvard Law Review* 102 (1989): 1667–68 nn. 49–51.

In *Jantz* v. *Muci* (1991), the plaintiff was an applicant for a position as a public school teacher who had claimed that he was denied the position because of the principal's perception that he had "homosexual tendencies."

Defendant's motion for summary judgment was denied because there was a material fact as to why plaintiff was not hired. In so holding, the district judge found the classification of those with a homosexual orientation to be inherently suspect. Finding homosexuals as a class to be powerless politically, the Jantz court criticized the Ninth Circuit for its contrary holding in *High Tech Gays*.

The basis of this criticism was the Ninth Circuit's citation of various state statutes which were taken from some footnotes in the *Harvard Law Review* piece cited above. The *Jantz* court complains that the Ninth Circuit ignored the text of that piece which said, among other things: "Unfortunately, very little legislation protects gay men and lesbians from discrimination in the private sector. No federal statute bars discrimination by private citizens or organizations on the basis of sexual orientation. Nor do the states provide such protection: only Wisconsin has a comprehensive statute barring such discrimination in employment."

In the first place, *Jantz* is a decision against the teaching of its own Court of Appeals for the Tenth Circuit. In *Rich v. Secretary of the Army*, classifications based on choice of sexual partner were held not to be suspect. Secondly, and more to the point, just because some students in Cambridge, Massachusetts say it, does not make it so. Based on the evidence of legislation, ordinances and obvious political trends, both *High Tech Gays* and this decision are justified in their conclusions that homosexuals are gaining in political stature, despite opinion to the contrary.

7. In *Cleburne*, Justice White gave an indication of what was meant by political powerlessness. The mentally retarded were held not to be "politically powerless in the sense that they have no ability to attract the attention of lawmakers."

8. The most significant policy separating the sexes in the Navy is that which excludes women from combat. The so-called "Combat Exclusion Rule," 10 U.S.C. § 6015 (1988), which mandates separate categories for men and women to serve on combat vessels in the Navy, did not violate equal protection under either rational basis review or strict scrutiny.

Part of the modern rationale underlying the combat exclusion rule is the avoidance of sexual conduct and pregnancy interfering with combat missions. It stands to reason that the categorical exclusion of those with a homosexual orientation from the Navy is, at least in part, while aimed at keeping good order, a way of keeping sexual conduct and desires from interfering with combat duties.

9. DOD Directives 1332.14 and 1332.30 were promulgated before the HIV epidemic became a matter of great public concern, or an influence on policymakers or legislators. Health-related issues such as the HIV or AIDS were not, as a matter of historical fact, considered when these directives were given.

10. This report was brought to the attention of respective counsel by the Court during final argument on November 7, 1991. Each was afforded the opportunity to comment. Plaintiff's counsel indicated at oral argument that he did not believe health-related issues to be in the case. Defendants' counsel filed a short comment within a week expressing the view that health-related issues were not originally part of the military's policy of excluding homosexuals, but that they would be considered if re-evaluated.

11. Again, this is not to imply that all persons are not potentially at risk of being infected with the HIV, but merely to point out the relative risks. The fact remains that 59% is a much larger risk category for men who engage in homosexual activity than the 10% or so of all persons, male or female, who have the HIV from heterosexual activity.

INDEX

abnormal hormonal states, 64–67
abortion, 71
Abzug, Bella, 114
ACLU ratings, 119
ACT-UP (organization), 207n.5
Adam (O.T. character), 46
Adam, B. D., 128
Administrative Procedures Act, 7, 35, 36, 38, 205n.3
adrenal gland, 64, 69
advertisers, 109, 113
affection values, 89, 96
AFL-CIO COPE ratings, 119
African Americans: campaign contributions by, 106; churches of, 112; demography of, 93; Department of Defense on, 203–4n.1; Hate Crime Act and, 100; in House of Representatives, 118; medical theories on, 129; in military service, xx, 5–6, 25, 27–29, 30, 32, 142, 162; pigmentation alteration by, 165; psychological stress on, 134; public feelings for, 98–99; segregated schools and, xviii; stereotypes attributed to, 128; as suspect class, xvi; violence against, 16, 21–22, 103, 128–29; mentioned, 130, 169
aging persons, 181–82
AIDS (Acquired Immune Deficiency Syndrome): fund raising for, 106; Gasch on, xxi, 180, 185, 187–88, 207n.5, 208n.9, 209nn. 10 and 11; gay rights and, 114; Helms Amendment and, 117; House of Representatives and, 115; in LeVay's subjects, 172–73; public attitudes toward, 95–96; safer sex and, 138; mentioned, 93, 116
Aircraft Owners and Pilots Association PAC, 107
allied military forces, 5, 26, 146–49
allied social groups, 87, 90, 113–15
American Heritage Dictionary of the English Language, 54
American Medical Association PAC, 107

American Psychiatric Association, 16, 129, 133
American Psychological Association, 16–17, 80–81, 121, 133
American Samoa, 115
anal intercourse. *See* sodomy
ancient sexual ethics, 41–44
androgen-insensitivity syndrome, 65
androgens, 62, 64–65, 67, 71
anti-abortionists, 97
anticipatory avoidance procedure, 75
Antony, Marc, 43
anxiety relief, 75, 77, 130
apocopation, 51
Arab countries, 28
Aristotle, 85
Artemidorus Daldianus, 43
ascetics, 45
Asian-American sailors, 142
AT&T PAC, 107
Athenians, 44, 85
attitudes. *See* social attitudes
Augustine, Saint, 45
Augustus, Caesar, 43
aunts, 61
authoritarianism, 124
Auto Dealers and Drivers for Free Trade PAC, 107
aversion therapy, 75–78, 80

Bayer, Ronald, 129
Beard, Charles, 86
behavior. *See* heterosexual conduct; homosexual conduct
"behavior" therapy, 74–81
Belgian armed forces, 148
Ben-Shalom v. *Marsh* (1989): Gasch on, 176, 177, 181, 183; Justice Department on, 156, 157–58, 159; Wachtell, Lipton, Rosen & Katz on, 162, 163–64
Berg v. *Claytor* (1977), 5, 32
Bérubé, Allan, 134–35, 144
"Betty K.," 126
Bieber, I., 71–72

Mediterranean city-states, 41, 46, 85
men, 67–69, 125–26, 172. *See also* boys;
male bisexuals; male heterosexuals;
male homosexuals; uncles
Menninger, William, 135
mental illness theory of homosexuality,
16–17, 129, 132–35
mentally retarded persons, 23, 163, 164,
166, 181, 208n.7
Michigan, 118
midshipmen, uncommissionable, 7, 37,
151, 159–60, 168–69, 206n.3
military allies, 5, 26, 146–49
military ban on homosexuals. *See* U.S.
Department of Defense—Directives
1332.14, 1332.30
military camps, 187
military judgment, 6, 30, 33–35, 152, 153–
55, 167–68, 186
military officers, 26, 37, 141, 142–43, 144,
183
"military order, discipline, morale" argument: Defense Department on, 204n.2;
Gasch on, 183; Herek on, 131; Wachtell,
Lipton, Rosen & Katz on, 5, 6, 26–27,
37–38; Wolinsky on, 167
Minnesota, 118
minorities: allies of, 90, 113; campaign
contributions by, 106; cultural ideologies and, 127; federal gay rights bill
and, 115; Helms Amendment and, 118;
homosexuals as, 122–23; immutable
characteristics of, 165; majority tyranny and, 86- 87; in Navy, 142; psychological stress on, 134; public feelings
for, 97; stereotypes attributed to, 18;
U.S. v. *Carolene Products Co.* on, xv, 14–
15; violence against, 103. *See also* racial
discrimination
Missouri, 118
monkeys, 63–64
monozygotic twins, 58, 59–60, 61
Montgomery County Republican Club, 101
Moore, G. D., 9
"morale, order, discipline" argument. *See*
"military order, discipline, morale" argument
morality. *See* ethics
mothers. *See* pregnancy
municipal legislation, 207n.6
murder investigations, 103
musicality, 30

"mutable" homosexual orientation. *See*
"immutable" homosexual orientation
mystery cults, 42

NAACP, xviii, 32
NARAL-PAC, 106–7
National Abortion Rights Action League
PAC, 106–7
National Association for the Advance-
ment of Colored People, xviii, 32
National Committee for an Effective Con-
gress, 107
National Conservative Political Action
Committee, 108
national crises, 26
National Education Association PAC, 107
National Election Studies, 96–99
National Opinion Research Center (Uni-
versity of Chicago), 92, 95, 99, 120
National PAC, 107
national security concerns. *See* security
concerns
National Security Political Action Com-
mittee, 106
NATO countries, 28
Nazi Germany, 21, 103, 129, 191n.3
Negroes and the New Southern Politics
(Matthews and Prothro), 106
Netherlands armed forces, 148
New Jersey, 118
Newsday, 52, 53
newspaper coverage. *See* media coverage
Newsweek, 53
New Testament, 44
New York City Gay and Lesbian Parade,
207n.5
New York City St. Patrick's Day Parade,
52, 180
New York State, 100, 112, 113, 115, 118,
119
New York Times, 52, 53, 103
Noelle-Neumann, Elisabeth, 92
Norris, William A.: *Ben-Shalom* and, 158;
on congressional intent, 33–34; on
criminalization, 19; on powerlessness,
20- 21; on private biases, 164; on secu-
rity risks, 33; on sexual reorientation,
17–18; mentioned, xvii, 15, 178
Norton v. *Macy* (1969), 24–25
Norwegian armed forces, 148–49
numerosity, 90–95
Nunn, Sam, xxi